THE NEW ASTROLOGY

THE ART AND SCIENCE OF THE STARS

THE NEW ASTROLOGY

THE ART AND SCIENCE OF THE STARS

Nicholas Campion
Steve Eddy

Trafalgar Square Publishing

First published in the United States of America in 1999 by

Trafalgar Square Publishing
North Pomfret, Vermont 05053

Printed in Singapore by Tien Wah Press

Library of Congress Catalog Card Number: 99-60333

ISBN 1-57076-152-3

10 9 8 7 6 5 4 3 2 1

DESIGN JANE FORSTER

ILLUSTRATIONS
STEVEN DEW p. 139, p. 206, p. 218, p. 224, p. 225, p. 239, p. 245

PICTURE ACKNOWLEDGEMENTS

Anglo-Austrian Observatory/ Royal Edinburgh Observatory: p. 30
T. Murtagh/R. Griffin/Armagh Planetarium: p. 150
Bridgeman Art Library, London: Agnew and Sons p. 88/ Bargello, Florence p. 81/ John Bethell p. 192/ Bibliothèque Nationale, Paris p. 34, p. 50, p.73, p. 87, p. 224/Bonhams, London p. 55, p. 202/ British Library p.22, p. 36, p. 54, p. 60, p. 105, pp. 248–9, p.253/ British Museum pp. 32–3, p. 128, p. 171, pp. 184–5, p. 197, p. 261/ Castello del Buonconsiglio p. 58, p. 94/ Châpel of the Planets, Tempio Malatestiano, Rimini p. 65, p. 111/ Château de Versailles p. 59/ St Neots, Cornwall p. 40/ Collection of the Earl of Pembroke, Wilton House p. 38/ Egyptian National Museum p. 66/ Forbes Magazine Collection, New York pp. 192 –193/ Galleria degli Uffizi, Florence p. 154/ Galleria dell'Academia, Venice pp. 74–5/ Guildhall Library, Corporation of London p. 43/ Hermitage, St. Petersburg p. 49/ Kunsthaus,

Zurich p. 47, Kunsthistorisches Museum p. 24/ The Louvre, Paris p. 15, p. 80, p. 135, p.136, p. 138, p. 152, p. 272/ Roy Miles Gallery, London p. 198/ Musée Archeologique, Sousse p. 191/ Musée Condé, Chantilly p. 18, p. 86, p. 251/ Musée de la Tapisserie, with special authorization of the city of Bayeux pp. 256–7/ Museo Merano p. 215/ Musée des Beaux-Arts p. 122/ Musée d'Orsay p. 25/ Musée Granet, Aix-en-Provence p. 172/ Museum of Mankind, London p. 121/ Museo de Santa Cruz, Toledo pp. 90 –91/ National Gallery pp. 164–5, p. 221/ National Gallery of Ireland pp. 112–113/ National Museum of India p. 41, pp. 208–9/ Naturhistorisches Museum, Vienna p. 159/ Oriental Museum, Durham University p. 203, p. 244/ O'Shea Gallery, London pp. 222–3/ Pinacoteca Capitolina, Palazzo Conservatori p. 164/ Prado, Madrid p. 107, p. 179/ Private Collection pp. 8–9, p. 64, pp. 96–7, p. 180, p. 263/ Rafael Valls Gallery, London p. 219/ Stapleton Collection pp. 70–71, p. 92/ Tate Gallery p.

229/ Victoria and Albert Museum p. 11, p. 115
Mary Evans Picture Library: p. 186
Fortean Picture Library: p. 270
Ronald Grant Archive: pp. 268–9
Hutchison Library: pp. 264–5
Images Colour Library: p. 17, p. 27, p. 48, p. 71, p. 82, p. 98, p. 104, p. 110, p. 119, p. 123, p. 124, pp. 126–7, p. 130, p. 137, p. 141, p. 145, p. 146, p. 147, p. 155, p. 160, p. 163, pp. 174–5, p. 216, p. 230, p. 232, pp. 236–7, pp. 238–9, p. 241, p. 242, pp. 246–7, pp. 254–5, p. 258, pp. 266–7, pp. 274–5.
NASA: pp. 30–31, pp. 62–3, p. 102, pp. 116–117, pp. 118–119, p. 130, pp. 132–3, p. 134, p. 142, p. 143, p. 144, p. 149, p. 156, p. 157, p. 161, p. 162, p. 167, pp. 168–9, p. 170, p. 176, p. 177, p. 178, p. 182, p. 184, p. 188, p. 189, p. 194, p. 195, p. 199, p. 206–207, p. 213, p. 226, p. 227, p.234, p. 274
Science Photo Library/ Frank Zullo p. 78/ Dr Luke Dodd p. 200–201/ Pekka Parviainen p.212

PERMISSIONS

Extract from *Phaenomena* by Aratus, translated by G. R. Mair, Harvard University Press, 1977, reprinted by permission of the publisher.

Extract from *Moralia,* by Plutarch, translated by F. C. Babbitt, Harvard University Press, reprinted by permission of the publisher.

Extract from *Manilius: Astronomica,* translated by G. P. Goold, Cambridge, Mass.: Harvard University Press, 1977, reprinted by

permission of the publishers and the Loeb Classical Library.

Extract from *Ptolemy: Tetrabiblios,* translated by F. E. Robbins, Cambridge, Mass.: Harvard University Press, 1940, reprinted by permission of the publishers and the Loeb Classical Library.

Extract from *The Yavanajataka of Sphujidhvaja,* translated by D. Pingree, Cambridge, Mass.: Copyright © 1978 by the

President and Fellows of Harvard College, reprinted by permission of the publishers.

Extract from *Book of the Hopi* by Frank Waters. Copyright © 1963 by Frank Waters. Used by permission of Viking Penguin, a division of Penguin Books Inc.

Extract from *The First Men in the Moon* by H. G. Wells, reprinted by permission of A. P. Watt Ltd on behalf of the Literary Executors of the Estate of H. G. Wells.

CONTENTS

INTRODUCTION

Among the qualities that distinguish us as human beings from every other species on Earth is our desire to reveal, describe and investigate the world around us. For as long as humans have roamed the planet, they have wondered about the nature of their relationship with the cosmos. They have been awestruck by the brilliance of the Sun's rise and the beauty of a blue sky, and moved by the mysteries of the New Moon and the patterns made by the stars.

For thousands of years, storytellers have created legends that express their feelings and fears about the cosmos, weaving myths that tell of sky gods and goddesses, of the stormy relationship between the Sun and the Moon. Some speak of the upheavals that accompanied the creation. Others tell of beings from the sky, angels or creatures from other planets, coming to Earth to teach us wisdom. Many prophesy the end of the world, the last giant cataclysm after which existence as we know it comes to an end, and humanity is reclaimed by heaven – or by empty space.

From the beginning, our views of the cosmos have shaped our beliefs about our place and purpose. Scientists, priests, mystics, poets, architects, musicians and mathematicians have looked to the stars for inspiration, or for an explanation of human life.

To the first known astronomers – the builders of the great ancient monuments such as Stonehenge and the Egyptian pyramids – the Earth was the centre of the universe. Modern space exploration has shown that we live on one planet among thousands, perhaps millions. Are we, then, no longer special, but just one species on one small inhabited planet at the edge of an insignificant galaxy?

We are taught that science and myth are opposites, that one reveals the truth while the other is fantasy. Yet myth is a means of describing truths that cannot be reduced to science; and science itself is increasingly entering realms that defy the imagi-

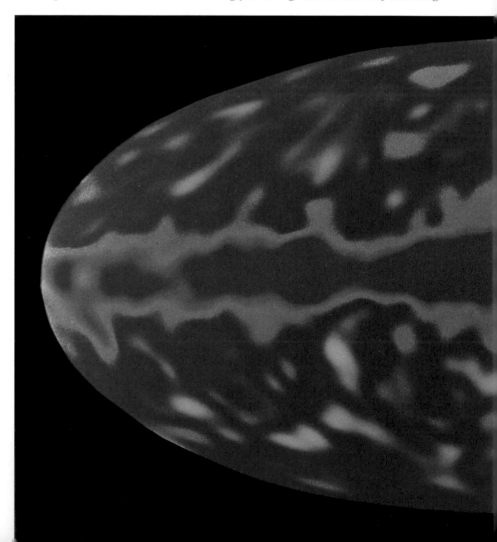

'The universe is not only queerer than we suppose,
but queerer than we can suppose.'

J.B.S. Haldane (1892–1964) *On Being the Right Size*

nation. Modern cosmology has travelled a long road
from the shamans who use magical rituals to merge
their spirits with the stars to the world of the space
shuttle and the Galileo space probe. Yet theoretical
physicists have themselves conjured up a universe
in which matter and energy are interchangeable,
space and time can be bent, and parallel universes
compete to occupy the same 'space'.

Modern science is raising more and more questions about the boundary between consciousness
and matter. As it does so it revives long-forgotten
problems such as where individual consciousness
ends and the universe begins. If the Sun has a physical impact on our lives, what is its psychological
role? And if the Sun has a role, what about the
planets and stars? Or are our views of the universe
determined by the limits of our imagination? And if
in subatomic physics, the very presence of the
observer influences the outcome of the experiment,
does the universe evolve to match our myths?
From the spread of newspaper horoscopes and
rumours of alien abduction to the first tentative
steps toward space exploration, from traditional
folklore to the most advanced technology we have
ever created, the stars retain the power to move us
to vast feats of the imagination.

There are common threads linking the physicist
Stephen Hawking to the ancient Sumerians, Albert
Einstein to the ancient Egyptians, and modern
astronomers to ancient astrologers. These are the
threads we must trace if we are to tell the full story
of humanity's relation-
ship to the stars, and
the ways in which now,
as in ancient times,
we continue to 'invent'
the heavens.

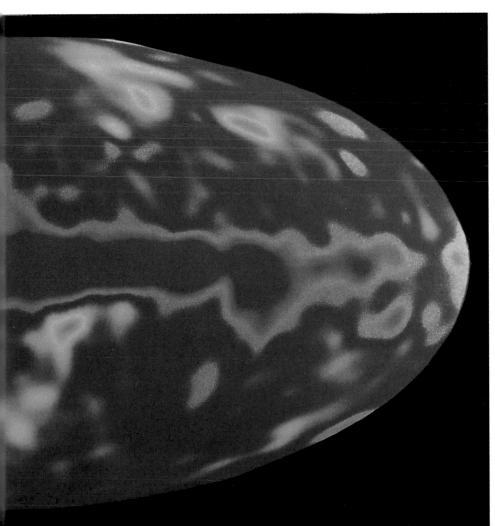

**Echoes of the early
universe: a microwave
map of the sky
using false colours to
illustrate variations in
temperature. Blue areas
are cool, deep blue are
average, and pink and
red are warmer, while
the red band across the
middle is radiation from
the Milky Way. These
variations in radiation
are thought to be the
remnant of the Big Bang
which it is believed gave
birth to the universe
between 10 and 20
billion years ago.**

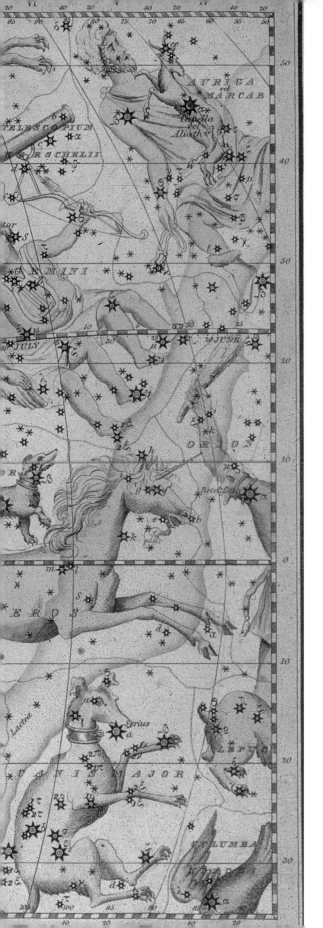

THE ZODIAC

According to ancient Greek belief, the entire universe was alive, and the planets and stars were the visible faces of the gods. 'Zodiac' is a Greek word meaning 'pertaining to animals', sometimes translated as 'circle of animals'. The Greek word *zoon* (pronounced 'zoh-on') can mean either a picture or a living creature: the original Greek zodiac was therefore much more than a set of animal pictures – like the universe, it was considered to be alive.

The zodiac is perhaps best known as the band of twelve 'signs' along the ecliptic (the Sun's annual path as seen from Earth) which are used in Western astrology. However, a zodiac may consist of more or fewer than twelve signs or constellations, and may be placed anywhere in the sky – Arab astrologers and astronomers sometimes used zodiacs based on the equator. A zodiac does not even have to be in the sky; ancient and medieval mystics believed that the principles embodied in the twelvefold zodiac occurred throughout nature, and that individuals contained the zodiac within themselves.

Each of the twelve signs of the zodiac used in the West is named after one of the constellations. A constellation is a collection of stars imaginatively linked together to represent an animal or object; in this way the heavens are organized into some recognizable form. Although we are not really sure why they were named as they are, it is likely that mythological figures and symbolically important creatures were allocated a place in the sky by the astronomer-priests of ancient religions. Some were included, some left out – for example, the pig found a place in Chinese astronomy, but not in the West. Being a variety of shapes and sizes, constellations are not useful for exact time-keeping, nor for pinpointing planetary positions, except to say that a particular planet is in a particular constellation.

A 19th-century celestial chart, engraved by John Emslie, showing constellations prominent in the spring in the north. Leo, Cancer and Gemini are noticeable, above Hydra, the Serpent, and Monoceros, the Unicorn.

ZODIACS

The first known attempts to bring order to the sky occurred before *c*.2000BC. In Babylon the path of the Sun was divided into three sections according to the seasons. In months one, six, seven and twelve the Sun was in the central region, known as the Way of Anu (the sky god); in months two to five it was in the northern section, the Way of Enlil (god of the air and wind); and in months eight to eleven it was in the southern section, the Way of Ea (the water god).

The earliest division of the sky into possibly equal divisions was based not on the modern twelve signs, but on 36 sections of 10 degrees each, known as 'decans'. Both the ancient Egyptians and Babylonians are known to have used this method of division before *c*.2000BC, probably with minor variations; the Babylonians had a list of 36 important stars, while the Egyptians divided the day into 36 sections, each relating to a sky section. The Greeks doubled this number and catalogued 72 constellations.

THE TWELVE ZODIAC CONSTELLATIONS

Around 700BC the Babylonians began to use the zodiac belt, incorporating eighteen constellations. These included the Pleiades (which later became part of the constellation of Taurus); the Great Swallow (whose stars are now included in Piscis and Pegasus); and the goddess Annitum (which is now in Piscis and Andromeda). The Babylonians included three constellations despite the fact that the Sun did not pass through them (a prerequisite for a zodiacal constellation) but probably because they rose over the horizon at the same time as Aries and Taurus: these were Orion, Perseus and Auriga. By *c*.500BC the number of zodiac constellations in Babylonian astronomy had been reduced to twelve.

The conventional solar zodiac operated alongside a lunar zodiac in ancient Babylon. This consisted of 28 divisions, which came to be known in medieval Western astronomy as 'mansions'. The Arabs and the Chinese also used lunar mansions, and they still survive in modern Indian astrology.

'Heaven is inhabited by twelve zodiacal gods, which show themselves in the zodiac. He that is born under Aries has much cattle, much wool and besides, a brazen face and crooked head, which is certain to wear the cuckold's horns. There are many scholars, lawyers, and horned beasts come into the world under this sign. Now, Taurus gives birth to football players, herders and such as can shift for themselves. Under Gemini are coach horses, oxen, baubles and those who claw. I myself was born under Cancer and therefore stand on many feet and have large holdings both on land and on sea – since Cancer suits both. Under Leo are born spendthrifts and bullies; under Virgo, women and those who wear iron garters. Under Libra, butchers, slip-slop makers and men of business. Under Scorpio, poisoners and cutthroats. Under Sagittarius, those who are goggle-eyed, herb-women and bacon stealers. Under Capricorn, poor helpless rascals, to whom nature gave horns so that they might defend themselves. Under Aquarius, cooks and potbellies. Under Pisces, caterers and orators. And so the world goes round like a mill wheel and is never without mischief, that men be either born or die. It is an egg, a honeycomb – with all good things in it, for those who know....'

Petronius, *Satyricon*, 1st century AD

THE SIDEREAL AND TROPICAL ZODIACS

The solar zodiac was more convenient than the lunar for measuring planetary positions, and, *c.*500–400BC, Persian astronomers began to organize the twelve unequal constellations into twelve equal-sized 'signs' of 30 degrees each, a system now known as the sidereal ('star-based') zodiac. The advantages of the new system, which first appears in 419BC, were clear, for the twelve signs could be matched with the twelve months, and the entry of the Sun and planets into each could be forecast in advance. The system was borrowed by the Greeks and survives in India to this day. The sidereal zodiac's disadvantages are that it moves with the constellations, and that the divisions between the constellations are essentially arbitrary. There is therefore no single agreed sidereal zodiac. In July 1928 the International Astronomy Union (IAU) introduced a new set of divisions, but Indian astrologers continue to use the system based on the ancient Persian model.

The tropical zodiac, used by modern Western astrologers, begins at the First Point of Aries – the point in the sky occupied by the Sun at the northern spring equinox (the autumn equinox in the southern hemisphere), usually on 21 March. It is therefore tied to the seasons rather than to the stars. As the constellations gradually shift their positions the two zodiacs, tropical and sidereal, move out of alignment. They last coincided *c.*AD100 and will line up again in approximately 23,000 years.

Each of the tropical zodiac's twelve signs runs for 30 degrees along the zodiac, while the zodiac belt traditionally extends for about 8 degrees on either side of the ecliptic. The Sun spends about

An illustration of the twelve signs of the Zodiac, from Sri Lanka. The sidereal and the tropical zodiacs use the same signs and imagery, and share their mythology, although the two zodiacs are not synchronized.

four weeks in each of these signs, and this has become the basis of modern popular Western astrology.

Whenever most Western astrologers refer to signs of the zodiac they mean the signs in the tropical zodiac. The tropical signs share the mythology of the twelve zodiac constellations, but they are not the same. The difference is simple: tropical zodiac signs are based on the seasons, constellations and sidereal signs on the stars.

The variance between the tropical and sidereal zodiacs is known by the Sanskrit word *ayanamsha*. It is generally agreed that 0 degrees Aries in the sidereal zodiac is currently about 5 degrees Pisces in the more familiar tropical zodiac, an *ayanamsha* of 25 degrees.

A THIRTEENTH SIGN?

The ecliptic now passes through a thirteenth constellation, known as Ophiucus (the Serpent Bearer), which was added to the twelve traditional zodiac constellations in the IAU's reorganization of 1928 (see p.11). Around 1971 a number of astrologers began to use Ophiucus, and in January 1995, the story that astronomers had 'discovered' a thirteenth sign became headline news around the world – a testimony to media interest in astrology in the age of astrophysics and space travel. However, most astrologers do not regard Ophiucus as a true sign of the zodiac.

THE CHINESE ZODIAC

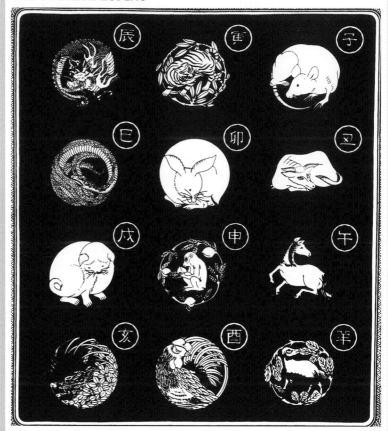

RAT: Charming, intelligent, sociable, fun-loving, good memory
18.2.12 5.2.24 24.1.36 10.2.48 28.1.60
15.2.72 2.2.84 9.2.96

OX: Methodical, stable, determined, tenacious, dutiful
6.2.13 24.1.25 11.2.37 29.1.49 15.2.61
3.2.73 20.2.85 7.2.97

TIGER: Competitive, courageous, reckless, charismatic, proud
26.1.14 13.2.26 31.1.38 17.2.50 5.2.62
23.1.74 9.2.86 28.1.98

RABBIT: Sociable, compassionate, modest, sensitive, creative
14.2.15 2.2.27 19.2.39 6.2.51 25.1.63
11.2.75 29.1.87 16.2.99

DRAGON: Charismatic, outgoing, independent, decisive, volatile
4.2.16 23.1.28 8.2.40 27.1.52 3.2.64
31.1.76 17.2.88 5.2.00

SNAKE: Seemingly wise, yet naive, reserved, subtle, prudent
23.1.17 10.2.29 27.1.41 14.2.53 2.2.65
18.2.77 6.2.89 24.1.01

HORSE: Sociable, energetic, strong-willed, opinionated, sporty
11.2.18 30.1.30 15.2.42 3.2.54 1.1.66
7.2.78 27.1.90 12.2.02

GOAT: Persevering, sensitive, idealistic, conservative, fussy
1.2.19 17.2.31 5.2.43 24.1.55 9.2.67
28.1.79 16.2.91 1.2.03

MONKEY: Active, agile, inventive, restless, plausible, stubborn
20.2.20 6.2.32 25.1.44 12.2.56 30.1.68
16.2.80 4.2.92 22.1.04

ROOSTER: Artistic, practical, shrewd, alert, extravagant, showy
8.2.21 26.1.33 13.2.45 31.1.57 17.2.69
5.2.81 23.1.93 9.2.05

DOG: Loyal, honest, friendly, reliable, needing affection
28.1.22 14.2.34 2.2.46 18.2.58 6.2.70
25.1.82 10.2.94 29.1.06

PIG: Contented, home-loving, practical, sincere, hard-working
16.2.23 4.2.35 22.1.47 8.2.59 27.1.71
13.2.83 31.1.95 18.2.07

LEFT The most familiar feature of Chinese astrology in the West is probably its allocation of twelve signs to each year in a twelve-year cycle. There is, however, no correspondence with the twelve Western signs. Starting dates for the animal years (day, month, year; 1912–2007) are shown, together with the characteristics ascribed to each sign. These images are Japanese, from Heishici Kotany's 'Family Crests', Kyoto, 1915.

BELOW The elaborately carved Aztec Sun Stone, showing the 52-year calendar cycle, was originally located on one of the pyramids at Tenochtitlán, Mexico. It is 3.6m (12ft) in diameter and weighs 23 tons.

CENTRAL AMERICA

The great civilizations of Central America, such as the Maya and the Aztecs, evolved their own calendar systems and with them an astrology quite different from that found in the West, India or China. The Aztecs used a ritual year of 260 days, known as the

THE CHINESE ZODIAC

Chinese astronomy and astrology developed in almost total isolation from that in the rest of the world – India, Babylon, Egypt and Greece. None the less, there are some connections, and some Indian astrology appears to have crossed the Himalayas with Buddhist missionaries.

Chinese astrology is immensely complicated, incorporating many different systems. It divides the solar year into 24 periods known as *Ch'i*, which are fixed to the solar year. Two *Ch'i* correspond to one sign in the Western tropical zodiac.

The main Chinese calendar is based on the Moon, so the lunar zodiac of 28 divisions is also an essential element of Chinese astrology. Most familiar are the twelve 'branches', each

tonalpohuali, alongside the usual 365-day solar year. This ritual year was subdivided in two ways: into thirteen periods of twenty days, with each day named after an animal; and into twenty periods of thirteen days, with every day given a number between one and thirteen. Astrologers based their prognostications on the animal and number that ruled each day, also taking into consideration the day's ruling deity and the most important planetary cycles. Unfortunately, the Spanish conquistadores of the 16th

one symbolized by an animal. Although it is very rare for sophisticated Chinese treatises to use these animal names, they underpin popular astrology and provide an important focus for the annual new year celebrations. Each year is symbolized by an animal (see box opposite), and children born during that year are believed to share its basic characteristics. Each year also corresponds to one of the five elements (water, fire, metal, wood and earth). Thus, among people born as a Snake (wise yet naive), one might be a Water Snake, another might be a Metal Snake and a third an Earth Snake, so that the Snake characteristics are correspondingly modified by the element. The whole cycle takes sixty years to complete.

century plundered and destroyed Aztec civilization, and enormous amounts of information relating to the elaborate culture of the Aztecs have thus been lost.

The Maya, who flourished in Central America *c.*AD300–900, developed an extremely precise calendar system. They accurately calculated the orbit of Venus, and new evidence suggests that they also tracked Mercury and Mars. This, combined with indications that they divided the sky into constellations, suggests that they might have placed planets in constellations, in the manner of Western and Indian astrology.

OMENS AND INFLUENCES

The word 'astrology' may be loosely translated from the Greek as 'the word of the stars', and loosely defined as the study of any relationship, whether symbolic or scientific, between events on the earth and in the heavens. There is no one astrology, but a number of different astrologies, which rest on different assumptions. Astrology is described as a religion or faith, a science, a form of psychology or a system of myth. In the past it was often used to guide initiates along the path to spiritual enlightenment. Although astrology is based on astronomical data, it relies on personal interpretation too much to be considered a science in the modern sense – most astrologers call it an 'art'.

THE ASTROLOGICAL UNIVERSE

Astrology is found in many ancient cultures. The Hebrew prophets searched the sky for signs of God's pleasure or warnings of his anger; Babylonian priests used it to advise their kings; and Greek philosophers believed it could take them closer to God. The forms that evolved in Europe, the Middle East and India are all linked, but other cultures, such as Central America and China, developed quite different systems.

Astrology rests on two premises. One is that, as the entire universe is interconnected, one part can be examined to shed light on another even when the connections are not apparent. The other is that a certain time possesses a certain quality. Therefore, by looking at the patterns of stars and planets at any one moment, the astrologer makes deductions about life on Earth at corresponding times.

> In the Hebrew Scriptures (Old Testament) God spoke to the prophets through celestial omens: 'And I will give portents in the heavens… The Sun shall be turned to darkness, and the Moon to blood, before the great and terrible day of the Lord comes.' (Joel 2.30–31)
>
> In Islam, although astrology was frowned on by some theologians, astrologers found support from various passages in the Koran. In one, Allah appears to criticize those who ignore his celestial portents: 'We spread the heavens like a canopy and provided it with strong support, yet of its signs they are heedless.'

ASTROLOGY AS LANGUAGE

Most modern astrologers describe astrology as a symbolic language, an idea dating back to ancient Babylon, where the movement of the stars was thought to be the gods' writing in the sky. The Greek philosopher Plato (c.427–347BC) extended the Babylonian notion that the planets represented words, asserting that they represented ideas. According to this doctrine, everything in the physical universe was a copy of an original 'idea' which existed in the mind of God. The entire universe was an imaginative exercise conducted by God; all physical reality was an illusion; and there were no distinctions between matter and spirit, or the Earth and the stars. Plato believed that the study of astronomy and astrology took the individual on a direct path to God.

The concept that the stars

could be read like a book survived among the Sufis (Muslim
mystics), who described the
world as the Koran of creation,
believing God spoke to humanity
via nature. This idea was taken
up by medieval astrologers in
Europe. The 17th-century herbalist Nicholas Culpeper insisted
that there were two books the
pious should read to understand
God: the book of the scriptures –
the Bible – and the book of the
creatures – the zodiac.

**The ancient Egyptian zodiac at
Dendera, dating back to the 1st
century BC or early 1st century AD,
depicts the twelve signs as we know
them today. It is carved into the
ceiling of a small chapel from the
temple of Hathor.**

'The course of the stars indicates what is going to happen in particular cases, but does not itself cause everything.'

Roman philosopher Plotinus,
On Whether the Stars are Causes, 3rd century AD

THE STARS AS CAUSES AND INFLUENCES

The belief that the stars and planets 'cause' events on Earth is due to a modern misunderstanding of Aristotle's theories of planetary motion. Aristotle, who was a pupil of Plato, believed that God's ideas descended from heaven to Earth via the planets. The primary cause was God, and the secondary causes were the planets, through whom God's ideas passed, providing a link in the chain of communication between humanity and heaven. When astrologers talk of the planets 'causing' events on Earth they are using a shorthand derived from Aristotle. In the Middle Ages Aristotle's theories were elaborated until it was thought that everything in the universe was linked in an intricate set of connections and correspondences, the 'Great Chain of Being'.

The idea that the stars exerted physical pressure on the Earth was put forward by Pliny the Elder in the 1st century AD, but was disputed by his contemporaries. Even before Pliny, Cicero had argued that the planets were much too far away to exert any influence on the Earth. However, developments in modern astrophysics are begin-

ning to show that the influence of bodies in space upon one another may not be as impossible as was previously thought. For example, Percy Seymour, Senior Lecturer in Astronomy at Plymouth University, England, has proposed electromagnetic fields (see pp.247, 249) as a possible means by which planetary alignments could affect life on Earth. (See also box opposite.)

SYNCHRONICITY

Modern astrologers often justify astrology by reference to Carl Jung's theory of synchronicity, in which events are linked if they occur at the same time. One version of the theory – held by most astrologers – argues that there are real connections between events occurring at the same time. For example, if a child born with Mars rising over the eastern horizon is lively and energetic, then the child's personality and the position of Mars are connected through time in a way known as 'acausal' – that is, Mars does not *cause* events on Earth. Rather, astrologers see *correlations* between its movements and related developments.

Another version of the theory, supported by a minority of astrologers, places the emphasis on *meaningful* coincidence. In

this version two events are linked only if the astrologer endows them with significance. Jung developed this idea after a session in which he was psycho-analyzing a patient, placing great emphasis on a dream in which a golden scarab beetle had appeared. As the patient was speaking Jung heard a tapping at the window; opening it, he found a rose-chaffer beetle – a northern relative of the Egyptian scarab. The shock of the coincidence between dream and reality provided a moment of illumination and became the turning point in the patient's treatment.

The point about this story is that the beetle was only significant because both Jung and his patient made the link between its appearance and the dream. Without them there would have been no link. Thus true synchronicity does not exist in the absence of a human observer. As applied to astrology this means, simply, that there is no astrology without the astrologer.

ASTROLOGICAL INTERPRETATION

Most academic study assumes that to a greater or lesser degree human life is subject to pressures outside individual control and that personality is shaped in part by social influences, chemical processes and childhood conditioning. Astrology tends to share the assumption that life is broadly determined by outside pressures unless individuals become conscious of their

The earliest known horoscope for the United States, by Ebenezer Sibly, published in London in his *New and Complete Illustration of the Occult Sciences* (1790). Sibly combined the planetary positions on 4 July 1776, when the US Declaration of Independence was agreed, with the moment on 20 March 1776 when the Sun entered Aries, beginning the astrological year. While the American revolutionaries had no interest in astrology, many of them were freemasons, deeply interested in mystical cosmology.

motives and learn how to make free choices.

The astrologer's main tool is the horoscope ('marker of the hour'). This is a diagram set to indicate the positions of the Sun, Moon and planets in relation to the Earth at any particular moment. These are positioned in the twelve zodiac signs. Twelve other divisions, six above the

BELL'S THEOREM

In 1964 the British physicist John Bell proposed that two particles that had once been connected would forever be connected, even if they became widely separated. In the early 1980s, experiments at CERN, the European particle accelerator, showed that Bell was correct. The hypothesis states that an unknown force, of which space, time and motion are all aspects, continues to link separate parts of the universe that were once united. Given that, according to Big Bang theory, the entire universe evolved from a single point, this suggests that every single part of the universe must be connected to every other single part.

horizon and six below, are known as houses and indicate specific areas of life such as business, career, family and relationships. Each planet has a set of meanings shaped according to the sign of the zodiac in which it falls, and applied specifically to the house in which it is found. For example, if Venus indicates emotions, then when it is in Scorpio it denotes intensity, and when in the sixth house (representing work) it indicates the effort that the individual might put into building partnerships.

The distances between the planets are also significant. For example, two planets found on opposite sides of the zodiac are usually seen to be in conflict, provoking tension. These distances are known as aspects. Predictive techniques rely mainly

> 'Now that is the wisdom of a man, in every instance of his labor, to hitch his wagon to a star, and see his chore done by the gods themselves. That is the way we are strong, by borrowing the might of the elements.'
>
> Ralph Waldo Emerson (1803–82), 'Society and Solitude'

on looking at the planets' future positions – or aspects – in relation to a past horoscope. There are also symbolic ways of moving the planets, known as progressions or directions.

Modern psychological astrologers typically describe the birth chart – the diagram of planets and signs of the zodiac for the time of birth – as indicating potential which it is then up to the individual to develop. At the end of the 19th century Alan Leo, the founder of modern astrology, popularized the aphorism 'character is destiny', by which he meant that each individual makes his or her own future. In his opinion, and that of many modern astrologers, prediction is therefore misleading. The astrologer should concentrate on helping individuals to understand their personalities.

LEFT An Italian manuscript painting of the zodiac, from the Portolan (book of sailing directions and charts) of Admiral Coligny, dating from the early 16th century.

SIGNS OF THE ZODIAC

The twelve signs are divided up in several ways, providing a basis for interpretation, as well as having cosmological and philosophical significance. In the individual sections that follow, these basic divisions are noted at the start, then elaborated under the 'Astrological' headings.

The principal division is into the four elements. Fire (Aries, Leo, Sagittarius) is said to be enthusiastic, active and emotionally warm. Earth (Taurus, Virgo, Capricorn) is cautious, practical and realistic. Air (Gemini, Libra, Aquarius) is intellectual, communicative and at home in the realm of ideas. Water (Cancer, Scorpio, Pisces) is emotional, sensitive and able to empathize. In the medieval doctrine of the four humours (see p.252) fire signs were hot and dry, earth cold and dry, air hot and moist, and water cold and moist. In Carl Jung's classification of the signs, fire is the intuitive type, earth the sensation type, air the thinking type and water the feeling type.

The second division is into the qualities – cardinal, fixed and mutable. This reflects the idea, present in Hinduism and Buddhism, that everything is involved in a continual cycle of coming into being, consolidation and dissolution. Cardinal signs (Aries, Cancer, Libra, Capricorn) are associated with initiative; fixed signs (Taurus, Leo, Scorpio, Aquarius) with resistance to change; and mutable signs (Sagittarius, Virgo, Gemini,

Pisces) with adaptability, restlessness and openness to change.

The third division is into the polarities of masculine–feminine (positive–negative), related to yin and yang in Chinese philosophy. Broadly, masculine signs are self-expressive, feminine ones receptive, and the terms 'masculine' and 'feminine' should be understood symbolically rather than literally. They alternate around the zodiac, beginning with masculine Aries.

When a sign is said to be 'ruled' by a certain planet, it is thought to have a particular connection with that planet. Gemini is 'ruled' by Mercury, and astrologers regard Geminis as being mercurial – quick-witted, lively and changeable. The drive embodied by each planet will be expressed according to the nature of the sign in which it is placed. For more information see individual planets (pp.116–199).

The twelve signs are often called 'birth' or 'star' signs, and individuals are frequently described as being, for example, 'an Aries': born with the Sun in Aries. However, people may also be 'Arien' if that sign features strongly in their horoscope as a whole, even if they were born with the Sun in another sign.

Each sign has its weaknesses, as well as its strengths. These are dealt with in the following sign sections under 'The Shadow'. This, in Jungian terms, also represents the aspects of personality that an individual is least likely to acknowledge.

ARIES

The Sun enters the tropical zodiac sign of Aries around 21 March and leaves around 20 April. Its entry marks the spring equinox (autumn equinox in the southern hemisphere), when the length of day and night are exactly equal. In traditional astrology Aries is a hot, dry, cardinal, masculine sign, a member of the fire element, and ruled by Mars. The Sun is exalted (strong) in Aries, and Saturn debilitated (weak). Its colours are white and red, its guardian angel is Malchidael and its symbol is the Ram.

The ancient Sumerians knew the constellation as Lu Hunga and the Babylonians knew it as Agru, both of which mean 'hired man'. To the Greeks and the Romans it was Krios and Aries respectively (both meaning 'ram'). In India it is known by the Sanskrit Mesha ('ram'); to the Hebrews it was Tala ('lamb') and to the Arabs al-Kabs ('the ram'), or al-Hamal ('the lamb'); in China it corresponds to the months Ch'un Fen ('spring equinox') and Ch'ing Ming ('clear and bright'). There is some confusion as to how the hired man became the ram. The Greeks may have mistranslated either the Sumerian sign *lu* or the Babylonian *agru* as 'sheep'. Or perhaps the hired man himself could have been a shepherd (see p.23).

In the ancient Alban (pre-Roman) calendar, which comprised ten months of 36 days each, April came first. Tradition records that Romulus, the legendary founder of Rome, placed it second, while Numa Pompilius, his wise successor, placed it fourth in his twelve-month year, with 29 days. Under his reformation of the calendar, Julius Caesar gave April an extra day, making thirty.

April, or Aprilis, may be named after Aphrilis, from Aphrodite, the Greek goddess of love (whom the Romans equated with Venus); the first day of the month was the festival of 'Veneris et Fortunae Virilis' ('Virile Love and Fortune'). Some suggest that it was named after the Latin *aperio* ('I open'), after the opening of the buds. The Anglo-Saxons knew April as Oster-monath, perhaps because it was the month of the east wind. This is one possible origin of the term 'Easter'.

ARIEN STARS

The constellation Aries contains 28 visible stars, including Gamma Arietis, which was one of the first double stars to be discovered. It was discovered accidentally by the English scientist Robert Hooke in 1664 when he was tracking a comet.

Aries contains few other stars of note, and those that are notable tended to have unfortunate reputations. Classical astronomers believed that Hamal (the Lamb) combined the characters of Mars and Saturn, and

'The first sign is commonly pictured as a Ram, said by the ancients to be the head of Time. Its domains are the paths of goats and sheep, caves, mountains, thieves, fire, mines and gems.'

Indian astrologer Minaraja, 4th century AD

RIGHT **Aries contains the Sun at the spring equinox in the north, long seen as the start of the year, giving us the sign's connection with new beginnings and powerful initiatives.**

caused violence, cruelty and premeditated crime. A Roman astrologer who spotted it rising before dawn would predict loss and disgrace, although we may imagine that such forecasts were made with great discretion.

In 431BC the Greek astronomers Meton and Euktemon defined the point occupied by the Sun at the spring equinox as the First Point of Aries. Around AD120 the astronomer Claudius Ptolemy established the First Point as the beginning of the 'tropical' zodiac, used by Western astrologers to this day (see p.11).

THE END OF THE WORLD

The Greek philosopher Plato, writing *c*.400BC, believed that when all seven known 'planets' – the Sun, the Moon, Mercury, Venus, Mars, Jupiter and Saturn – formed a conjunction at the positions they had occupied at the creation, the universe would come to an end. Plato did not specify which sign of the zodiac would contain this unique planetary line-up, but later commentators assumed that he meant Aries. However, since Aries was the sign of the spring equinox and Plato believed in endlessly recurring cycles, it was

The month of April, from an English book of hours known as the Golf Book (*c*.1520). A pair of lovers is pictured in a garden, surrounded by typical spring pursuits, including games.

> 'The sign of Aries as a whole is characterized by thunder and hail. Its leading part is rainy and windy, its middle temperate and the end hot and pestilential.'
>
> Ptolemy, *Tetrabiblos*,
> 2nd century AD

considered inevitable that as soon as the universe had wound down and come to an end, it would begin all over again.

A similar concept involving a repetitive cycle of destruction and creation has now been adopted in modern physics by Big Bang theorists, some of whom believe that the universe expands to its limit and then contracts to a single point, only for the whole process to begin again (see pp.207–8).

THE SPRING EQUINOX

Of the four major stations of the Sun in the calendar (the spring and autumn equinoxes and the summer and winter solstices), the spring equinox has long been considered the most important. Its official significance survives in the modern secular calendar in some countries as the beginning of the financial year and other administrative conveniences.

The theme of spiritual liberation following a mythical descent into hell or bondage was central to the religious rites practised around the equinox. The earliest-known equinox festival was the

twelve-day Zagmuk, or Akitu, which was celebrated in Mesopotamia from before *c*.2000BC, and which in its earliest forms commemorated the mythical death and resurrection of Dumuzzi (also known by the Hebrew name of Tammuz), the solar/vegetation god, and later of Marduk (similar to the Greek Zeus and Roman Jupiter), the chief of the gods. The Jewish Passover takes place on the Aries Full Moon, celebrating the beginning of the biblical Exodus and the Hebrews' liberation from the 'winter' of bondage in Egypt. Easter itself has been celebrated on different dates by different churches at various times, but always between 21 March and 25 April. The most usual choice is either the date of the annual Full Moon in the sign of Libra, which takes place when the Sun is in the tropical sign of Aries, or the following Sunday.

THE GOOD SHEPHERD

To the Sumerians, Aries was Lu Hunga, the Hired Man. However, given Aries' religious importance after *c*.2000BC as the sign of the

spring equinox, it seems unlikely that this image is as lowly as it may appear. It is possible that the 'hired man' was originally Dumuzzi, the Middle Eastern god of vegetation and creative forces, who according to legend began life as a shepherd and later became one of the great kings of Sumer before the flood. The Jewish king David followed a similar path, having been a shepherd as a youth. Christ himself was simultaneously the spiritual 'king of the Jews' and the ultimate good shepherd.

Classical astronomy preserved Aries' image as a man, and the Roman poet Ovid knew it as Phrixea Ovis, while others knew it as either Phrixus or Portito Phrixi. In Greek myth, Phrixus was the heroic son of King Athamas of Boeotia, who fled on the back of a ram to escape the wrath of his step-mother Ino. The myth relates how Ino resented her stepchildren and arranged a plot to have them killed. She began by parching the wheat, causing a crop failure and bringing the threat of famine. Athamas

> 'I sawe Phoebus thrust out his golden hedde upon her to gaze;
> But when he sawe, how broad her beames did spredde, it did him amaze,
> He blushed to see another Sunne belowe,
> Ne durst againe his fyrye face out showe;
> Let him, if he dare,
> His brightnesse compare
> With hers, to have the overthrow.'
>
> 'April' from Edmund Spenser's *The Shepheardes Calendar*, 1579.
> Phoebus is the Sun, and the 'other Sunne' is the Moon.

Abraham sacrificing Isaac by Andrea Mantegna (*c.*1490–95). The ram that is eventually sacrificed in place of the boy is seen on the left.

which he ordered him to sacrifice his own son, Isaac. As Abraham was about to strike, God intervened, telling him to spare the boy. Abraham looked up and saw a ram caught by its horns in a nearby thicket, which he then sacrificed to God as a burnt offering, in place of his son.

The appearance of a ram as the instrument of salvation in each case serves as a reminder that (in the north) Aries is the sign that brings winter to an end. The astronomical myth acts as a vehicle for a deeper religious moral, which is that one must be prepared to serve God no matter what he orders, but that in submitting to fate, the individual paradoxically achieves freedom.

THE QUEST

Arien myths, such as that of Jason and the Golden Fleece, speak of the naive enthusiasm, unthinking courage and wilfulness of the Arien type. Jason is told by his usurping uncle that he can have his share of the kingdom if he brings back the Golden Fleece, which came from the ram on which Phrixus had escaped (see above). Jason builds a ship (the famous *Argo*), gathers a band of heroes (the Argonauts), and embarks on his journey. After a series of heroic

appealed to the oracle at Delphi but Ino bribed messengers to bring back a false reply that Phrixus must be killed to save the harvest. Athamas took Phrixus to the top of the mountain overlooking his palace and was about to sacrifice him to Zeus, when Nephele, Athamas' first wife and Phrixus' real mother, intervened, sending from heaven a winged ram with a golden fleece. Phrixus and his sister Helle climbed on to

the ram's back, but as they made their escape Helle fell into the narrow strip of sea that connects the Aegean to the Sea of Marmara and was drowned. The sea was thereafter known as the Hellespont.

The same myth occurs in a different form in the Hebrew Scriptures (Old Testament). The book of Genesis relates that God devised a test for Abraham, the first great Hebrew patriarch, in adventures, he is told by King Aeëtes that he may have the fleece if he can harness a plough with two wild bulls who have hooves of bronze and breath of flame, and use it to plough a field and plant it with dragons' teeth. He succeeds in this task with the help of the king's daughter, the sorceress Medea; when her father goes back on his word, she also helps Jason to subdue the dragon guarding the fleece. She then cuts her brother's throat and delays her father's pursuit by strewing the path with pieces of her brother's dismembered body.

Jason is a solar hero, and the fleece and the bulls represent Aries and Taurus respectively. There may be a mythical reference here to the passage of the spring equinox from the constellation of Taurus to that of Aries c.2000BC. A psychological interpretation presents Jason as a hero in search of his true self (represented by the fleece), undergoing numerous trials along the way. The equation of the self with the Sun is clear – the fleece is golden, and gold is the traditional metal of the Sun.

Jason and Medea by Gustave Moreau (1865). In classical art and literature Medea was typically represented as a woman struggling with the conflict between her love for Jason and her equally strong attraction to magic. It was owing to the powers of her sorcery that Jason retrieved the Golden Fleece and was able to escape.

THE ASTROLOGICAL ARIES

The spring equinox is a time of growth and emergence. New life asserts itself, pushing out of the ground with blind determination. As a masculine, cardinal fire sign ruled by Mars, and as the first sign of the zodiac – and therefore the seed-point of the yearly cycle – Aries is traditionally seen as a strong, active, vital sign. As one of the two Mars-ruled signs (the other being Scorpio) Aries is assertive. Not for nothing is its image the Ram – think particularly of the battering ram.

Ariens like a challenge to which they can rise, because in so doing they define themselves in the world. They explore their boundaries, discovering the limits of what is and is not permissible.

Another typical Aries feature is egotism; not that Aries is deliberately selfish – rather, it is preoccupied with its own aims. One expression of this is that Ariens are often surprised to meet other Ariens – as if they thought themselves the only one in the world! On the other hand,

when it occurs to them, they can be generous, chivalrous, and even self-sacrificing, taking on another's problem as their personal cause with an almost militant zeal.

Ariens are competitive, needing desperately to be the best at whatever they do, yet frequently lacking the application to put in the long-term effort required to develop their talents. Often they learn to accept their limitations and strive simply to produce their personal best.

THE SHADOW

One of the classic fairy-tale images that surface in Arien myths is the knight in shining armour – the King Arthur archetype. Yet all heroes contain a tragic flaw. For Aries the fatal weakness is an inability to understand that once a decision has been taken, it must be implemented in line with practical circumstances. When the Arien shadow emerges, arrogance and impatience take over. The flawed hero fails to consider the consequences of his or her actions, and hopes and dreams unravel, just as in Arthurian legend the knight Lancelot's inability to control his passions destroyed Camelot.

'It is a Masculine, Diurnall Signe, movable, Cardinall; in nature fiery, hot and dry, cholericke, bestial, luxurious, intemperate and violent; the diurnall house of Mars, of the Fiery triplicity and of the East.'

English astrologer William Lilly, 1647

RELATING

Aries is quick to initiate social activity. Headstrong, impulsive, passionate and dynamic, but with little thought for the future, Aries falls in love at first sight – but gets bored easily.

Ariens take a ready interest in others and make friends easily. Often popular on account of their vitality and apparent (sometimes flimsy) self-confidence, they are basically loyal though often neglectful; quick to defend their friends but not willing to make great personal sacrifices for them; impulsive gestures of generosity come a lot easier than long-term commitment.

At best Aries is warm, affectionate and unpossessive. At worst, Ariens' competitive approach to life may make them regard a partner as a trophy that demonstrates their success to the world – a sort of human Golden Fleece.

IN THE WORLD

Aries is the sign of the born leader. Yet Ariens also have a reputation for being short-tempered – not an ideal leadership quality. This impatience, traditionally associated with Mars, can be the downfall of Aries, who hates having to wait for things to happen, wants instant results, and cannot resist the challenge of an impossible deadline – provided it is not too far ahead.

Perhaps the truth is that Ariens have a limited number of leadership qualities. They may be inspiring, in their enthusiasm and fiery determination, and in their easy dismissal of obstacles. Yet they are more likely to lead by example than by coaxing or assistance, since they lack the patience to wait and see if their followers are keeping up.

Aries was said by the Romans to rule Britain, Germany and France, the warlike nations of northern Europe. Perhaps they had never forgotten the sacking of Rome by the Gauls in 390BC, or the legions of Varus being wiped out by the Germans in AD9, or the rebellion of the Britons led by Boudicca in AD60. Ptolemy's view that the Arien Britons were 'fierce, headstrong and bestial' was typical.

An Arabic image of Aries, the Ram, from an 18th-century manuscript in the collection of Dar at Athar al-Islammiyah, Kuwait. Aries has traditionally been depicted as a ram or a lamb in Western astrology since the time of the ancient Greeks.

TAURUS

The Sun enters the tropical zodiac sign of Taurus around 21 April and leaves around 21 May. Taurus is ruled by Venus and is the sign of Mars' fall – where Mars is at its weakest. The Moon is exalted (strong) in Taurus, and ancient images often blend the bull's horns with the horns of the crescent Moon. Taurus is a cold, dry, feminine, fixed sign and a member of the earth element, and its colour is white (sometimes mixed with lemon) or green. Its guardian angel is Asmodel and its symbol is the Bull. The Babylonians knew Taurus as Guanna, the Bull of Heaven. In China it corresponds to the months Ku Yü ('grain rains') and Li Hsia ('summer begins'). In ancient Greece it was Tauros and in India Vrisha or Vrishabha ('bull').

May was the second month in the Roman calendar and was named in honour of the Maiores – the senate, or major branch of the Roman legislature. According to another version, it was named after Maia, a Roman goddess worshipped on 1 May and 15 May. The Anglo-Saxons knew the month as Tri-Milchi, a reference to the improved condition of cattle in the spring pasture, when they could be milked three times a day.

THE STARS OF THE BULL

The constellation of Taurus used to be represented by the front portion of a bull – according to Sumerian myth, its hind quarters had been torn off by the goddess of fertility, Inanna (associated with the planet Venus). Taurus contains some of the most prominent stars in the sky, as well as some of the most interesting astronomical features – including the Crab Nebula (see pp.30–31), a supernova (the gaseous remnant of an exploded star). This was first noticed in 1054 and was named in the mid-19th century by Lord Rosse, who decided that its extended filaments resembled a crab's pincers. The first asteroid ever to be sighted was Ceres, discovered in Taurus on New Year's Day 1801 by the Italian astronomer Giuseppe Piazzi.

> 'Taurus is an Earthly, Cold, Dry, Melancholy, Feminine, Nocturnal, Fixed, Domestical or Bestial Sign, of the Earthly Triplicity, and South, the Night-house of Venus.'
>
> English astrologer William Lilly, 1647

Taurus contains another significant group of stars, the Pleiades (known as M45 to modern astronomers), which were once classed as an entirely separate constellation. The Babylonians were intrigued by the Pleiades more than 4,000 years ago; the fact that there are seven stars in the group probably gave them added importance, seeming to connect them to the seven planets and the seven days of the week.

The most famous star in Taurus is Aldebaran (the bull's eye), which rose with the Sun at the spring equinox c.3000BC; tradition records that it became one of the four 'royal' stars of Persia. Classical astrology recorded that it was one of the most propitious stars, signifying

RIGHT **The Bull is one of the zodiac's most powerful images. The Bull was seen as a terrifying creature, as in the Babylonian Bull of Heaven, but one that could be overcome, as in Minoan bull-leaping.**

honour, intelligence, eloquence, loyalty, integrity, popularity and courage – exactly the qualities looked for in a wise monarch. Aldebaran is about 65 light-years away from the Earth, which means that the light it sends out now will not reach us until the second half of the 21st century. The star is moving away from the Earth at about 48 kilometres (30 miles) per second.

The two other notable stars in Taurus are El Nath, which is situated on the tip of the northern horn, and in classical astrology was considered fortunate, and Alcyone, the brightest of the Pleiades, associated with love and blindness.

Taurus also contains another distinct group of stars, the Hyades, which were among the few stellar objects mentioned by the 8th-century BC Greek poet Homer. Classical astronomers included between three and seven stars in this group, but modern telescopes reveal several hundred. In Greek myth they were the daughters of Atlas and Aethra, and half-sisters of the Pleiades. Their main use was in weather forecasting, when their rising with the Sun supposedly indicated rain.

Perhaps the most interesting star in Taurus, about 450 light-years away, is HH30. It was only seen as a blur until the 1990s, when it was photographed by the Hubble Space Telescope, but now we know it is blasting a jet of material into the air at hundreds of kilometres per second. The jet contains blobs that are thought to be stars or even planets in the process of formation. For the first time we may be witness to a solar system being born.

CENTRE **The Crab Nebula, a supernova, the most distinctive astronomical feature in the constellation Taurus.**
RIGHT **The Pleiades, once one of the most important constellations, is now a part of Taurus. Its seven stars are sometimes known as the Seven Sisters.**

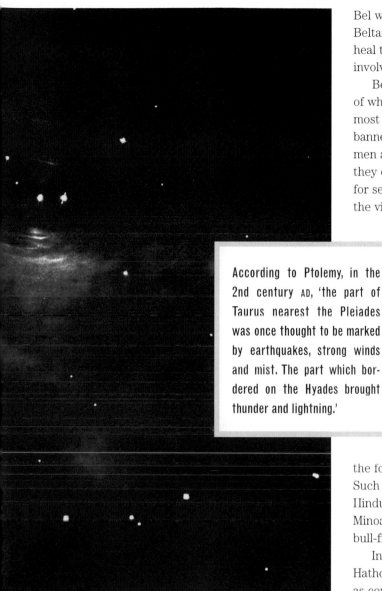

Bel was a fire-god, worshipped by the Druids, and Beltane was a fire-purification festival, designed to heal the ills of winter. One of the main Celtic rituals involved driving livestock between two fires.

Better known are the fertility rituals of May Day, of which dancing around a maypole is perhaps the most famous. In 17th-century Britain the Puritans banned the May Day festivities, alleging that young men and women spent too long in the woods, where they engaged in 'pleasant pastimes' – a euphemism for sex. The tradition of crowning the fairest maid of the village as Queen of the May survives in modern beauty pageants, the original calendar significance long forgotten. In 1889 May Day was designated a socialist festival (Labour Day), and in the 20th century the parades in the Soviet Union and other Communist countries provided some of the most spectacular political theatre the modern world has seen.

According to Ptolemy, in the 2nd century AD, 'the part of Taurus nearest the Pleiades was once thought to be marked by earthquakes, strong winds and mist. The part which bordered on the Hyades brought thunder and lightning.'

THE COW MOTHER

Taurus is one of the earliest and most important constellations. The Sun rose in Taurus, marking the spring equinox, from c.4000 to c.2000BC, and bulls were the focus of much early myth and religious ritual. Such reverence for the bull survives now only in Hinduism, which holds cows sacred, while ancient Minoan bull leaping may be the origin of modern bull-fighting.

In Egypt the goddesses Nut (see p.185) and Hathor (see p.120) were both sometimes portrayed as cows. Statues of Hathor, the better-known goddess, present her as a woman (sometimes with a cow's head) with cow's horns holding the disc of the Sun between them. Although sometimes described as the daughter of the Sun god Ra and wife of Horus, the solar falcon, she is also Horus' mother; her name can be translated as 'dwelling of Horus'. It was believed that every evening at dusk the Sun was enclosed in her breast, to be reborn every morning.

The Greeks identified Hathor with Aphrodite, the goddess of love, and hence with the planet

MAY DAY

May Day, the springtime festival of 1 May, was originally Beltane, an ancient Celtic festival held between the spring equinox and summer solstice. We know from the astronomical alignments of certain megalithic sites in Britain that the festival was observed as early as c.3000BC. The name may be related to 'Baal', the Phoenician or Canaanite word for god (literally 'lord'), as well as to 'Bel', one of the Babylonian names for Jupiter. To the Celts,

Venus, which they believed 'ruled' Taurus. Hathor was the protector of women and enjoyed immense popularity as the goddess of joy and love. Every year before dawn on New Year's Day, Hathor's birthday, the priests at her main sanctuary at Dendera carried her statue out to be bathed in the rays of the rising sun. This began a day of carnival, ending in intoxication in honour of the goddess.

FATHER BULL

Bull myths were common in the ancient world. The 'Bull of Heaven' first appears in the Babylonian epic of Gilgamesh, dating to before *c*.2000BC when the Sun rose at the spring equinox in the constellation Taurus. The epic tells of the legendary king Gilgamesh, whose feats may be seen to mirror the Sun's journey through the year. Gilgamesh is himself repeatedly described as a bull; he is violent, impulsive, lustful and strong. The epic also relates how Ishtar sends the Bull of Heaven to kill Gilgamesh, but he and his companion Enkidu instead kill it.

The central bull-cult of the Roman Empire was Mithraism. Mithras himself was a solar hero who

The goddess Hathor placing the magic collar on the pharaoh Seti I, a painted limestone relief from Seti I's tomb (*c.*1300BC) in the Valley of the Kings, Egypt.

A Roman mosaic depicting Europa's abduction by Zeus (the bull), from the 1st-century AD Roman villa at Lullingstone in Kent, England.

In some versions Europa is the daughter of Phoenix, a solar symbol. If she is the daughter of the Sun, the myth becomes an allegory for the Sun's domination by the Bull during his passage through Taurus. It also reverses the story in the Babylonian epic of Gilgamesh, in which the goddess Ishtar uses the Bull as an instrument of her vengeance. In the Greek version, the maiden is on the receiving end of sexual violence, so that Taurus becomes the archetype of the aggressor rather then the victim.

THE BEAST WITHIN

In the Greek myth of the Minotaur, King Minos promised a white bull to the god Poseidon, but was persuaded by greed to keep the animal. Poseidon punished him by causing Pasiphaë, wife of Minos, to be filled with desire for the bull. She copulated with it and gave birth to the Minotaur – half man, half bull, whose hunger was only satisfied by human flesh. The Minotaur's human nature is driven by the 'beast within'.

Desires of the flesh are a strong feature of the Taurean temperament. But sensuality does not have to emerge in lust and appetite; the sign also has an affinity with beauty and a talent for creating beautiful objects.

had been important in Persian religion. In the Roman Empire, his cult became a sophisticated zodiac religion in which the passage of time was the central focus of the sacred rites, an essential part of the soul's salvation. Members of the cult passed through a series of initiations, focusing first on the Moon and then on each of the planets. The cult also involved bull-sacrifice and worship of Mithras as bull-slayer. Sacrifice of the sacred bull was meant to ensure the fertility of the universe; full initiation into the cult was meant to ensure the immortality of the individual.

THE RAPE OF EUROPA

Zeus, the supreme god of the Greeks, also appeared as a bull. The story relates how Europa, the beautiful daughter of Agenor, King of Phoenicia, was gathering flowers at the water's edge. Zeus, seized with desire for the maiden, transformed himself into a bull and concealed himself amongst Agenor's herd, which was grazing nearby. Struck by the bull's beauty, Europa began to caress him. When he knelt at her feet Europa sat on his back. The bull sprang up and carried Europa over the sea to Crete, where he raped her.

THE ASTROLOGICAL TAURUS

Taurus is the second sign of the zodiac, and the Sun passes through it at the time when in the northern hemisphere spring is establishing itself. The life that started with Aries is now being consolidated. In terms of the development of human consciousness, if Aries is the egotism of the infant as yet undifferentiated from its world, Taurus is the infant whose self-awareness has awakened to possessions and ownership: the 'mine' phase. It is associated in astrology with the second house, which rules money, possessions and evaluation.

Taurus is a 'feminine' sign, and more introverted than extroverted. It is also a fixed earth sign, ruled by Venus. Fixed signs take up where cardinal signs leave off; their special forte is getting things firmly established and keeping them that way – preservation rather than initiation. Hence Taurus is rather slow to enter into any project, through a combination of caution, inertia and a simple lack of initiative, but equally slow to abandon it. Taureans hate changes in the status quo, and if change is inevitable, they prefer other signs to make the first move.

Taurus is practical, well-rooted and materialistic though not necessarily greedy, concerned with stability, security and values, more at home in the tangible world of the senses than in the nebulous realm of ideas.

'Is not thilke the mery moneth of May,
When love lads masken in fresh aray?
…Youghtes folk now flocken in everywhere,
To gather may baskets and smelling brere.'

'May' from Edmund Spenser's *The Shepheardes Calendar*, 1579.
Spring should be a time of love and merrymaking.

A 16th-century Turkish manuscript depicting Taurus. The figure on the cow may be Venus, Taurus' ruler; in the centre below is the Moon, exalted in Taurus.

Ancient astrologers believed that Aries and Taurus did not get on because they were next to each other; the 1st-century AD Roman poet Manilius wrote that 'sympathy between them is blunted because the sight of each other is denied them'.

RELATING

Taurean people, it is said, like to know what is theirs by right – what they can rely on – and hang on to it with great tenacity. Not for them the 'open marriage'. They are sensual, which can make them great lovers (and also big eaters!), though often sexually conservative; but they are also possessive.

Taurus is one of two signs ruled by Venus. The other, air sign Libra, is more intellectual and rationalistic, but both are especially concerned with harmony. Venus is the goddess of love and beauty. It follows that true Taureans work hard to preserve peace and harmony in a relationship. And, as an earth sign, they are particularly sympathetic to their partners' physical needs, making sure that they eat well, wrap up warm in winter, and get enough sex.

Taureans tend to be reliable and long-suffering in a relation-

'Shall we set about some revels? What shall we do else? Were we not born under Taurus?'

Shakespeare, *Twelfth Night*, c.1601

ship. They are usually patient and slow to anger. However, like the Bull of Heaven, the normally placid Taurus will eventually turn to anger if goaded for long enough.

Taureans can be reliable friends, perhaps not always financially generous – because they are too worried about their own material security – but willing to help out in practical ways. They tend to stay in touch with old friends for years, if not for life, even if in many ways their interests and circumstances have diverged. Some Taureans find themselves exploited by less reliable friends, either financially or emotionally.

THE SHADOW

Taurus' strongest quality is its stability. Jung classified it under the 'sensation' type and the sign is at home in the realm of the senses. It survives emotional storms, intellectual whirlwinds and physical danger. Yet stability can give way to extreme obstinacy, and this often emerges in the form of rigid ideas and fixed notions regarding what should be done, or about the way the world works. When the Taurean shadow emerges it is utterly and totally incapable of change, no matter what the consequences may be.

IN THE WORLD

As a worker the typical Taurean is dependable, persistent, patient, practical, sensible, realistic and cautious – qualities that stem from the sign's fixed-earth nature. However, Venus introduces artistic flair to complement these solid virtues. Taurus on its own does not tend to produce original artistic genius, but it does bring appreciation of form, an awareness of harmony in colour and in music, and general good taste – without which originality is likely to express itself as mere revolt or eccentricity. Taureans may therefore find themselves particularly at home in the arts, in design or in fashion.

Traditionally Taurus is also connected with all types of occupation involving money and property, such as banking and stockbroking; indeed, in Stock Exchange parlance, a 'bull' is someone who buys at a lower price, hoping to sell at a much higher price later. Bull markets are those in which prices rise rapidly, offering the shrewd investor the chance of making substantial profits.

'If Taurus is in the ascendant one should do things pertaining to cows, ploughing, property, treasure, games, friends, women, beds and acquisitions.'

Indian astrologer Sphujidhvaja, c.AD270

GEMINI

The Sun enters the tropical zodiac sign of Gemini around 22 May and leaves around 21 June. Gemini is ruled by Mercury. In classical astronomy Jupiter is considered to be debilitated (weak) in this sign. It is a hot, moist, masculine, mutable sign and a member of the air element. Its colour is white, sometimes mixed with red, and its guardian angel is Ambriel. It is symbolized by the Twins.

The Babylonians knew Gemini as Mastabba.galgal, meaning 'great twins'. The corresponding Chinese months are Hsiao Man ('grain fills') and Mang Chung ('grain in ear'). The Greek name was Didumoi ('twins') while in India it is known as Mithuna ('couple' or 'boy and girl'). Australian Aborigines called it the Young Men, while South African San (Bushmen) know it as the Young Women.

According to one version, June was named in honour of the Juniores, the junior branch of the Roman legislature, although the poet Ovid claimed it was the month of Juno, wife of Jupiter and the queen of the gods.

THE STARS OF GEMINI

The constellation Gemini contains 47 visible stars, although some astronomers have counted more than 100. The most notable are Castor and Pollux, marking the heads of the twins. Castor is not actually a star at all, but a system of three double stars (six in all), held together by their common gravitational pull. Pollux is an 'orange giant' 35 light-years from Earth.

'The arms of the Twins are forever locked in mutual embrace. One of the twin brothers imparts blossom and springtime, so the other brings on thirsting summer. Both are unclad. One feels the heat of ageing spring, the other of approaching summer.'

Roman poet Manilius, *Astronomica*, 1st century AD

ABOVE **The Twins, illustrating May, from the Bedford Book of Hours (*c.*1423).**
RIGHT **Gemini is represented by pairs of twins, sometimes seen as compatible, sometimes as opposites.**

Gemini is an 'aerial, hot moyst, sanguine, Diurnal, common or double-bodied humain Signe; the diurnall house of Mercury; of the aery triplicity, Westerne, Masculine'.

English astrologer William Lilly, 1647

Leda and the Swan by Cesare da Sesto (1477–1523). From the two eggs at the feet of Leda and Zeus (the swan) have hatched two pairs of twins, Pollux and Helen, and Castor and Clytemnestra.

In Greek myth, the twins Castor and Polydeuces (more commonly known by his Roman name, Pollux) were traditionally the sons of Zeus and Leda and the brothers of Helen of Troy and Clytemnestra, and were born after Leda's rape by Zeus in the form of a swan. Pollux was the son of Zeus, and therefore immortal, but Castor was the son of Leda's husband. Castor was a famed horseman and warrior who taught Heracles to fence; Pollux was a champion boxer. The twins joined Jason and the Argonauts in search of the Golden Fleece (see pp.24–5). Jason was a solar hero and the twins represented the Geminian element in the quest for the Arien fleece.

The Greek astronomer Ptolemy considered that Castor had a Mercurial nature, and concluded that it signified a sharp mind. He also linked Castor to Apollo and Pollux to Heracles, two of the sons of Zeus.

Biblical writers described the twins as the sons of Rebecca, Esau and Jacob, whose story is related in the book of Genesis; or as David and Jonathan, who may not have been brothers but were inseparable friends; or even as Adam and Eve. Other cultures portrayed them as animals – a pair of peacocks in Persia – or, in Egypt, two sprouting plants.

One other Geminian star, Propus, was used in astrology, and was said to share the natures of Mercury and Venus and to confer good fortune, although it was never as influen-

---

The poet Dante was born on 14 May 1265 with the Sun in Gemini. He acknowledged the sign gratefully in his *Paradiso*:

'O stars of glory, from whose light on high
A mighty virtue poureth forth, to you
I owe such genius as doth in me lie ...'

---

tial as Castor and Pollux.

The southern part of the constellation lies in the Milky Way, while the boundary of the zodiac itself runs between Castor and Pollux. Gemini was the site of two of the most important modern astronomical discoveries: in 1781 William Herschel discovered Uranus not far from Propus, and in 1930 Clyde Tombaugh discovered Pluto in the constellation.

THE CELESTIAL TWINS

A number of the most important ancient myths feature sets of twins as the most convenient means of representing opposing possibilities. Sometimes one is female and the other male; for example, the Adam and Eve tale is a variation on the twins theme. Frequently one is good, the other wicked. In many cases one is responsible for the death of the other. Twins myths frequently tell stories concerning the primeval split in the universe, the rupture between earth and heaven, or water and earth, which usually occurs during the earliest stages of the creation.

In cases where one twin was

demonized, the rivalry between the two frequently became a perpetual battle between good and evil. In the Sumerian creation myth the god Apsu, the primordial sweet water, and Tiamat, his female salt-water counterpart, were originally lovers; their offspring were the gods. One of their sons, Ea, slew Apsu, causing Tiamat to attack him and the younger gods with a horde of monsters. Tiamat was eventually killed by Marduk; her body was split in half, the two pieces forming the sky and the earth. By the time of the first Babylonian empire, c.1800BC, Tiamat had become a demon of chaos and destruction.

The ancient Persians believed that the history of the universe was shaped by the struggle between Ahriman, the god of darkness, and Ahura Mazda, the god of light. Egyptian mythology was dominated by the daily battle between the Sun and the forces of the underworld. In the Christian world the rivals became God and Satan or Christ and Antichrist.

'Geminians are thoughtful and intelligent in all things, especially in the search for wisdom and religion.'

Ptolemy, *Tetrabiblos*, 2nd century AD

The biblical twins Cain and Abel, from a stained glass window in a church at St Neots, Cornwall, England. The tale in which Cain kills Abel is one of the classic twins myths in Western culture.

All such myths have a common feature; the eventual triumph of the forces of good, light and order, representing the healing of the catastrophic split at the creation. Karl Marx believed that they described the alienation of humanity from the natural environment, and a central feature of the Communist revolution was to be a reconciliation between humanity and nature.

Modern psychologists take a different line, and argue that the opposing forces represent the archaic split between consciousness and unconsciousness which occurred at the dawn of civilization. Some see the forces of cosmic darkness and chaos as representing the 'other' or the 'shadow', those aspects of our personalities that we find unacceptable and repress. Carl Jung argued that the more we bury these characteristics, the deeper they bury themselves in the unconscious. Eventually they erupt in an uncontrolled manner.

The two classic twins myths in Western culture are the stories of Cain and Abel (the sons of Adam and Eve) and of Romulus and Remus, the legendary founders of Rome. In each case one twin slew the other – Cain killed Abel and Romulus killed Remus. The murderer's punishment is to survive, living with the guilt of his crime. Neither myth offers a solution, only a comment on the alienation of humanity from its 'other'.

In Indian astrology, the heavenly twins of Gemini become the Mithuna, or divine male–female couple:

'Third is the Couple, holding a vina [a stringed instrument] and a club, the region of the shoulders and arms of the Lord of Creatures. Its domains are dancing and singing, craftsmen, the sports of women, love's pleasures, and gambling.'

Indian astrologer Minaraja, 4th century AD

THE ASTROLOGICAL GEMINI

Traditionally, Gemini's character was seen in the seasons. In the northern hemisphere in May and June, life and movement return to nature, before the onset of full summer. In human development, Gemini represents the phase where the child becomes mobile and begins to investigate the world with intense curiosity.

Carl Jung defined Gemini as one of the 'thinking' signs. By this he meant that it embodies the principle of logical thought. It probes, inquires, looks at the facts and comes to rational conclusions.

Gemini's ruler is Mercury, messenger of the gods, and Gemini is associated very much with the gathering and dissemination of information – anything from the most inconsequential gossip to the most erudite treatise. The typical Gemini is said to use words with great ability, whether persuading, cajoling or entertaining.

As a 'masculine' sign, Gemini is relatively outgoing. In research in the 1970s, the psychologist Hans Eysenck (1916–92) included it as one of the 'extroverted' signs – those that interact actively with their environment. First impressions may be different, especially in the case of those Geminians who love nothing better than to be left alone with their thoughts or with a good book. Its mutability makes it

This terracotta carving from Kausambi, India, dating from the 2nd century BC, portrays the Geminian twins as lovers – known in Indian astrology as the Mithuna, or divine male–female couple (see also box opposite).

adaptable and versatile, and difficult to pin down – like quicksilver; also typical of a mutable sign, it is changeable, restless and not renowned for staying-power.

Gemini's wonderful flexibility and curiosity helps to prevent mental ageing and to retain a thirst for knowledge, a desire to communicate and a readiness to embrace change. This youthfulness, and the wisdom that can come to Gemini with age, are both represented in the Indian tale of the Ashvins (see box).

RELATING

Although there is debate about the precise nature of Gemini's approach to relating, it is agreed that Gemini people are initially attracted to a partner's mind. They relish verbal exchange and move progressively from light banter to deep discussions on the meaning of life. Gemini is often flirtatious but rather unemotional, and has a boredom threshold so low as to be almost non-existent. Gemini often plays the impartial observer, endlessly fascinated by how people work, yet frequently unwilling to express personal emotions.

> 'If Gemini is in the ascendant one should do things pertaining to sons, one's wife, money, the traditions, the crafts, advice, affection, and fine arts such as singing.'
>
> Indian astrologer Sphujidhvaja,
> c.AD270

THE ASHVINS AND CYAVANA

According to Hindu myth, once there was a beautiful young woman called Sukanya who was given in marriage to the sage Cyavana, whose great wisdom was equalled only by his age and ugliness. The divine twins the Ashvins thought that Sukanya ought to be married to one of them, not to an ugly old man, but she refused to leave her husband. However, the twins offered to make Cyavana as youthful and good-looking as them if she would then choose a husband from among the three of them.

Cyavana bathed in a lake with the twins, after which he looked exactly like them. Even so, Sukanya managed to choose him as her husband, and the grateful Cyavana repaid the twins by persuading the great god Indra to grant them full status as gods.

The Gemini approach to sex is similarly often one of enthusiastic though rather detached curiosity. There may be a lot of interested sexual experimentation, and in the past the sign has sometimes been associated with bisexuality. A typical Gemini is quite capable of enjoying sex without any particular depth of feeling. Or if there is feeling, it may be swiftly transferred when something more interesting comes along. Geminis may be more concerned with how they can get away with an extramarital affair than with whether the affair is a good idea in the first place.

It may seem that Geminis are captivating but rather lightweight – sexual butterflies flitting from one flower to the next. While there may often be an element of truth in this, there can be a deeper or at least more complex side to Gemini as well.

THE SHADOW

Gemini rationalizes its emotions, finding convenient excuses and explanations for everything, often misleading itself and others in the process. If Geminians have one task it is to face up to their feelings, to their desires, needs, jealousies, fears, longings and passions, rather than projecting them on to others. The shadow Gemini is the mad scientist, so obsessed with reason and logic that he or she is incapable of seeing the moral or social consequences of his or her actions.

IN THE WORLD

Not all Geminis are super-intelligent communicators. However, their curiosity and the ease with which they handle facts and figures gives them special skills. Gemini is likely to be most at home in an occupation involving variety, contact with people, and the handling of information.

The Great Fire of London by Philippe de Louthebourg (1799). Myth recounts that London was founded by the twin giants Gog and Magog, and medieval astronomers held the city special to Gemini. In the 17th century, astrologers worked out that London was founded with the Sun at 25 degrees Gemini, using a system that surveyed planetary positions at the times of past plagues and fires. Using the same system, William Lilly is said to have forecast the Great Fire of 1666 – he was even investigated under suspicion of having started the fire.

Gemini's willingness to experiment and adapt accordingly, and to respond to new circumstances and information, is a huge asset in many occupations, especially transport, teaching, advertising, the media and medicine. Geminis are society's brain-workers, its writers, thinkers, clerks and professors.

Some ancient astrologers thought that northern Greece and India were ruled by Gemini. Manilius wrote that 'you brothers, does Thrace worship and farthest Ganges which waters the fields of India'. Some thought that Egypt was Geminian; the unity of 'upper' and 'lower' Egypt reminded them of the bond between the twins. By the 17th century, Wales was also thought to be under Gemini; comparisons were made between Gemini's rulership of the throat and Wales' reputation as the home of preachers and poets. By the early 19th century, North American astrologers added the USA to the list. Joan Quigley, Ronald Reagan's astrologer, used a chart with Gemini rising to offer advice on American policy during the president's meetings with Soviet leader Mikhail Gorbachev.

CANCER

The Sun enters the tropical zodiac sign of Cancer around 21 June and leaves around 22 July. Its entry marks the summer solstice, the longest day in the northern hemisphere, after which the days begin to grow shorter. In the southern hemisphere it marks the winter solstice and the shortest day. Cancer is ruled by the Moon. Jupiter is exalted (strong) in Cancer; Mars and Saturn are debilitated (weak). Its colours are green and russet and its guardian angel is Muriel. It is a cold, wet, cardinal, feminine sign, a member of the water element, and its symbol is the Crab.

THE STARS OF CANCER

As the ruler of midsummer, Cancer had an importance in the ancient world which belied its lack of bright stars. The constellation contains about 23 visible stars, but the most interesting object is not a star at all. This is M44, known as the Praesepe or the Beehive cluster. The first astronomer to distinguish individual stars in M44 was Galileo (1564–1642), who wrote about them in his great work *Sidereus Nuncius*.

The tropic of Cancer, marking the northern limit of the Tropics, falls at latitude 23 degrees north, passing through Mexico, the

Cancer was known as Al'lul (the Crab) to the Sumerians before *c*.2000BC and as Alluttu by the Babylonians after *c*.1800BC. The constellation was widely known; in West Africa the Hausa knew it by their name for crab, Kaduwa. The constellation had a particular importance in Egypt, where it signified the annual flooding of the Nile. In China it corresponds to the months Hsia Chih ('summer solstice') and Hsiao Shu ('slight heat'), and in India it is known by the Sanskrit word for crab, Kataka.

July, Cancer's month, was originally Quintilis, the thirty-day fifth month of the Roman calendar. Julius Caesar had a special regard for it as the month of his birth and added an extra day, making 31; after his untimely death the month was renamed July in Caesar's honour. The Anglo-Saxons knew July as Hey-monath – the month when hay was harvested.

Cancer 'is the only house of the Moon, and is the first Signe of the Watry, or Northerne Triplicity, is watry, Cold, Moyst, Flegmatick, Feminine, Nocturnal, Moveable, a Solstice Signe, mute and slow of Voyce, Fruitful, Northerne.'

English astrologer William Lilly, 1647

RIGHT **The Crab is the central Cancerian image. Here it is accompanied by the Moon, its planetary ruler, the stars of the constellation and the fires of the midsummer celebrations.**

'And now the Sonne hath reared up his fyrie footed teme,
making his way betweene the Cuppe, and golden Diademe,
The rampant Lyon hunts he fast,
with Dogge of noysome breath,
Whose balefuyll barking brings in hast
pyne, plages and dreery death.'

'July', from Edmund Spenser's *The Shepheardes Calendar*, 1579.
The Sun moves from Cancer into Leo, the Lion, in July, and the rising of the
Dog Star, Sirius, in Canis Major, initiates the 'dog days'.

Sahara, northern India and southern China. This is the latitude at which the Sun is directly overhead at noon on 21 June, marking the start of summer in the northern hemisphere.

In ancient Babylon, for the two months before the solstice and the two months after, the Sun passed through the Way of Enlil – the domain of heaven conceived as special to Enlil, god of the wind. Enlil was one of the great creator gods, but when he sent powerful winds he was also a god of destruction, swooping from the sky to punish humanity.

July's stifling heat led the Romans to worry that midsummer warmth could produce not only disease but also a wider social malaise, a corruption in the body politic. They identified the hottest period as that during which Sirius, the Dog Star, in the constellation Canis Major, the Greater Dog, rose over the eastern horizon before dawn. This period, between 3 July and 11 August, came to be known by the term 'dog days'.

THE BEGINNING AND THE END

Cancer was often known as 'the birthday of the world', in a tradition that has its roots in the astral mysticism of Egypt in the centuries before Christ. It was believed that when the world was created the Moon, Mother of All, was in Cancer. But what gives life can also take it away.

In *c*.280BC Berossus, a priest of Bel (associated with the god and planet Jupiter) moved to the Aegean island of Cos to teach ancient Babylonian wisdom to the Greeks. He took with him a prophecy that when the Sun, Moon, Mercury, Venus, Mars, Jupiter and Saturn all met in Cancer the world would be destroyed by fire. The Romans were influenced by this forecast, and the belief was propagated by some of their greatest writers, including Pliny the Elder in the 1st century AD. When the first Christians predicted that Jesus would return in fiery splendour they found a receptive audience.

THE MIDSUMMER FESTIVAL

Since time immemorial the summer solstice has been one of the great fire festivals, an excuse for midsummer madness. Midsummer's Day was celebrated on 24 June, and on Midsummer Eve (the previous day) bonfires were lit across Europe. Shakespeare's comedy *A Midsummer Night's Dream*, a tale of magic, sorcery and confusion, is a fantasy in which Titania, the queen of the fairies, falls in love with Bottom, a man with the head of an ass – a story taken from festivities that would have been familiar in the 17th century. The ancient tradition of midsummer well-dressing, in which the village well is decorated with flowers and greenery, survives today in some country areas such as the Peak District in England.

As it did with many pagan festivals, the Church took over some of these ancient practices, and Midsummer's Day is also the feast of St John the Baptist, a time for healing rituals, religious devotion and cleansing, a preparation for the autumn. In 1876 an

'The fourth, Karkin, known as the chest area, has the form of a Crab resting in water. It dwells in flooded fields, reservoirs and sandbanks and the resorts of the celestial women.'

Indian astrologer Minaraja,
4th century AD

old woman in Ireland recalled how as a child she had been taken to the local well on Midsummer Eve to be cured of whooping cough. She wrote: 'I shall never forget the spectacle of men and women, creeping on their knees, in voluntary devotion, or in obedience to enjoined penance, so many times round the well.'

In Spain, the eve of the nativity of St John (23 June) is celebrated with hilltop fires, dancing and religious parades. In the town of San Pedro Manrique people walk barefoot across red-hot ashes, often carrying a child on their back. In the town of Corpino the statue of Our Lady of Corpino is carried around the church, shedding her healing powers on the heads of kneeling believers. Such ritual acts, whether pious or riotous, enable entire communities to make a mental and emotional break with the past, setting their sights on the future.

This painting, by Henry Fuseli (1741–1825) depicts the awakening of the fairy queen Titania, surrounded by her attendant fairies. Fuseli was inspired by Shakespeare's *A Midsummer Night's Dream*, the greatest dramatization of midsummer madness.

THE GREAT MOTHER

Classical astronomers designated Cancer a feminine sign. Counter to most tradition, they defined its ruling planet, the Moon, as female. Added to their classification of Cancer as a water sign, this gives the complete Cancerian personality: sensitive, nurturing, emotional, delicate, artistic and compassionate.

In traditional astrology Cancer and Leo occupy special positions in the zodiac since they do not share their ruler with another sign, as do the other signs. Leo is the sign of the Sun, the celestial Father, and Cancer that of the Moon, the cosmic Mother. Cancer, then, is the supreme representative of the Cancerian principle, the perfect foil to its neighbour, Leo.

Through the Moon, Cancer is associated with the archetype of the Mother, and Cancers of either gender are said to be very caring and nurturing. In Western society such qualities have traditionally been considered to be desirable in women, but taboo for men. However, times have changed, and the typical Cancerian male may be the modern 'new man' – displaying qualities, such as emotional sensitivity, that are conventionally associated with women.

Cancer, from the temple of Hathor at Dendera, Egypt (*c.*1st century BC–1st century AD). The Crab is surrounded by its neighbouring constellations, including the Geminian twins.

THE ASTROLOGICAL CANCER

A well-known characteristic of the crab is its sideways scuttle. This is reflected in Cancers by their tendency to approach things in a roundabout, circumspect way. As a cardinal sign, Cancer takes the initiative – but with caution, even with extreme anxiety. Yet a well-developed imagination encourages artistic endeavour, and enables the more aware Cancer to empathize with others.

It is said that Cancerian people tend to have good memories and to be interested in history, or at least in tradition. According to most astrologers, Cancer is the most family-oriented and clannish sign of the zodiac. This is why, by the 17th century, English astrologers had agreed that Scotland, with its system of family clans, was a Cancerian country.

Such an attachment to the past has a number of consequences. Cancers may find it hard to uproot themselves from familiar circumstances. They may be sentimental about the past, too, and find it hard to let go of it. They are sometimes unwilling to let go of old possessions, being great hoarders of pots, jars, old clothes, and general bits and pieces that others would throw out, as well as items of sentimental value, such as children's toys when the children have grown up. The simple lesson is that all things must pass.

THE SECOND ROME
One of the greatest events to take place under Cancer was the foundation of Constantinople by the Roman emperor Constantine in AD326. Although he was the first Christian emperor, Constantine continued with the traditional use of astrology to probe into the mind of God and the nature of time, and ordered his astrologers to choose the time for the city's inauguration, which they did 'at the hour of the Crab', when Cancer was rising over the eastern horizon, on 26 November 326. The city became the capital of the Eastern Roman (Byzantine) Empire, which lasted until 1453.

The Founding of Constantinople, a tapestry from the 17th-century 'History of Emperor Constantine' series made by the Raphael de la Planche Factory, Paris. The tapestry portrays the Roman emperor Constantine consulting his astrologer.

'If Cancer is in the ascendant one should do things pertaining to gems, ornaments, water, women, fields, beds and all sorts of flowers.'

Indian astrologer Sphujidhvaja, *c.*AD270

Cancer, from a 16th-century Turkish manuscript. The character in the bottom left-hand corner is the Moon, Cancer's ruling planet. Cancer is the only one of the twelve signs to be ruled by the Moon, and as such has a profound association with the archetype of the cosmic Mother.

Cancers like the security of home and family, and some only really come out of their shell in the family setting. The sensitive, deeply emotional Crab hides its true nature inside a defensive shell, except with family or friends it can truly trust.

They are also reputed to have retentive memories – they certainly think they do. Indeed, they do tend to remember family birthdays, as well as just how good a relationship was when it first began. How they love to reminisce! On the other hand, they are quite willing to drag up their version of the past in perfect detail every time there is an argument.

In Jung's system of psychological types Cancer is a 'feeling' sign, living in the world of emotions, swept by waves of hope, fear, desire and love. They can be deeply hurt and carry emotional wounds around for years, never revealing them to other people, even to those to whom they are closest. Cancerian people certainly experience emotions, but often they need to find ways to express them in an appropriate manner.

RELATING

Romantic, idealistic and convinced that love is the ultimate panacea, Cancerians are held back only by their low self-esteem. Similar to the sideways-walking crab, they take two steps forward and one back, reluctant to come out of their shell and expose themselves, prepared to get the ball rolling but in a cautious and roundabout manner.

Such caution has sound reasons. So vulnerable and romantic a sign must protect itself lest its hopes be dashed amidst humiliation and rejection. At their best, Cancerians are sensitive to the needs and feelings of others, especially their partner and other loved ones; at their worst, when hurt, they are too concerned with their own problems to notice anyone else's. The contented Cancer is enormously supportive, but when the Crab feels wronged its pincers snap. The vengeful Cancer strikes deep and never misses.

Cancers are often reliable friends. Slow to build up intimacy and trust, but equally reluctant to forget friends once this has been established, they take their more privileged friends into the bosom of the family.

THE SHADOW

The Cancer is a deeply sensitive and compassionate person, yet when wounded the Crab withdraws into its shell, fearful and anxious, placing security above all else. The shadow Cancer is a cold creature, overly defensive and often sarcastic, carping, critical, quick to blame others and resentful of their success. If the fairy-tale Cancer is the princess or prince who lives happily ever after, the shadow is the old maid, or crusty old man, dried out and devoid of feeling.

IN THE WORLD

Cancer's key asset at work is a combination of caution and enterprise. This can be valuable, for example, in management, although attachment to the past can make the classic Crab slow to embrace new technology and discard outdated practices. On the other hand, Cancers are imaginative, which is valuable in many occupations, and able to empathize – which is useful for anyone dealing with the public, and almost essential in jobs with a counselling or therapeutic component. Healing and the arts are considered special to Cancer.

Matters and persons associated with the Moon, Cancer's ruler:
'All things which abound in moysture, the Sea, Rivers, Study of Histories, Embassayes, Navigations, long Journeys, Water, Fishing; brewing Ale or Beer, boyling of Allum, making Salt, etc. Queens, Empresses, Princesses, Widowes, the Commonalty or vulgar People, who are in continuall motion; Saylors, Footmen, Messengers, Embassadours, Fishermen, Vagabonds, faint hearted people, Watermen, the Mistresse of the house, the Mother.'

English astrologer William Lilly, 1647

LEO

The Sun enters the tropical zodiac sign of Leo around 24 July and leaves around 23 August. Leo is ruled by the Sun, but Saturn is debilitated (weak) in the sign. In traditional astrology it is a hot, dry, fixed, masculine sign and a member of the fire element. Its traditional colours are red and green, its guardian angel is Verchiel and its symbol is the Lion. Above all it is the royal sign, the sign of kings and heroes.

Leo was known as Ur.gul.la (the Lion) to the Babylonians, Leon to the Greeks and Simha (Sanskrit for 'lion') in India. In China it corresponds to the months Ta Shu ('great heat') and Li Ch'iu ('autumn begins'). The Greeks and Romans connected the constellation to the myth of Hercules and the Nemean Lion, and sometimes called it Neameaus, Nemeas Alumnus, Nemeaum Monstrum and even Cleonaeum Sidus after Cleonae, the town where Hercules slew the lion. The Romans also sometimes called it Bacchi Sidus ('star of Bacchus'), after the god of wine and ecstasy, who frequently dressed in a lion's skin and sometimes transformed himself into a lion; or Jovis et Junonis Sidus, after Jove (Jupiter) and Juno, who were the lion's protectors.

> 'If Regulus stands inside the Moon's halo: this year woman will give birth to male children.'
>
> Assyrian astrologer Nabu-Iqisa, *c.*8th century BC

In China some of Leo's stars constituted the Red Bird and, later on, some were the Horse. In the 16th century the Chinese adopted Leo itself, calling it Sza Tzse, while its western half was joined with Leo Minor to become a Yellow Dragon, mounting upward and marked by the line of ten stars from Regulus through the Sickle. The Chinese also considered it one of the Heavenly Chariots.

In the old Roman calendar August was the sixth month, Sextilis. When Julius Caesar reformed the calendar in 45BC, he added one day, making thirty . When Caesar's great-nephew and heir, Octavian, became emperor and changed his name to Augustus, he added another day to Sextilis and called it August in his own honour. Amongst the Celts, the midsummer festival – the feast of Lammas – was celebrated on 9 August.

THE STARS OF LEO

The constellation Leo can be identified from the shape of a lion roughly visible in its brightest stars. Some astronomers have described it as a mouse or a rat, although such creatures scarcely live up to its glorious mythology.

Leo has about 52 visible stars, twelve of which were named by ancient astronomers. Of these, three – Denebola, Zosma and Regulus – were put to use in their astrological work. Regulus was the most notable, and is one of the most important stars in astral mythology. The twenty-first brightest star in the sky, it is in fact a triple star (three stars close together) and is relatively close to the Earth, being only about 84 light-years away. Also known as Cor Leonis, the Lion's Heart, it was one of the four 'royal' stars of the Persians,

RIGHT **The Lion represents royalty and courage. Leo's association with the Sun and all things magnificent derives from before 2000BC when it was the sign the Sun occupied at the summer solstice.**

thanks to the fact that it had marked the summer solstice before c.2000BC.

Ancient astronomers considered that Regulus combined the warlike qualities of Mars with the wisdom of Jupiter, and would forecast great honour for any child born with Regulus rising before dawn. If they saw it prominent in the birth chart of a prince they would predict a glorious reign – as long as it was not overwhelmed by destructive stars. If Regulus was prominent this was a sure sign to a Babylonian astrologer that his predictions should involve the king. Some time around 700BC the astrologer Rasil warned the Assyrian emperor: 'If a planet comes close to Regulus: the son of a king who lives at my border will make a rebellion against his father but will not seize the throne.'

The 13th-century astrologer Guido Bonatus, who was kept in almost permanent employment giving military counsel to the warring towns of northern Italy, advised: 'See whether Cor Leonis be in the Ascendant, this alone signifies that the Native shall be a person of great note and power, too much exalted.'

The other two notable

Leonine stars, Denebola and Zosma, were responsible for the sort of bad fortune that results from arrogance and the abuse of power. Both could be used as warnings against unwise actions by kings. In one Egyptian tradition, the Sun rose near Denebola at the creation, so Leo became the House of the Sun. According to Greek mystics, the Sun was in Leo at the moment of creation – they reasoned that it could be nowhere else, for Leo was the Sun's own sign. They never attempted to work out a date for the creation, since ultimately it was impossible to see into the mind of God. To Egyptian and Greek astrologers this meant that when the Sun was in Leo it was stronger than in any other sign.

The most notable celestial

> 'The Lion on the mountain, the heart area of the Lord of Creatures, they call the fifth. Its domains are forests, crags, caves, woods, mountains and outland places.'
>
> Indian astrologer Minaraja, 4th century AD

Jnfoz leonis fut ftelle. 2/1. vioz. 2 æ magnitudine prima. 2. æ seda. 6. æ ma. g. æ qrta. g. æ g

An Egyptian bas-relief limestone stele showing the lion-headed goddess Sekhmet with the god Heka (c.2nd century BC).

event in Leo is the Leonid meteor shower, which peaks around 17 November, when tens of thousands of meteors enter the atmosphere every hour. However, not every year guarantees a good show, and the Leonids are particularly active every 33 years or so. Magnificent displays were seen in 1799, 1833, 1866 and 1966, and large showers are also due around 2033.

THE CELESTIAL LIONESS

In ancient Egypt the lion was a terrible beast, and it was natural for Sekhmet, the goddess of war and mother of the Sun, to take the form of a woman with the head of a lioness. Sekhmet had a celestial connection with Hathor,

LEFT A medieval English manuscript painting depicting Leo. In the Middle Ages there were moves by the Church to replace the zodiac's classical images with Christian ones, and it was suggested that Leo be renamed 'One of Daniel's lions' after the biblical story of Daniel in the lions' den.

the cow-headed solar–sky goddess (see pp.31–2). Hathor was an embodiment of Taurus, originally the constellation of the spring equinox, while Sekhmet was an embodiment of Leo, the constellation of the summer solstice prior to c.2000BC. Both goddesses were therefore different aspects of the sky, one manifested through the equinox, the other through the solstice. Sekhmet's name, which simply means 'the powerful', is also the title given to Hathor on the occasion when, in the form of a lioness, she hurled herself against the men who had rebelled against Ra, the Sun god.

THE HERO

As a fixed fire sign, the embodiment of royalty, Leo is said to be a preserver of the status quo rather than an initiator or revolutionary. Fixed qualities are reliable, persistent and slow to adapt. Fire is enthusiastic, warm, generous and creative.

In Western astrology both Leo and the Sun represent the active, masculine principle. Witness the heroic nature of solar myths, in which the hero descends into the underworld, conquering darkness, death, or the forces of the unconscious, and returning to the world of light. In addition the lion is associated with heroism.

The myth of Hercules and the Nemean Lion is a standard calendar story representing the triumph of human over animal strength. A similar tale occurs in the Hebrew Scriptures (Old Testament): 'Then Samson went down with his mother and father to Timnah.... And behold a young lion roared against him; and the Spirit of the Lord came mightily upon him, and he tore the lion asunder as one tears a kid.'

Samson puts a riddle to the Philistines: 'Out of the eater came something to eat. Out of the strong came forth something sweet.' Samson's Philistine wife, Delilah, entices the answer from him (out of the lion came forth honey) and betrays him. Samson forgets his loyalty to his people and, above all, to God. Theologically Samson's legend speaks of one individual's struggle, torn between doubt and faith.

The calendar aspects of the tale are reinforced by repeated use of the numbers seven (the week, the planets) and thirty (the month). Samson reveals his secret after a seven-day feast; he tells the riddle to thirty 'companions', promises them thirty linen garments if they guess the answer, and kills thirty men after he is tricked.

The myth has a clear moral, pointing to the weaknesses in Samson's solar-Leonine character. Though physically strong he is complacent and morally weak. At the moment of greatness his fatal flaw is revealed. Samson's human tragedy becomes an analogy for the Sun's annual motion: as soon as it reaches its triumph at midsummer it begins to retreat to midwinter.

As one of his Twelve Labours, Hercules killed the Nemean Lion with his bare hands, thereafter wearing its skin as a trophy and to show that he had taken on its courage and strength. The Hindu god Vishnu in his *nrisimha* (man-lion) incarnation dethrones the demon Hiranyakasipu. Hollywood has taken the hero myth and made it its own. Hercules, shorn of his religious power, has become Superman. In modern myth, rock stars and film stars are Leo-type super-heroes, vanquishing evil or strutting on the stage in return for the adulation of the masses.

The classic Leo is supremely dignified, refusing to do anything demeaning. Leos tend to be open and honest: after all, no true king stoops to deception. However, they can also be proud, and this, when combined with the fixity of the sign, can make them truly stubborn.

Psychologically Leo is an extroverted sign, reaching out to control its environment. In the Jungian system it is one of the 'intuitive' signs, which means that those born under this sign are able to sense possibilities that pass other people by.

Leos are often thought of as bossy, which can indeed be the case. However, this does not stem from a simple desire to get their own way (as in Aries) or a need to control others (as in Capricorn). Rather, it derives from Leo's self-image as a natural ruler who always knows best and should not be contradicted.

Leos love to be appreciated and hate to be ignored. But they are not necessarily vain: they set themselves high standards and need the encouragement that comes from having their successes acknowledged.

LEFT *Samson Slaying the Lion* by Gustave Doré, from his Bible Illustrations (1866). The biblical tale of Samson, like the classical legend of Hercules and the Nemean Lion, functions as a calendar myth (see box opposite).

Medieval astrologers considered that the Leonine Italians, like the Arien British and Germans and the Sagittarian Spanish, were freedom-loving, industrious, manly warriors. They followed Claudius Ptolemy, who wrote that 'they are without passion for women and look down upon the pleasures of love, but are better satisfied with association with men'. Not only did these astrologers not bother to consider the women of those countries, but they were also deeply influenced by the myths of warlike Romans, Celts and German tribes.

THE SHADOW

Leo is the great 'I', the Ego. What Leo wants Leo must have. The Leonine principle must be obeyed. The Leo is on a hero's, or heroine's, quest for the Holy Grail, the symbol of true self-understanding, or at least of a better life. While pride and generosity are the virtues of the warm-hearted Leo, when the self-centredness that is necessary to the mythical heroic quest tips over into petty vanity and selfishness, the Leo makes impossible demands which cannot be fulfilled.

RELATING

In relationships Leos are determined to have only the best and never to put up with a relationship that is in any way second-rate, underhand, secretive or seedy: they would rather be alone.

In spite of their apparent enthusiasm, Leos may sometimes be slow to initiate relationships; they cannot bear the humiliation that might come with making a fool of themselves or being rejected. They are equally slow to give up on a relationship – out of loyalty and commitment, generosity, reluctance to admit having made a mistake, or a simple fear of change. The true Leo remains loyal to old friends, even when their views and lifestyles have drifted apart over the years.

Usually they are sociable people and the typical Leo has many friends. Sometimes they prefer crowds of hangers-on,

Places signified by Leo include 'Woods, Forrests, Rocks, both steep and cragged, Castles, Forts, Parks, and all inaccessible places, also Kings-Pallaces, and in Houses; such places as where fire is, or hath been kept, as Chimneys, Stoves, Furnaces and Ovens'.

Henry Coley, 1676

The Month of August, a 15th-century fresco from Castello de Buonconsiglio, Trento, Italy.

'All as the Sunnye beame so bright,
hey ho the Sunne beame,
Glaunceth from Phoebus face forthright, so love into thy
hart did streame:
Or as the thunder cleaves the clouds, hey ho the Thunder,
Wherein the lightsome levin shroudes,
so cleaves thy soule asunder.'

'August' from Edmund Spenser's
The Shepheardes Calendar, 1579

acquaintances to whom they are not truly close, in spite of appearances. They like to hold court, and hate to be ignored or overlooked. They are very enthusiastic and inventive when it comes to recreation, and often throw good parties. Perhaps the greatest example was Louis XIV, the Sun King, who was born with the Moon in Leo and turned his palace of Versailles into an endless parade of ritual and colour.

It has been said that all of life is a theatrical event to a Leo. When they act ostentatiously it is because they need other people to provide an audience in which they see their own behaviour reflected. Only then can they judge themselves.

Sometimes a relationship is an extension of the Leo's creative urge, and they attempt to mould partners in their image. Or it may be an extension of the desire to perform, so that having a relationship can be a public statement. At best Leos are romantic, playful and passionate; at worst they make demands that cannot be met by a mere mortal.

RIGHT **The Triumph of King Louis XIV of France** by Joseph Werner (1637–1710), from the Palace of Versailles. Louis XIV was born with the Moon in Leo, and was the last French king to consult astrologers.

'If Leo is in the ascendant one should do things pertaining to battles, the use of swords, fire and kings.'

Indian astrologer Sphujidhvaja, *c.*AD270

IN THE WORLD

Clearly, Leonine people's high self-esteem disinclines them toward menial positions of any sort. A Leo in a lowly job might fantasize about promotion, develop delusions of grandeur, or find someone even lower down the scale to dominate.

Leo is traditionally associated with kings and the nobility. Since not everyone can be in these categories, Leos must content themselves with work in which they personally can be king – or queen. The best way for them to do this is to find a role that allows them scope for their creative inspiration. Leo is at home in the world of entertainment – whether promoting, producing, directing or performing, in positions that entail handling big budgets, and in jobs with a certain amount of glamour and exposure to the public eye.

The regal tastes that Leos enjoy make it hard for them to live on a small income. Whereas some signs, such as Capricorn, will put up with distasteful work for the sake of money and prestige, Leos must enjoy their work. Otherwise their lack of enthusiasm will take its toll on their standing with the boss – not to mention on their health.

VIRGO

The Sun enters the tropical zodiac sign of Virgo around 24 August and leaves around 23 September. Virgo is ruled by Mercury. Venus and Jupiter are debilitated (weak) in Virgo. Virgo is a cold, dry, mutable, feminine sign and a member of the earth element. Its colour is black specked with blue, its guardian angel Hamaliel and its symbol the Virgin.

To the Babylonians, Virgo was Ab.sin; this means 'furrow' but may also be translated as 'corn seed', for in the great Babylonian star catalogue, the *Mul Apin*, the astronomers wrote: 'The star Ab.sin is the corn-ear of the goddess Shala.' In Greece, Virgo was Parthenos ('virgin') and in India Kanya (Sanskrit for 'virgin'). In China it corresponds to the months Ch'u Shu ('limit of heat') and Pai Lu ('white dew').

> 'The Fishes and the limbs of the Virgin fly in opposition but cherish the bonds they share, and their bond triumphs over circumstances.'
>
> Roman poet Manilius, *Astronomica*, 1st century

In the Roman calendar, when the year began in March, September was the seventh month, named after the Latin for seven, *septem*. The name has stuck even though it is now the ninth month. The Anglo-Saxons knew it as Gerstmonath, or Barley month; barley was sacred to Virgo and the source of both bread and beer, the staples of the medieval diet.

THE STARS OF VIRGO

Virgo is the second-largest constellation, and includes about 58 visible stars, of which the best known is Spica ('ear of corn'). The Babylonians regarded the star as so important that they named the entire constellation after it (Ab.sin). Spica is the sixteenth-brightest star in the sky, and is about 220 light-years away from the Earth, which means that we are seeing Spica now as it was before the French Revolution (1789).

According to Greek astronomers, Spica combined the nature of the planet Venus with a small dose of Mars. They saw Venus as sweetening Mars' rough

ABOVE **Virgo, from the Bedford Book of Hours (*c.*1423).**
RIGHT **Virgo's mythical origins go back to the Earth goddesses of archaic religion. Connected to Mercury, seen at the top of the picture, Virgo is a sign of wisdom.**

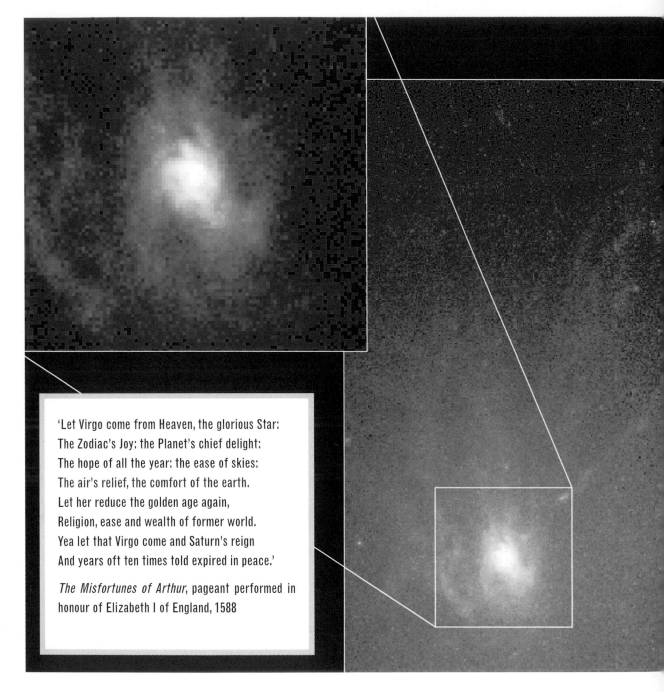

'Let Virgo come from Heaven, the glorious Star:
The Zodiac's Joy; the Planet's chief delight:
The hope of all the year; the ease of skies:
The air's relief, the comfort of the earth.
Let her reduce the golden age again,
Religion, ease and wealth of former world.
Yea let that Virgo come and Saturn's reign
And years oft ten times told expired in peace.'

The Misfortunes of Arthur, pageant performed in honour of Elizabeth I of England, 1588

character and Mars as toughening Venus' gentle nature, with near perfect results. If Spica was rising or culminating (overhead) at birth astronomers forecast 'unbounded good fortune, riches, happiness, ecclesiastical preferment, unexpected honour or advancement beyond one's hopes or capacity'.

Medieval astronomers took it for granted that Spica was a fortunate indication and only if there were thought to be considerable problems arising from other stars would its benefits be denied. The Sun currently occupies the same zodiacal degree as Spica on 14–16 October.

A view of M87, the giant elliptical galaxy in the Virgo cluster, the best known of all galaxy clusters. M87 spews out a glowing jet of material that extends almost 5,000 light-years into space.

The other prominent star in Virgo is Vindemiatrix, a bright yellow star found on the constellation's right wing. In the classical world it was also known as Vindemiator, the Gatherer of the Grapes, and represented Ampelus (Greek, 'vine'), the son of a satyr and a nymph. It is said that Bacchus (Dionysos), as a sign of his affection, gave Ampelus a vine which grew up the trunk of an elm. One day, while gathering grapes, the young man fell and broke his neck. The grieving Bacchus, as a mark of his undying love, placed him in the heavens as the star Vindemiatrix. It was an important calendar star, mentioned by Aratus, court astrologer to the Macedonian king Antigonus II in the 3rd century BC. Its visible rising before the Sun in August marked the beginning of each year's grape harvest. Perhaps Ampelus' fall and death served as a reminder of what might happen to those who drank to excess.

The Greek astronomers thought that Vindemiatrix combined the natures of Mercury and Saturn, planets which when found together would be associated with hermits and scholars. They emphasized the negative qualities of the combination – worry and loss – and if the star featured in an astrological consultation they would advise kings to be cautious and merchants to avoid all risks.

In the north, not far from the boundary with the neighbouring constellation, Coma Berenices, lies an area once known as 'the realm of the nebulae'. The main feature of this area is the Virgo cluster, perhaps the best known of all galaxy clusters. The Virgo cluster includes about 2,500 individual galaxies, including the celebrated 'Sombrero' galaxy, and the enigmatic M87, which appears to be ejecting an enormous jet of material from its nucleus. In terms of intergalactic distances, the Virgo cluster is relatively close to the Earth – only about 50–60 million light years away.

Virgo also includes 3C273, the brightest quasar (starlike source of energy) in the sky and the first whose position was precisely established, in 1963. 3C273 is approximately 3,000 million light-years from the Earth, a distance that grows by the day as it rushes away from us at 16 per cent of the speed of light.

THE GODDESS OF WISDOM

In Greek mythology Virgo is identified with Dike, the goddess of justice and daughter of Zeus and Themis. Dike lived during the first great period of life on Earth, the Golden Age, when disease, violence and unhappiness were unknown, and men and women lived together in perpetual bliss. This was the Greek equivalent of the Garden of Eden. Dike dispensed wisdom and justice, on behalf of Cronos (the Roman Saturn), ruler of the gods, maintaining peace and harmony.

However, central to all myths of a primeval paradise is the idea of the flaw that inevitably triggers decline and collapse. When Cronos was overthrown by his son Zeus, history began to pass through a sequence of ages, each constituting a Great Year, modelled on the Sun's passage through the seasons; history itself had a spring, summer, autumn and winter. Zeus' reign inaugurated the Silver Age, in which humanity became subject to death and disease. This was followed by ages of bronze, of heroes and of iron, each of which was worse than the others. Eventually, unable to bear life amongst humans any longer, Dike spread her wings and withdrew first to the mountains and then to heaven.

Psychologically this myth comes in the class that deals with

the Fall, the alienation of humanity from heaven and its progressive separation from God. The desire to restore this severed connection underpins most of the world's major religions.

Another version of Dike's parentage portrays her as Astraea, the daughter of Astraeus (father of the stars) and Eos (goddess of the dawn). In their longing for the restoration of Dike's golden age the Romans forecast her imminent return; about thirty years before the birth of Christ, the poet Virgil wrote that 'the great line of the centuries begins anew. Now the Virgin returns, the reign of Saturn returns, now a new generation descends from heaven on high.' The Romans were receptive to the Christian notion of the virgin birth and when, in the 5th century, the Church declared Mary's perpetual virginity, it represented an absorption of the ancient classical myth. The Astraea-Virgin myth was particularly popular in the Renaissance, when there was once again the hope that a golden age had returned. Astraea was made a model of the wise monarch, and the English compared her to Elizabeth I, the 'Virgin Queen', exploiting the fact that Elizabeth was born with the Sun in Virgo.

A number of other notable goddesses were linked to Virgo, including the Greek Demeter (the Roman Ceres), whose abduction to the underworld by Hades (Pluto), was an important calendar myth, symbolically documenting the beginning and the end of winter; Tyche, the Greek goddess of fortune; and Atargatis, the Syrian fertility goddess.

Virgo's myths, connected to the universal religious symbolism of the Virgin, often extended beyond the limited confines of the sign or constellation. According to one 16th-century poem:

'Thus, sacred Virgin, Muse of chastitie,
This difference is betwixt the Moone and thee:
Shee shines by Night; but thou by Day do'st shine:
Shee monthly changeth; thou dost nere decline.'

Richard Barnfield, *Cynthia*, 1595

ABOVE **Virgo represented by Ceres, from a zodiacal relief by Agostino di Duccio in the Tempio Malatestiano, Rimini (*c.*1450).**
LEFT **Elizabeth I of England, the 'Virgin Queen', in the so-called 'Armada Portrait'. It is thought that Elizabeth was warned of the Armada by her astrologer John Dee.**

THE WISE VIRGIN

The individual goddesses associated with Virgo were not important in the classical pantheon, yet the constellation's wider mythic connections mark it out as possibly the most important of all. In their broader role Virgoan divinities are related to the mighty Earth goddesses who stood at the centre of Middle Eastern religion before *c.*2000BC, such as the Babylonian Ninhursaga, and the many female characters, human or divine, who copulated with the sky god to conceive the world saviour. The Egyptian Isis, wife of Osiris and mother of Horus, is one such figure. Leto, the mother of Apollo in Greek and Roman myth is another. The greatest representative of this tradition in recent history is Mary, the virgin mother of Christ and queen of heaven in Roman Catholic mythology.

Between *c.*3000BC and the beginning of Christianity, the Mother deity evolved from being the universal fertility goddess and creator of life to the pure Virgin who conceived without sexual contact – still a bringer of life, but strangely removed from the physical world. Originally in Greek a *virgo* was a young woman, not necessarily a virgin, and the word had deeper meanings as 'intact and self-contained'. The word also has the same root as *virago*, heroine or warrior, and the Virgoan approach to the world and to relationships is connected more with self-possession and self-control than with sexual virginity; the Earth Mother embarked on the ultimate heroic task, the creation of life from within herself.

An Egyptian tomb painting showing a departed soul standing before the goddess Isis, with Osiris and Thoth (*c.*2850BC).

THE ASTROLOGICAL VIRGO

The popular conception of Virgo is a person of painstaking, careful, even nit-picking attention to detail, conservatism, shyness, prudery and humble service. However, the conventional view fails to do justice to this complex sign.

Whereas air sign Gemini's curiosity is directed toward information and ideas, Virgo is supremely practical and more interested in how things work – be it gadgets or social systems. And whereas Sagittarian restlessness focuses on distant goals, the Virgoan variety is concerned with perfection.

One very strong feature of the typical Virgo approach to life corresponds closely to an aspect of mentally oriented, fact-finding messenger god Mercury: a remarkable capacity for analysis. Without a gathering of data and a rational assessment of it, there can be no analysis. The Virgo mind gathers information, separates the wheat from the chaff (hence the Virgin's winnowing fan), and sorts it into categories.

RELATING

The question the classic Virgo faces is: are relationships truly necessary? This is why Virgo is said to be critical and choosy. The typical Virgo is not wildly outgoing, but is not necessarily prudish or virginal. However conventional the sign appears at first, Virgo plays by its own rules, finding its own unique path. When considering prospective partners, Virgos carefully weigh up all their assets and failings before making a decision, and emotional considerations are matched with practical. Once a choice has been made their sense of what is right and proper makes for fidelity and a determination to see through the bad times in order to enjoy the good.

Virgo is not averse to playing a supporting role, happy to be of real assistance to a partner, concerned for their health and well-being, and even screening out undesirable characters who might make their loved one unhappy. As a mutable sign, one of Virgo's assets is adaptability, and the typical Virgo is very amenable, rarely so attached to a plan that it cannot be changed.

THE SHADOW

Virgo inhabits the realm of the senses and takes as its priority the careful management of the material world. In this it excels. Yet it has difficulty expressing emotions, seizing the initiative and receiving attention and rewards. Virgo is a perfectionist.

> Virgo is an 'Earthy cold Melancholly, Feminine, Nocturnal, Southern Signe, the House and Exaltation of Mercury'.
>
> English astrologer Henry Coley, 1676

It desires only the best, whereas in the real world it must compromise. To compromise over principles may be unbearable and the pure Virgo will turn his or her back on the world. Although the central theme of the Virgoan life is service, to individuals, to groups and to the world, a willingness to serve can become an openness to exploitation – which can lead to resentment

IN THE WORLD

Virgoans have a need to feel that they are doing work that is useful. They are conscientious, practical and reliable, and even if not actually capable of putting up a shelf or servicing the car, they are likely to be highly organized and to know the score when it comes to getting someone else to do the job. Furthermore, they will not overlook shoddy work, even if they find it hard to insist on its being remedied. In a work context this means that Virgo would find it easier to be an inspector than a manager.

As a Mercury-ruled sign, Virgo is capable of sound analytical work, and of communicating results effectively. Virgoans take easily to work involving accounting, systems analysis, computing, education, health and the media. Many are drawn to handicrafts, particularly those involving precision.

LIBRA

The Sun enters the tropical zodiac sign of Libra around 23 September and leaves around 23 October. Its entry marks the autumn equinox in the northern hemisphere (spring equinox in the southern hemisphere), when the day and night are of equal length. Libra is ruled by Venus; Mars and Saturn are both debilitated (weak) in the sign. It is a hot, moist, cardinal and masculine sign, a member of the air element; its colour is black, dark crimson or tawny and its angel is Zariel. It is symbolized by the Scales.

Babylonian astrologers, who advised some of the most powerful monarchs in the ancient world, believed that planets in Libra indicated events in Elam, the east. The Romans are responsible for the later belief that China is Libran. This connection seemed to make sense as later scholars felt that the principles of harmony in Chinese beliefs such as Taoism could be compared to Libran balance.

To the Babylonians Libra was Zibanitum ('scales'), in Greece Zugos ('yoke'). In India it was Tula or Tulam ('balance'), or Juga or Juka after the Greek, and was sometimes represented as a man bending on one knee and holding a pair of scales. In China it corresponds to the months Ch'iu Fen ('autumn equinox') and Han Lu ('cold dew'). Originally the Chinese called it Show Sing ('longevity'), but they later renamed it Tien Ching, the Celestial Balance; they also portrayed it as a Crocodile or Dragon.

October was the eighth month in the Roman calendar, named after the Latin for eight, *octo*. The Anglo-Saxons knew it as Wyn-monath – Wine month, a designation perhaps borrowed from the grape-growing areas of Germany and France.

THE STARS OF LIBRA

Libra is not the most dramatic constellation. The 3rd-century BC Greek poet Aratus described it as important but dim. Under the modern International Astronomy Union boundaries it ranks only twenty-ninth in size, covers 1.304 per cent of the sky and contains just 35 visible stars.

One story – completely false but widely repeated – holds that Virgo and Scorpio were originally next to each other, and that the Romans then carved Libra out of Scorpio to make a twelfth sign of the zodiac. The truth is rather less dramatic. Around 700BC the Babylonians used *qaran zaqaqipi* ('scorpion's horns') as an alternative name for Libra. The Greeks, who borrowed all their zodiac signs from Babylon, preferred this name, and generally called Libra Chelae ('claws'). Confusion was caused when the Greek cosmographer Eratosthenes included the Scorpion and the Scorpion's Claws in one constellation in the 2nd century BC, although generally they were regarded as separate and distinct. Perhaps to draw a proper distinction

'The Man, holding merchandise in his Scales in the market, stands as the place of the hips and navel. His domains are people of pure purpose, vinas [stringed instruments], coins, cities and roads, all clothing, and tall crops.'

Indian astrologer Minaraja, 4th century AD

RIGHT **In Egypt the scales were crucial to the rites of passage of the dead. It is from these ancient origins that we derive our images of justice held in the balance.**

'If the Scales position is stable: there will be reconciliation and peace in the land.'

Letter from Assyrian astrologer to the emperor, *c.*700–600BC

between the two constellations the Romans reverted to Libra, though they continued to use Chelae and Yugum ('yoke') as alternatives. The confusion continued almost to the present day, and in the 17th century the English astronomer John Flamsteed referred to Libra's stars as *in jugo sive chelis* ('in the Yoke or the Claws').

Alpha Librae, Libra's brightest star, is traditionally known as Zubenelgenubi, a word derived from the Arabic for 'southern claw' (*al zuban al janubiyyah*), a reminder of the constellation's ancient link with the scorpion. Zubeneschamali (Beta Librae) is the northern claw. Beta Librae also has one intriguing peculiarity – many observers claim it has a distinctive green tint.

Libra also contains the globular cluster N.G.C.5904, 5 M, which was discovered in 1702. William Herschel, the discoverer of Uranus, studied this cluster with his 12-metre (40-foot) reflector and counted over 200 faint but discernible separate stars.

THE SCALES

Libra is the only constellation of the zodiac that is represented by an inanimate object – the Scales. The Romans rationalized this connection by claiming that, as the sign of the autumn equinox, Libra balanced the two halves of the year.

The symbol of the scales has Babylonian origins, but the clue to its mythical significance may lie elsewhere, perhaps in ancient Egyptian religion, in which the scales figure prominently in the passage of the dead to the

Rome, the 'eternal city', was said to be Libran. About 100BC an astrologer named Lucius Tarrutius cast a horoscope for Rome based on the traditional date of foundation by Romulus and Remus, 21 April 753BC. He calculated that the Sun was in Taurus and the Moon in Libra. His calculations were wrong but the belief that Rome was Libran stuck, and around the time of Christ the poet Marcus Manilius argued that Rome and all of Italy were ruled by Libra, and hence had the power to either subdue other peoples or set them free as the balance swung. He wrote: 'Italy belongs to the Balance, her rightful sign: beneath it Rome and her sovereignty of the world were founded, Rome which controls the issue of events, exalting and depressing nations placed in the scales.' Manilius found support in the fact that the emperor Tiberius was born with the Moon in Libra. He was not to know, though, that on 13 October AD54, when the court astrologers chose the time for Nero, the most notorious emperor of all, to be proclaimed, they were to do so with the Sun exactly overhead in Libra.

BELOW *The City of Rome*, woodcut from the *Nuremberg Chronicle* by Herman Schedel (1493). Astrology was an integral part of life in imperial Rome. Some emperors, including Hadrian (ruled AD 117–138), were themselves astrologers. (See also box, left.)

ABOVE In Egypt the scales played a central part in the soul's passage from one life to the next. In this illustration from a papyrus Book of the Dead, the jackal-headed god Anubis weighs the dead man's heart in one scale, balancing it against a feather, symbolizing truth, in the other scale. The ceremony took place in the Hall of Double Justice, in front of the deceased and the assembly of gods and goddesses, presided over by the ruler of the Underworld, Osiris. Thoth recorded the results and if they were satisfactory Osiris admitted the deceased to eternal life. If they were not, the heart was consumed by a beast, the Devourer.

underworld. It may be that the survival of the Scales in Egypt, as opposed to the preference for the Scorpion's Claws in Greece, made it possible for the Romans to restore it to their zodiac. It appears in several places, including the famous zodiac at Dendera (see p.15), as a scale-beam, a symbol of the Nilometer (which measured the rise of the Nile during the annual flood). But it was more than a simple measuring device – to the Egyptians their entire land was a mirror of heaven and the Nile was the sacred river by which the gods gave them life. Observing the rise and fall of its waters was therefore an act of religious devotion.

> 'Abandon then the base and viler clowne,
> Lyft up thy selfe out of the lowely dust;
> And sing of bloody Mars, of wars, of giusts,
> Turne thee to those, that weld the awful crowne.
> To doubted Knights whose woundless armour rusts,
> And helmes unbruzed wexen dayly browne.'
>
> 'October' from Edmund Spenser's *The Shepheardes Calendar*, 1579. In October the Sun moves from Libra, where Mars is weak, to Scorpio, where it is strong. The poet is evoking Mars as a means of resisting the Sun's move into winter.

THE ASTROLOGICAL LIBRA

> 'The sign of Libra is changeable and variable. But its leading and middle portions are temperate, the end watery, the northern parts windy and the southern moist.'
>
> Ptolemy, *Tetrabiblos*, 2nd century AD

Libra is an extroverted sign, and classical astronomers classified it as cardinal. Both these labels express the same notion – that Libra is strong and capable of controlling the environment around it. Jungian astrologers, on the other hand, class it as a 'thinking' sign, able to analyze and weigh up possibilities.

The Sun enters Libra at the autumn equinox, when the seasons hang precisely in the balance. This theme of balance runs throughout the Libran personality. Librans are inclined to weigh everything up, to see both sides of any story. They can become expert strategists, like generals who precisely weigh up their forces against those of the opposition. On the other hand, they may appear to 'sit on the fence' in an argument, seeing the pros and cons on both sides, reluctant to be partisan and give unqualified support to either.

Many successful leaders were born with the Sun in Libra, including Mahatma Ghandi, General Eisenhower, Winston Churchill, Margaret Thatcher and Lech Walesa. Libran leadership tends to be marked by diplomacy, an ability to manipulate both people and circumstances.

The tendency to see both sides is the basis of the popular view of Librans as indecisive

RIGHT **Libra, from a 16th-century Turkish manuscript, depicted with the Libran scales in each hand.**

characters. The person who sees both sides of an argument may find it hard to choose in favour of one side or the other. Libra is a sign of contradictions and paradoxes. Its balances represent opposites. One is life, the other death; one conscious, the other unconscious. One is peace, the other war.

Libra is the peacekeeper. More than

'If Libra is in the ascendant one should do things pertaining to foreign lands, litigations, jewels, buying and selling.'

Indian astrologer
Sphujidhvaja, *c.*AD270

any other sign of the zodiac, it knows the importance of harmony, dialogue, equality and justice. However, when faced with hard choices or with the reality of conflict it may sometimes collapse. If there is something particularly Libran about leading a country in war, it is that conflict involves assessing the balance of power, weighing up

The great 17th-century English poet John Milton referred to Libra's peaceful qualities in *Paradise Lost* when he wrote:

'The Eternal, to prevent such horrid fray,
Hung forth in heaven his golden scales, yet seen
Betwixt Astraea and the Scorpion sign.'

Milton was paraphrasing Homer who, almost 2,500 years earlier, had written:

'The Eternal Father hung
His golden scales aloft.'

the other side's position. Libra fights war precisely in order to create peace.

Librans might be more at ease with their contradictory nature if they were to see it in the sense of dialogue. They are often fluent communicators who can become very good at saying challenging things without giving offence, and are frequently adept at settling differences between opposing factions. They can become highly successful diplomats and mediators.

Libra's feel for harmony may be seen to emerge in tasteful dress and charming manners. Many Librans have an artistic streak, and even those who do not actually create art themselves will probably have the capacity to appreciate it and be able to express opinions on it. Their tasteful homes are often havens of peace in a troubled world.

RELATING

Libra is a sociable sign, and Librans are on the whole pleasant, tactful and communicative, so they usually have a wide circle of friends. Their anxiousness to keep the peace may make them appear to support one person and one viewpoint one minute, and another person and a different viewpoint the next. Libra's desire for harmony can come out in a reluctance to 'upset the apple-cart' or cause a scene. It will try to avoid discord, even if this sometimes means sweeping issues under a carpet of denial.

At its heart Libra's myths concern the reconciliation of opposites: light and dark, active and passive, male and female. Libra does not merely have relationships: it eats, drinks, thinks and breathes relationships. The fact that Libra is ruled by Venus, the goddess of love (the Greek Aphrodite), points to the fact that this is a particularly romantic sign. It wallows in the myths of romantic love, of gentle ladies and chivalrous knights. However, it should be remembered that Aphrodite was not made entirely of sugar and spice: she was born from the sperm of Ouranos' severed genitals, and it was her vanity and high-handedness in the name of love that led to the Trojan Wars. Love can lead to despair and disaster, just as in Arthurian myth, Guinevere's desire for Lancelot spelled catastrophe for the kingdom of Camelot.

THE SHADOW

The Libran shadow emerges in two forms. There is the extremist who, unable to cope with continual choices, takes refuge in simple answers, often the certainty of religious belief or political dogma. Then there is the flirt, for whom life is but a game, the seducer and heart-breaker, all smiles, smart clothes and wit. The Libran fairy-tale is one of absolute beauty, but when appearances are deceptive and when the tale goes wrong, beauty is a Siren that lures the unwary to their doom.

IN THE WORLD

The typical Libran is a 'people person' who enjoys working in a team and excels at any sort of negotiation or arbitration. Decisions may not come particularly easily to them, although they may be good at helping others to make up their minds by providing them with the necessary information. They usually thrive in professional partnerships. Venus, Libra's ruler, is associated with money, so that balancing the books, banking, or business will generally appeal. In Indian astrology Libra was traditionally associated with merchants. Libra may also find an expression in jobs that seek to establish balance between people, such as diplomats in government or mediators between individuals.

Balance in a slightly different sense is involved in a sense of justice and fair play – which Librans usually have in abundance. Hence many Librans find their way into the legal profession. The same principle on an aesthetic level draws Librans to the arts, to interior design and to the fashion world.

Triptych representing Justice, by Jacobello del Fiore (d.1439). The Libran scales are often used to symbolize justice, as in the famous statue above the Old Bailey lawcourts in London, England.

SCORPIO

The Sun enters the tropical zodiac sign of Scorpio around 23 October and leaves around 22 November. In traditional astrology Mars rules Scorpio and Venus is debilitated (weak) in it. Scorpio is a cold, wet, fixed, female sign, and a member of the water element. Its colour is brown, its ruling angel Baraluel and its symbol the Scorpion. Modern astrologers tend to regard Scorpio as being ruled by Pluto, either on its own or jointly with Mars.

Scorpio is the eighth sign of the zodiac. The Latin Scorpius is used to denote the constellation in modern astronomy, to distinguish it from the the zodiacal sign, Scorpio. The constellation was called Gir.tab or Zuqaqipu ('scorpion' or 'stinger') by the Sumerians 5,000 years ago. The Greeks called it Scorpios while the Romans sometimes used the North African name Nepa or Nepas. In early China, Scorpio formed part of the mighty Azure Dragon of the East and in later days the constellation was the residence of the heavenly Blue Emperor. In the time of Confucius it was Ta Who, the Great Fire. It also corresponded

According to the Australian Aborigines a young initiate was seduced by a girl, and when the pair were discovered they fled to the sky, chased by their teachers. They all became the stars of Scorpio, which now stands in the sky as a reminder that a newly initiated man should not have sexual relations with a woman until after he has been purified.

to the Chinese months Shuang Chiang ('hoar-frost descends') and Li Tung ('winter begins'). In India it is known as Vrischika, Sanskrit for 'scorpion'. The Arab name, al-Akrab, also means 'scorpion'. Pious Christian astronomers later tried to replace the Scorpion with the Apostle Bartholomew or the Cardinal's Hat. However, even the Maya of Central America saw the constellation as a scorpion.

November was the ninth month of the Roman calendar (Latin *novem*, nine). To the Vikings and Anglo-Saxons it was known as Wint-monath or Blot-monath – the month when the gails blew and the ships were

laid up until the spring, and when much blood was shed as cattle were slaughtered and salted for the winter.

The ancient Celtic festival of Samhain, held on 31 October, marked the end of the year and the beginning of winter. It was celebrated with massive fires, designed to bring heat to the earth before the final onset of winter. The festival is the origin both of Hallowe'en, with its customs of dressing up and wearing a mask and overtones of the dead rising from the grave; and of the English Guy Fawkes Night, or Bonfire Night, when bonfires are lit in commemoration of the Gunpowder Plot of 5 November 1605.

'The eighth, which has the shape of a Scorpion in a hole, is called the region of the penis and anus of the Lord. Its domains are caves, crevices and holes, poisons, stones and hiding-places, ant-hills, insects, and snakes both big and small.'

Indian astrologer Minaraja, 4th century AD

RIGHT Scorpio is a sign of depth and secrecy. Its principal festival is Hallowe'en, which in the north provides a ritual preparation for the long, dark nights of winter.

'The sign of Scorpio as a whole is marked by thunder and fire. Its leading portion is snowy, its middle temperate and the end causes earthquakes. The north is hot and the south is moist.'

Ptolemy, *Tetrabiblos*, 2nd century AD

THE STARS OF SCORPIO

Although the constellation of Scorpius is part of the zodiac, the boundaries of the constellations were redrawn in 1928 and the Sun now spends only nine days passing through its stars. The remaining two-thirds of the month are spent in the constellation Ophiucus.

Scorpius used to be one of the largest constellations. The Roman poet Ovid wrote that it sprawled across two signs of the zodiac. The Greek scorpion was in two halves, one containing the body and sting, the other, known as Chelae, the claws. Under the Babylonians the Claws had been the Balance, a designation restored by the Romans (see pp.68–70).

LEFT **The Milky Way and the constellation of Scorpius. Antares is visible as the bright, reddish star at the centre right of the photograph. Antares is the 'heart' of the scorpion; its 'head' comprises the bright stars to the upper right of Antares and its 'tail' is the line of bright stars stretching away from Antares to the lower left of the picture.**

Scorpius can be identified by the curved stars of its tail, poised ready to sting. It contains 62 visible stars, of which the brightest is Antares, a name that comes from the Greek 'Anti Ares', meaning 'like Mars', or 'rival of Mars' (Ares was the Greek god of war, the equivalent of the Roman Mars; the Greeks knew the planet Mars as the star Ares). Antares is a giant, 400 light-years from the Sun and several hundred times its size. Its volume is a billion times that of the Sun, and if it were represented by a hot-air balloon the Earth would be no bigger than the full stop at the end of this sentence.

Antares also has a strange companion, Antares B, which is 100 times smaller and can just be made out with a small telescope. The two stars move around a common centre of gravity, although Antares B takes as long as 900 years to complete one orbit. Antares B also has one strange feature – it is green. Just why this is so is not known, although it is generally thought to be the result of an optical illusion.

Antares' association with Mars is derived from its reddish colour (Mars being the red planet). In ancient Persia it rose with the Sun at the autumn equinox and was one of the four 'royal' stars that marked the equinoxes and solstices. The

Greeks believed that its character combined the natures of the planets Mars and Jupiter, which meant that it was warlike, impulsive and potentially destructive. They believed that anyone linked to the star would achieve great honour through violence; a child might grow up to be a great general, although one who brought great bloodshed. When combined with the Moon, Antares was supposed to be favourable for business and domestic matters and to confer an interest in philosophy.

Most of the stars in Scorpius had an ominous reputation amongst the astronomers of ancient times, mainly because of the constellation's association with Mars, and were reputed to bring 'malevolence, fiendishness, repulsiveness, pestilence and contagious disease'.

The most notable astronomical events to take place in Scorpius are the Scorpiid meteor showers that occur annually on 3 May and 5 June. Scorpius also contains the strongest X-ray source in the sky. This is Scorpius X-1, which is a binary star – appearing as one star but actually two stars revolving

'If the sting of Scorpius surrounds the halo of the Moon at its appearance, the flood will come. If the Plough star comes close to Scorpius: the ruler will die from a sting of the scorpion.'

Assyrian Omens, *c.*8th century BC

The adventures of Gilgamesh illustrated the cycle of the seasons. This 8th-century BC Assyrian relief shows the hero holding a lion. Gilgamesh's encounter with the Scorpion-men is the earliest mythological account of Scorpio.

round each other. One of the two is probably a high-density neutron star. The X-rays are apparently caused by the acceleration of gas to speeds approaching that of light as it steams into the intense gravitational and magnetic fields near this star.

THE INNER JOURNEY

Before *c*.2000BC the Sun rose in Scorpio at the autumn equinox, around 21 September, and it often makes an important appearance in calendar myths. In the Babylonian epic of Gilgamesh (see p.32), Mashu, the great mountain that guarded the rising and setting Sun, and whose twin peaks were 'as high as the wall of heaven', was guarded by Scorpion-men. The myth describes them as: 'half-man and half scorpion; their stare strikes death into men, their shimmering halo sweeps the mountains that guard the rising Sun.'

After Gilgamesh meets the Scorpion-men he is sent on a journey into the dark for twelve leagues, during which 'his heart was oppressed and from the rising of the Sun to the setting of the Sun there was no light'. The twelve leagues are obviously the twelve hours of night but could also represent the six months from the autumn to spring equinoxes when the nights are longer than the days. In either case Gilgamesh's journey is an astronomical calendar myth. It does not attempt to explain why the Sun disappears at night or becomes cold during the winter, but describes the experience of being abandoned. The archetypal myth of the descent to the underworld was later to find expression in the Christian story of Christ's three-day torment in hell.

Gilgamesh, who himself embodies the Sun's heroic qualities of strength and courage, survives his ordeal and after eleven leagues he sees the light of dawn. After twelve leagues the Sun streams out and he finds himself in the garden of the gods, where he encounters Shamash, the Sun god.

To the ancient Sumerians and Babylonians

Gilgamesh's ordeal was a mystical and poetic account of the perils of night. Looking back from our current vantage point we identify a metaphor for the difficulties through which we pass and without which we cannot grow or mature. To modern psychotherapists this is a myth of individuation, in which we discover our true individual nature only after a long inner journey.

LIGHT AND DARK

The scorpion figured in Greek myth as the creature that stung Orion to death. Orion was a solar hero and his constellation sets as Scorpius rises. In one version of the story, Artemis, a lunar goddess, sends the scorpion to sting Orion after he tries to rape her. In another, the Earth sends the scorpion after Orion boasts that he could kill any wild beast; such pride could not go unchallenged. Scorpio becomes the instrument of vengeance but is perhaps a necessary corrective, bringing the cleansing of winter after the excesses of summer.

Hercules' battle with the Hydra is also said to be a Scorpionic myth (each of Hercules' twelve labours corresponds to a month and a constellation). This story finds Hercules encountering the

diabolical many-headed Hydra, one of the most fearsome dragons that ever lived. Hercules is charged with the task of killing the Hydra, but every time he cuts off one of its heads another grows in its place. Eventually Hercules puts his sword to one side and adopts more subtle methods. In one account he carries a flaming torch into the

Hydra's cave and in another he carries the monster out into the sunlight. The result is the same: the Hydra is killed by the light.

Psychotherapists see a clear psychological message in the myth: if we try to deal with our inner problems by denying them, others will grow in their place. Instead neuroses are healed by bringing them into the open.

Hercules and the Hydra, a bronze sculpture by Giambologna (1529–1608). The legend of Hercules' slaying of the many-headed Hydra is said to be a Scorpionic myth.

THE ASTROLOGICAL SCORPIO

Scorpio is courageous, tenacious, intense, secretive and intuitive. The scorpion is not everyone's favourite animal. After all, it hides in dark places and inflicts a painful sting on its prey or anyone who poses a threat. One story tells of the scorpion who persuades a reluctant frog to carry it across a river. Half-way across, the scorpion stings the frog. Just before they both die, the frog, uncomprehending, asks, 'Why did you do that?' The scorpion just has time to answer: 'It's in my nature.'

Scorpios get rather a bad press, though it is generally agreed that a Scorpio is a good person to have on your side if it comes to a fight. The Scorpio may be the nicest person in the world, yet is still inclined to hide under metaphorical stones, and when threatened or backed into corner will deliver a painful verbal or emotional sting. Scorpio knows its own vulnerability and seeks to protect itself at all costs.

Another Scorpio key word is survival. The Scorpio approach to the world is one of life and death struggle: survival at all costs. Scorpios may actually thrive on threat, but they have a great capacity to rise, phoenix-like, from the ashes of any disaster, and to help others to do the same.

'If Scorpio is in the ascendant one should do things pertaining to poison, fire, giving, obstructing, hindering, and dividing one's enemies.'

Indian astrologer Sphujidhvaja, c.AD270

The zodiacal sign of Scorpio, painted on the inside lid of an Egyptian mummy coffin (2nd century AD).

RELATING

Scorpio has a reputation for smouldering sexuality, passion, and a tendency to vow revenge when scorned. How accurate is this? As a fixed water sign, Scorpio is sensitive, emotional, slow to embark on a relationship but equally slow to leave, and always able to empathize with a partner's feelings. Mars, the sign's traditional ruler, signifies strong sexual desire, although this could be sublimated – for example in religious devotion. The sign's modern association with the relatively new planet Pluto represents a need for secrecy and self-protection, which makes the typical Scorpio difficult to get to know.

Scorpio gives undying devotion, but also demands it. Scorpios can be extremely romantic, and the sign is devoted to the ideal of love. But as with all great ideals its opposite is always present. When its love is not requited it can turn in on itself in the self-punishment of the puritan. When it is rejected or betrayed, its pain can be transformed into anger.

Once it is unleashed, Scorpionic love has no limit. The typical Scorpio will go to the ends of the earth in search of undying commitment and when it loves it does so with a single-mindedness that occasionally amounts to obsession. With the right person Scorpio can be as passionate as its reputation promises, but with the wrong person, or at the wrong time, or if hurt, it can freeze over like a lake in winter.

THE SHADOW

Possessive, jealous, unforgiving – when the Scorpionic shadow emerges it devotes itself to vengeance. The film *Fatal Attraction* (1987), in which a married man's jilted lover is determined either to have him or to destroy him and his family, is Scorpio myth in the making. The image has become predominantly feminine – the *femme fatale* – but is present equally in men, even if Hollywood fails to recognize it. The male equivalent is the habitual seducer – personified in James Bond. Shakespeare's *Romeo and Juliet* is pure Scorpio, with a plot containing passion, devotion, secrecy, violence, revenge and a final suicide scene in the darkness of the family vault: love that ends in tragedy is Scorpionic.

IN THE WORLD

Scorpio has some very marketable qualities, being pefectionist, hard-working, determined, brave, reliable and loyal with a great capacity to stick at a job and to concentrate closely on fine detail without giving way to distractions.

To Scorpio, information is power – power that is retained by holding on to information: Scorpios play their cards very close to their chest. They do particularly well in jobs demanding the rare combination of toughness and sensitivity, which right wrongs and heal the sick. Such qualities are put to good use in areas such as research, the police force, the armed forces, medicine, counselling and psychotherapy, or social and charity work. The sign's general weakness, however, is its tendency to keep secrets and conspire.

> Classical astronomers believed that the Scorpionic nature of parts of North Africa was revealed in its inhabitants' attitude to relationships. Claudius Ptolemy wrote that 'their marriages are brought about by violent abduction, while sometimes the women are common to all the men'.

> Scorpio signifies all 'Muddy, Morrish grounds and stinking Lakes, Ditches, and Quagmires, Gardens, Vineyards and Orchards, all Sinks in Houses, Wash-houses, ruinous houses, neer waters, all places where creeping and venemous Creatures frequent.'
>
> English astrologer Henry Coley, 1676

SAGITTARIUS

The Sun enters the tropical zodiac sign of Sagittarius around 23 November and leaves around 21 December. In traditional astrology Jupiter rules Sagittarius, while Mercury is debilitated (weak) in it. It is a dry, hot, mutable, male sign, and a member of the fire element. Its colour is yellow or green with a reddish tinge, and its guardian angel is Advachiel. Its symbol is the Archer, a Centaur with a bow and arrow.

The Babylonians called Sagittarius Pa.bil.sag, the Greeks knew it as Toxotës ('archer') and the Indians call it Dhanus ('bow'). In China it conforms to the months Hsiao Hsüeh ('little snow') and Ta Hsüeh ('heavy snow'). The Chinese knew the constellation not as a horse but as a tiger, or as Seih Muh, the Cleft Tree. After the Jesuits introduced Western astronomy to China, Sagittarius was known as Jin Ma, the Man-Horse.

> Being created from two creatures, man and horse, the Centaur links two seasons, possessing double powers.
>
> 'Milder autumn claims the smooth limbs and body of his human half. The animal portions in his rear prepare for a frosty winter.'
>
> Indian astrologer Minaraja, 4th century AD

Among the Jews Sagittarius as the Archer was the tribal symbol of Ephraim and Manasseh, and was also associated with Joash, the king of Israel, shooting arrows out of the 'window eastward' at the command of the dying Elisha. Other commentators have associated it with Ishmael or the apostle Matthew.

December was the tenth month of the Roman calendar (Latin *decem*, ten). The poet Martial (*c*.AD40–104) described it as *fumosus* (smoky), from the fires that were lit in Roman houses to keep out the cold, and *canus* (hoary), from the frosts and snow that settled on the high ground. The Anglo-Saxons knew it originally as Winter-monath, but later changed to Heligh-monath – Holy month – in honour of Christ's birthday.

SAGITTARIAN STARS

Sagittarius contains fifteen Messier objects (non-stellar objects such as nebulae) – the greatest number in any constellation. It is also the fifteenth-largest constellation, including about 65 visible stars; Sagittarius contains more variable stars (whose light varies, often in regular periods) than there are naked-eye stars in the entire sky. It also includes the

> 'The sign of Sagittarius as a whole is windy, but, taken by part its leading portion is wet, its middle temperate and its following part fiery. Its northern parts are windy, its southern moist and changeable.'
>
> Ptolemy, *Tetrabiblos*, 2nd century AD

RIGHT The Sagittarian Centaur combines the human and the bestial, the rational and the instinctive. In the north the Sun occupies Sagittarius as winter falls, though in the south it is a sign of summer.

Sagittarius is a 'fiery, hot, dry, masculine, cholerick, diurnal, Eastern, common, Bicorporeal sign, of the fiery Trigon.'

William Ramesey, 1653

centre of our galaxy, a radio-emitting source known as Sagittarius A, at which Galactic Latitude and Longitude both measure 0 degrees.

The 2nd-century BC Greek cosmographer Eratosthenes argued that the Centaurs were not archers, and described the constellation as a two-footed creature with the tail of a satyr. He identified it as Crotus, the son of Eupheme, who was nurse to the Muses, the nine daughters of Zeus. According to some accounts Crotus was the son of Pan, confirming the view that Sagittarius was a satyr, not a Centaur. However, mythical images are fluid and often blend into each other. Crotus himself invented archery and often went hunting on horseback. He was also popular amongst the Muses, who requested that Zeus put him in the sky in order to demonstrate archery.

RIGHT The zodiacal sign of Sagittarius, from a Persian manuscript. LEFT December, from the early 15th-century *Très Riches Heures du Duc de Berry* by the Limbourg brothers. Hunting wild boar is the seasonal pursuit. Sagittarius is on the left of the celestial sphere, Capricorn on the right.

The bright semi-circular row of stars in the neighbouring constellation of Corona Australis was thought of as a wreath discarded by someone at play, perhaps in Crotus' honour. The constellation has been called Croton and Crotos, but these names never stuck.

Some modern astronomers prefer to see Sagittarius as a teapot rather than a Centaur. Eight of its stars form the teapot and seven a spoon. Corona Australis is the slice of lemon, while the Milky Way is the steam rising from the spout. Others, particular in Asia, have retained the bow and arrow, but rejected the Centaur.

About twelve of Sagittarius' stars were used by Greek and Arabic astrologers, though none was of the first rank. One of the most pleasant was Ascella, a binary star located in the Centaur's armpit. Ascella was believed to confer good fortune and happiness, and if it was close to the Moon it signified 'new and influential friends, valuable gifts and the love of respectable women'.

Another of the constellation's stars, Sigma Sagittarii, is also known by the oldest star name in use, Nunki. The name was borrowed by modern navigators who found it in a list of Babylonian star names. The

The Fight between the Lapiths and the Centaurs by Jacob Jordaens (1593–1678). The painting depicts the scene that erupted when the Centaur Eurytus tried to abduct Hippodame, the bride of King Pirithous of the Lapiths.

original Nunki was a group of stars that was special to the Sumerian city of Eridu.

The Chinese noted an extraordinarily brilliant supernova in Sagittarius $c.$ AD1011, which the annals record was visible for three months. The most interesting recent discovery in Sagittarius is a dwarf galaxy which is colliding with our own galaxy, the Milky Way. Its present position is on the edge of one of the spiral arms. Over the time span of a human life the effect is negligible, but over hundreds of millions of years the collision could have a significant effect on the Milky Way's structure.

THE ARCHER

The earliest known image of a winged Centaur occurs on a boundary stone from the Kassite period of Babylon, $c.$1600–1150BC. Half-animal, half-human creatures were common in the ancient world, often representing constellations such as Leo or Taurus. The most famous monument is probably the Sphinx in Egypt; the best-known mythical creature the Cretan Minotaur. Sagittarius has even been called Taurus and Minotaurus, as well as Cornipedes ('horn-footed').

Such images represent humanity's dual nature, rooted half in the animal world, subject

to fate and uncontrollable passions, and half in the spiritual world, with access to reason, moral choice, enlightenment and salvation.

The Centaurs of Greek myth, half human and half horse, were a varied group. Early images show them as giants with hairy bodies; later they became half beast, perhaps to represent more vividly their animal nature. They were descendants of Ixion, son of the war god Ares (Mars), which accounts for their aggressive nature. Ixion committed the arrogant sin of coveting Hera, wife of Zeus and Queen of

Olympus, but to deceive him Zeus sent him a cloud in Hera's image. From this union was born Centaurus (who has his own constellation), who himself copulated with the mares of Pelion and fathered the Centaurs.

Etymologically *centaur* signifies 'those who round up bulls', which suggests that the Centaurs themselves may be a survival of earlier mythical figures based on the recurring themes of Taurus and the Bull of Heaven (see p.32). Their behaviour was gross, cruel, lecherous and drunken. They were wild, dangerous revellers, galloping out of the

woods intent on wine, rape and blood-letting; Hell's Angels have become a mythic equivalent in modern society. The Centaur Chiron, tutor to many heroes including Heracles and Achilles, was untypical in being kind, wise and civilized.

While the Centaur represents the baser qualities, the archer is a symbol of humanity's higher aspirations. The bow may be interpreted as divine inspiration, and the arrow as the unbending, directed will. In flight the arrow symbolizes the human quest for freedom, whether spiritual, political, intellectual or emotional.

THE ASTROLOGICAL SAGITTARIUS

Psychologically Sagittarius is an extroverted sign, confident and eager to interact with the world. In the Jungian system it is 'intuitive', able to see the possibilities which ordinary people miss. This is why its gaze is always fixed on the horizon.

In the northern hemisphere

> Places signified by Sagittarius include:
> 'A Stable of great Horses, or Horses for the Wars, or a House where usually great fourefooted Beasts are kept; it represents in the Fields, Hils, and the highest places of Lands or grounds that rise a little above the rest; in houses upper rooms, neer the fire.'
>
> English astrologer William Lilly, 1647

the Sun is in Sagittarius when the winter solstice is approaching and the coming darkness must be balanced by belief that light – and spring – will return. In Sagittarius the attacking sting of Scorpio becomes the flying arrow of hope, optimism, discovery and adventure. This is an outgoing sign, with all the enthusiasm of fire, the versatility and restlessness of mutability, and the largeness of vision, generosity and wisdom of Jupiter. The word 'enthusiastic', often used for the Sagittarian approach to life, is derived from a

Greek word meaning 'possessed by a god', which is appropriate for Sagittarius, a sign often associated with religious fervour.

Sagittarius' key theme is freedom, the attempt to transcend the limitations that most other people accept. The quests for spiritual revelation and philosophical enlightenment are Sagittarian, as are the great voyages of discovery, pushing back the boundaries of inner and outer space. Liberty is the Sagittarian rallying cry, yet when rules and responsibilities are abandoned, liberty gives way to licence, an insistence on individual freedom at the expense of collective rights.

Sagittarius is divided into two quite distinct natures: the

unbridled, pell-mell pursuit of animal appetite on the one hand; and the pursuit of knowledge, wisdom and enlightenment on the other. The drunken rugby player; the professor of philosophy; the guru – all are Sagittarian types.

Sagittarians are often said to be tactless, but if this is so, it is a product of the sign's optimism and of its focus on far horizons, so that minor details closer at hand are overlooked. There is also the fact that Sagittarians themselves tend to be very easy-going, and assume that everyone else is the same.

THE SHADOW

Sagittarius' shadow emerges not only from the Centaur – the crude, faithless braggart – but also from its more noble side. The Sagittarian is a believer. Many believe in themselves. Others believe in a religious or political cause. Yet so total is their belief that they can conceive of no other possibilities, and when the shadow emerges it does so as the dogmatist, the bigot, whose own freedom is won at the expense of other faiths and creeds.

RELATING

In classical astronomy the god associated with Sagittarius was Jupiter (the Greek Zeus). His mythology includes numerous accounts of his untiring pursuit of nymphs and maidens, and this chasing after successive conquests can be a feature of the Sagittarian approach to relationships. Yet Sagittarians can be romantic, especially in the initial excitement of the chase.

On the plus side, Sagittarians are lively and affectionate, bring fun and variety to a relationship, and are good at staying friends with ex-lovers. It is when a sense of adventure is lacking and, worse, when they feel hemmed in and tied down, that they seek stimulation elsewhere. They are

neither the most persistent of people nor the most dutiful, and often make promises that can never be kept and commitments that are instantly forgotten. To a Sagittarian, domesticity can be a death sentence.

IN THE WORLD

Sagittarius' great assets in any work situation are optimism, enthusiasm and the ability to go all out for a distant goal. Sagittarius' opposite sign, Gemini, is particularly gifted

Sagittarius is said to rule the thighs. In medieval astronomy the Sagittarian body was: 'streight wel proportioned, somewhat tall, of a loving cheerful countenance, high colour, Oval visage, a Ruddy, sanguine Complexion and brown hair.'

English astrologer Henry Coley, 1676

when it comes to gathering facts and figures, and fellow mutable sign Virgo works well with fine detail; Sagittarius, on the other hand, sees the big picture and interprets accordingly. Putting it another way, Sagittarius will see the wood despite the trees.

The down-side of this is that Sagittarius may overlook vital details, or miss out boring though essential stages of a process in its eagerness to reach the distant goal. Sagittarius is not a sign renowned for endur-ance in the face of tedium. This is an inspired but restless sign.

Traditional Sagittarian princi-ples – widening horizons, distant goals, the quest for freedom – are often associated with inspiration and vision, but not necessarily hard work. Sagittarian occupa-tions are said to include any that deal with ideas, including publishing, religion, the law and activity that spreads ideas far and wide. It is also connected to foreign travel, a broadening of mental horizons as well as geographical ones which was the urge behind the great voyages of exploration of land and space.

Sagittarians need to be at liberty to pursue their goals and interests, and hate being tied down to inflexible schedules. On the other hand, the sign is associated with organized reli-gion – as opposed to mysticism, which is associated with the other tradition-ally Jupiterian sign, Pisces. Religion is the basis of public morality and therefore of law, as well as in some sense of vision and inspi-ration, and here perhaps is the Sagittarian paradox: that laws protect indi-vidual freedom from the mayhem of the Centaur's unbridled animal appetite. The paradox extends to Jupiter, Sagittarius' ancient god, who was both the liber-tine and the law-giver of Olympus.

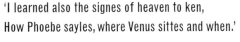

'I learned also the signes of heaven to ken, How Phoebe sayles, where Venus sittes and when.'

'December' from Edmund Spenser's *The Shepheardes Calendar*, 1579. The poet is using the dark winter days to discover the secrets of women and love – Phoebe is the Moon.

This detail from a 15th-century Spanish astrological tapestry shows the constellations. The figure of Sagittarius can be seen on the right-hand side.

CAPRICORN

The Sun enters the tropical zodiac sign of Capricorn around 21 December, and leaves around 20 January. Its entry marks the winter solstice and the shortest day in the northern hemisphere (the summer solstice and longest day in the southern hemisphere). Saturn rules Capricorn, Mars is exalted (strong) in it, and the Moon and Jupiter are debilitated (weak). It is a cold, dry, female, cardinal sign and a member of the earth element. Its colours are russet, dark brown and black. Its ruling angel is Hanael and its symbol the Goat-fish.

The tropic of Capricorn, 23 degrees south, is the latitude at which the Sun is overhead on the winter solstice (or summer solstice in the southern hemisphere). The tropic was named 2,000 years ago; these days the Sun is actually in the constellation Sagittarius.

The Babylonians knew Capricorn as Suhur.mas ('goat-fish'), the Greeks knew it as Aigokeros ('goat-horned') and the Indians called it Makara ('sea-monster'). The Roman Capricorn is from *caper* ('goat') and *cornu* ('horn'). In Chinese astrology it corresponds to the months Tung Chih ('winter solstice') and Hsiao Han ('little cold'), and was represented by the Ox. When the Jesuits introduced the Western constellations the Chinese adopted it as Mo Ki, the Goat-fish. The constellation was known to the Jews as Azazel, the scapegoat from Leviticus; and to

'The tenth is a Makara [a mythical water monster] with the front half of a deer, in the midst of water: they call it the knee-area of the Creator. It dwells in rivers, woods, forests, holes and the beauty of lotuses.'

Indian astrologer Minaraja, 4th century AD

ABOVE **Capricorn, a woodcut from the *Poeticon Astronomicon* by C.J. Hyginus (1485).**
RIGHT **Since the Sun approaches Capricorn at the winter solstice (summer in the south), one of the year's turning-points, the sign is connected to boundaries and gateways.**

THE STARS OF CAPRICORN

Capricorn is the smallest of the twelve traditional zodiacal constellations, and the fortieth in size in the complete list of constellations. It covers just 1.003 per cent of the sky and contains 31 visible stars.

Modern astronomers have identified other images aside from the goat. A smile (the 'smile in the sky') is easily traceable in the constellation's brightest stars, but some also claim to see a high-heeled shoe.

Greek and Arabic astronomers used about eight of Capricorn's stars in their astrological work, of which the most important was Deneb Algedi, a star 37 light-years away from Earth (and which actually falls in Aquarius in the tropical zodiac). Its importance was recognized when Claudius Ptolemy in the 2nd century AD claimed that it shared the qualities of Jupiter and Saturn. If it was overhead at birth Deneb Algedi was thought to signify 'great glory, fame, wealth, dignity and authority', assuming the rest of the horoscope supported this. Such Jupiterian benefits were replaced by Saturnine difficulties when Deneb Algedi was close to the Sun, including loss of property and position, probably through false friends.

Many classical myths were moral tales in which an individual born with great advantages achieved success but then succumbed to hubris (complacency, pride and arrogance resulting in eventual disgrace). Deneb Algedi represented both parts of this cycle, the rise and the fall, and as such was regarded as a window onto fate, bearing messages of humility, caution and devotion to duty for any great person born while it was prominently placed.

early Christians as the apostle Simon Zelotes.

It is said that the month of January was created by the second legendary king of Rome, Numa Pompilius (715–673BC), who added two months to the old ten-month calendar. January, was named after Janus, the god of doors; we might suppose that Janus' task was to open the door to the new year. Janus was also the god with two faces, gazing into both past and future, at that which was lost for ever and that which was yet to come. Janus' temple in the Forum in Rome was open in times of war and closed in peacetime and had two entrance gates, suggesting victory and defeat. Janus became a god of beginnings – symbolized by gateways – and Capricorn is the gateway to the year.

ABOVE **Janus, the double-headed god of doorways, after whom January was named.**
LEFT **A 15th-century fresco depicting January, from the Castello del Buonconsiglio, Trento, Italy.**

'You naked trees, whose shady leaves are lost, Wherein the byrds were wont to build their bowre, And now are clothd with mosse and hoary frost, Instede of blosmes, wherwith your buds did flowre: I see your teares, that from your boughes doe raine, Whose drops in drery ysicles remaine.'

'January', a time of care and mourning, from Edmund Spenser's *Shepheardes Calendar*, 1579

VÉRITABLE E RAIT DE VIANDE LIEBIG.

Le carnaval à différentes époque
Les Saturnales chez les anciens Romains. Avant-coureurs des fêtes du car

THE END OF THE WORLD

It was commonly believed in ancient Greece and the Middle East that, just as the planets each signified a different cycle of time and repeatedly began new cycles, so corresponding levels of existence on Earth were also continually renewed. This was obvious in nature, in which every year plants seeded themselves, blossomed and died. It was thought that the same principles extended to human society.

According to the Babylonian priest Berossus, writing at the end of the 3rd century BC, the Deluge, remembered in the flood myth of Noah, took place when the Sun, Moon, Mercury, Venus, Mars, Jupiter and Saturn occupied Capricorn at the same time. It is also thought that he expected there would be another deluge in the future when the planets reached exactly the same positions. This prophecy was popular amongst the Romans,

although they disagreed on the extent of the destruction.

Has there ever been such a conjunction? According to the French astronomer Nicolas Flammarion (1842–1925), Chinese astronomers observed five planets in conjunction in Capricorn in 2449BC. Yet the world is still here! Such prophecies raise interesting questions, however, for they sometimes seem to bring strange twists. In the Byzantine Empire, whose

capital was Constantinople, it
was prophesied that the world
would come to an end in 1492. In
that year, Christopher Columbus
sailed to the Indies and discovered the New World. The
medieval astronomer Cardinal

'If Capricorn is in the ascendant one
should do things pertaining to grain,
lotuses, metals, fields, water and fraud.'

Indian astrologer Sphujidhvaja,
*c.*AD270

**An impression of the Roman
festival Saturnalia, from an
early 20th-century French
advertisement.**

Pierre D'Ailly predicted the end
of the world for 1789 – the year
in which the French Revolution
took place. The world survived,
but Western society entered the
modern age of revolutionary
republics. In the 1980s some
forecasters looked at Berossus'
prediction in the light of planc-
tary transits through the sign of
Capricorn *c.*1989–92 and forecast
not the end of the world, but at
least a major political and
economic crisis. This time it was
the world of Soviet Communism
that came to an end.

SATURNALIA
The ancient festival of Saturnalia
was celebrated in December,
climaxing on or around 25
December, and was dedicated to
the god Saturn. A central characteristic of Saturn festivals was
the reversal of social positions, so
that slaves became masters and
lords served their slaves, as a
reminder that earthly goods and
status have no real meaning and
that the only true values are
eternal. There was much feasting
and drinking, presided over by a
'Lord of Misrule'. In 2nd-century
Rome Saturnalia acquired greater
solemnity as the 'Dies Natalis
Invicti Solis', the birthday of
the unconquered or risen Sun,
dedicated to Mithras, the solar
hero and representative of the
god of light.

In the 4th century, the
Christian festival of Christmas
was fixed on 25 December by
Pope Julius I (337–52). The
pagan traditions of Saturnalia
(and other pre-Christian traditions celebrating the winter
solstice) were incorporated into
the Christmas festivities, and the
Lord of Misrule survives in a
muted form in Father Christmas
(Santa Claus).

PAN AND PANIC
The Greeks identified the
constellation with Pan, the half-
man, half-goat god of the
countryside. A playful creature of
doubtful parentage, Pan spent
most of his days chasing females
and then taking siestas. One
attempted seduction, of the
nymph Syrinx, failed when she
eluded him by turning herself
into a handful of reeds. As Pan
clutched the reeds he was
enchanted by the sound the wind
made through them, so he
selected the best and made his
famous pan-pipes, or syrinx.
When Pan wished to frighten
people he uttered a loud shout –
the origin of the word 'panic'.

Capricorn's link with water
was not entirely severed. When
Gaia, Mother Earth, sent the
monster Typhon to attack the
Olympian deities, Pan took
refuge in a river, turning his
lower half into a fish. The point
of the Greek story is simple.
Capricorn could be represented
as a sensual, sometimes threatening creature, wallowing in the
pleasures of the flesh.

THE GOAT-FISH

The Goat-fish is one of the oldest zodiacal creatures and has been found in the Indus Valley civilization which flourished *c*.2000BC in Pakistan. In Babylon, the water god Ea was sometimes a half-man, half-fish figure. The Babylonians believed that Oannes, another fish-man, was reputed to have come from the waters of the Persian Gulf to teach wisdom to the first people. He in turn is linked to John the Baptist, the prophet who prepared the way for Jesus. Capricorn's watery nature is shared with its neighbour, Aquarius; Ea is also an early form of the Aquarian water-pourer. In Egypt Capricorn may have been connected to Chnum, the god of the waters, who was associated with the rising of the Nile and was depicted with a pair of goat horns.

Classical astronomers had different views on which countries best represented Capricorn. Some thought that the Goat-fish, half animal, half fish, ruled the Netherlands, which semed to them to be half land, half sea. Most agreed that Capricorn ruled India – perhaps the sign's innate conservatism suited one of the world's most ancient cultures.

A lithograph after a bas-relief in the Assyrian capital, Nineveh, depicting Oannes, the mythical half-fish, half-man, teacher of wisdom to the Babylonians. Oannes' dual nature indicated he linked the worlds of spirit and matter.

THE ASTROLOGICAL CAPRICORN

Psychology rates Capricorn as one of the introspective 'neurotic' signs, concerned more with its state of mind than with the outside world. Carl Jung, however, had a different perspective, classifying it under his 'sensation' function, giving it a sense of practical reality, at home in the world of the senses.

In the northern hemisphere the Sun's entry into Capricorn marks the winter solstice, the time of midwinter dormancy, when our ancestors survived largely on the supplies of food which they had put by earlier in the year. Capricorn is a sign renowned for common sense and planning, a fact underlined by its Saturnian rulership. Saturn, astrologically, always encourages a serious long-term view, often with short-term hardship.

The image of the goat – the sure-footed climber of mountains, able to survive on thistles if necessary – is an appropriate one for this sign. Capricorns are cautious, serious, methodical, realistic, determined to reach their personal peak and capable of sacrifice and endurance.

Many Capricorns remain earth-bound throughout their lives, but there is a more spiritual – even mystical – side to the sign, as suggested by the image described earlier, the sea-goat. The sea suggests the infinite potential of the spirit, and Capricornian ambition can apply itself to spiritual development, as well as to worldly achievement. Tradition holds that Christ was a Capricorn, and his birthday is celebrated just after the Sun's entry into the sign, at the lowest point of the solar cycle. This is also the point when the Sun begins its epic journey back to full strength at the summer solstice. Capricorn's planning and endurance could be seen as the qualities necessary for this journey.

RELATING

The typical Capricorn may well make the first move in a relation-ship, though in a far less obvious way than, for example, Aries; they may get the ball rolling with a discreet tap, but will not risk rejection or ridicule by chasing after it. Yet Capricorn expresses itself in different ways.

Serious and responsible to

According to an almanac from 1386, 'Whoso is born in Capcorn schal be ryche and wel lufd.'

the end, the typical Saturnine Capricorn is often limited to one or two serious relationships in a lifetime, or may settle down late in life. Searching for emotional and practical reliability in a partner, in extreme cases they may marry for money, status or security. Or they may remain in a marriage of convenience while conducting an affair in secret.

The Pan Capricorn, on the other hand, may be excessively flirtatious, giving way to earthy sensuality. These types are warm and sensual lovers. Yet Saturn never lets go, and for loyalty and commitment, Capricorns cannot be bettered. It takes a great deal to make them give up on a relationship.

Last is the Fish Capricorn, represented by the goat's tail. If water symbolizes the imagination then the Capricorn is a deep, sensitive, loving, compassionate creature, often confused by the depth of its desires. This is precisely why it often fails to express its feelings.

THE SHADOW

Through its connection with Saturn Capricorn is the sign of the patriarch – or matriarch. Responsibility and fidelity are virtues, but when social custom is inflated into religious duty the Capricorn shadow emerges as the puritanical disciplinarian. The tyrannical Victorian father, beating his children for no reason other than that it is good for them, is the very essence of the malfunctioning Capricorn. Others

'Cancer resists Capricorn, even though they are compatible signs, just as summer conflicts with winter. The one brings frost and ice and a countryside white with snow. The other brings thirst and sweat and parched earth.'

Roman poet Manilius,
Astronomica, 1st century AD

include the greedy capitalist, lording it over the workers and exploiting the environment, sacrificing other people and interests in the cause of wealth production; and the dull manager, whether in business or politics, who stifles initiative in the name of order.

IN THE WORLD

Capricorn is particularly concerned with status, and Capricorns like to feel they are respected. The emphasis is on practical achievement, but also central to the sign can be a desire for power and control, even if its motive is nothing more sinister than a need to feel secure – which may also be the drive behind Capricorn's long-term planning. The classic Capricorn rises slowly through the ranks of a conventional career, and is typically found in management posts, exercising authority within a well-defined structure. The self-made busi-ness executive is a Capricorn archetype, accumulating money and property. Capricorn is one of the signs of the successful risk-conscious capitalist.

AQUARIUS

The Sun enters the tropical zodiac sign of Aquarius around 21 January and leaves around 19 February. Aquarius is a hot, moist, fixed, masculine sign, a member of the air element. The Sun is debilitated (weak) in the sign. Its traditional ruler is Saturn, but modern astrologers regard it as being ruled by Uranus, either on its own or jointly with Saturn. Its colour is sky-blue, its guardian angel Gambiel and its symbol the Water Bearer.

The Babylonians knew Aquarius as Gu'la, which translates roughly as 'giant', but the Greeks knew it as Hydrokhoös ('water-pot') and the Indians called it Kumbha ('pot'). In China it corresponds to the months Ta Han ('severe cold') and Li Ch'un ('spring begins').

The Celtic festival of Imbolc, now Candlemas Eve, was celebrated on 1 February. Imbolc meant 'in the belly' and marked the time when ewes came into milk ready for lambing. Beating the bounds, an annual walk around the boundaries to establish territorial limits, was a typical Imbolc ceremony which still survives in some parts of rural Britain. Women who wished to conceive would make a cradle of hay and place it on the hearth as an offering to the goddess Brid. The clearing out of the remains of yuletide greenery and garlands is the origin of modern spring-cleaning.

Tradition records that February was one of the two months introduced into the Roman calendar by the legendary king Numa Pompilius some time before 672BC. Its root is the Latin *februum* ('to purify'); it was in this month that the 'Februa' took place – this was a Roman festival in which the faithful were purified after the depths of midwinter had passed. Ever since the emperor Augustus took a day from February and added it to August, in his own honour, February has suffered. Now it is the shortest month of the year, having only 28 days (29 in every leap year).

RIGHT The Aquarian Water Bearer represents the cleansing, nourishing qualities of water, symbolizing the spread of possibilities and potential, both anarchic and authoritarian.

'The ancients called the eleventh, the lower leg, a Water-pot emptied on the shoulder of a Man. Its domains are water-vessels, poor crops, birds, women, liquor-shops and gambling-halls.'

Indian astrologer Minaraja, 4th century AD

JANUARY

AQUARIAN STARS

The constellation Aquarius is the tenth largest, covering 2.375 per cent of the sky and including 56 visible stars. The most notable astronomical event within the constellation was the discovery of Neptune inside its boundary, by the German astronomer Johann Galle at the Berlin Observatory, shortly after midnight on 24 September 1846. The constellation's most interesting single body is NGC 7293, better known as the Helix planetary nebula (cloud of dust or gas). At about 700 light-years away, this beautiful object is the closest nebula to the Earth. As it is so near it also appears relatively large, almost the size of the Moon.

Classical astronomers gave only a few of Aquarius' stars any astrological significance. Sadalmelek, a pale yellow star on Aquarius' right shoulder, was named after the Arabic al-Sa'd al-Malik ('the lucky one of the king') and indicated occult and

PROMETHEUS

A number of modern astrologers have identified Aquarius with the figure of Prometheus in Greek myth. Son of Iapetos and Themis, half-brother of Atlas, Prometheus was a Titan, but was spared after the quelling of their revolt because he had supported the Olympians. In some stories it was Prometheus who made humans, moulding them out of clay. Zeus did not like them much, but he agreed that they could live provided they remained in ignorance. However, when Prometheus taught humanity to cheat the gods, Zeus retaliated by denying them fire. Prometheus risked the wrath of Zeus by stealing fire for humanity – and was duly punished by being chained to a rock on Mount Caucasus, where his liver was torn out by a vulture every day, only for it to heal at night so that the torture could be repeated.

mystical interests. It shared its meaning with Sadalsuud, from the Arabic al-Sa'd al-Suud ('the luckiest of the lucky'), a star that sits on the constellation's left shoulder.

A star with very similar meanings was Skat, which sits on the Water Bearer's right leg. There are two theories as to the origin of the name – it is either derived from al-Shi'at, the Wish, or from al-Sak, the Shin Bone. When it rises before the Sun it is supposed to signify 'sensitive, emotional and psychic people, subject to criticism and persecution from society but support from friends'.

According to the 1st-century AD poet Manilius, the Romans believed that Aquarians had a special relationship with Cancer and Sagittarius: 'The Waterman worships the Crab on high and contemplates the drawn bow of the Archer.'

THE WATER BEARER

The Greek figure that occupies the constellation Aquarius is not a major mythical character. The Greeks failed to appreciate the importance of the water-pouring god in earlier religion. Their water god, Poseidon (Neptune to the Romans), was a powerful figure, yet was responsible for the ocean rather than the rain.

The Babylonian Ea, on the other hand, was one of the four creator gods. He was venerated by the Sumerians before c.2000BC as Enki ('lord of the

earth'), and is often pictured pouring the waters of life over the land. A modern psychological perspective portrays Ea as a symbol of untapped potential. It was Ea's task to alert ordinary mortals to possibilities that they were ignoring. The Sumerians of the 3rd millennium BC would have had more immediate concerns, for without rain the rivers would dry up, the crops would fail and life would come to an end.

THE DELUGE

The Roman soldier and scholar Germanicus Caesar (c.16BC–AD19) identified Aquarius with Deucalion, the son of Prometheus, and one of the few men to escape the Great Flood. By pouring the waters of life he prevented a recurrence of the death-bringing deluge. There are a number of interesting twists to this tale. In the 9th century the Islamic astronomer Abu Ma'shar calculated that the rains that brought Noah's flood began at dawn on Friday 18 February 3102BC. He believed that all five planets known at that

A small part of the Helix Nebula, photographed by the Hubble Space Telescope. The tadpole-shaped objects result from instability in the interaction between gases and are known as 'cometary knots'. Each one is about twice as wide as our solar system.

'The sign of Aquarius is cold and watery. Taken part by part its leading portion is moist, its middle temperate and the last part is windy. The north brings hot weather but the south brings clouds.'

Ptolemy, *Tetrabiblos*,
2nd century AD

time, plus the Sun and Moon, were in the water sign of Pisces at that moment. In fact, if we calculate their positions in the tropical zodiac then the Sun, Moon, Venus, Mars, Jupiter and Pluto were in the sign of Aquarius. Had they known this, astronomers of the time would have considered this even more appropriate than Pisces.

On 5 February 1962 the Sun, Moon, Mercury, Venus, Mars, Jupiter and Saturn were in Aquarius. In India this provoked fears of a deluge and of the end of the world. In the West there was a different response. In the 1890s, perhaps aware of the coming alignments, a French hoaxer, Gabriel Jogand, had spread a rumour that the Antichrist would be born in 1962; on 5 February 1962 the American clair-voyant Jeanne Dixon had a vision of the birth of the Antichrist, destined to be a great world teacher and lead the world away from Christianity.

The Babylonians believed that the Assyrians, their northern rivals, were ruled by Aquarius, which meant that they had to watch out for an Assyrian invasion when Mars, the warlike planet, passed through Aquarius. The Romans thought that Russia was ruled by Aquarius. This tradition proved remarkably persistent, and in the 20th century some New Agers believed that the Russian Revolution heralded the Age of Aquarius.

ABOVE An 18th-century Arabic manuscript showing Saturn (on the left), the planetary ruler of Aquarius. RIGHT The early Christians associated the disciple Matthew with Aquarius – represented in this painting from the Lindisfarne Gospels (c.698AD) by an angel above his halo. Of the other gospels, tradition related John to Leo, Luke to Taurus and Mark to Scorpio.

THE AGE OF AQUARIUS

Around 1880 the idea that the world was soon to enter a new age of peace and fellowship became increasingly popular in esoteric circles. It was believed that this would take place when the constellations had shifted sufficiently for the Sun to rise against the background of the stars of Aquarius on the spring equinox. This, it is believed, will inaugurate the 2,160-year Age of Aquarius. Unfortunately, few agree when the Age will begin; it depends on how the constellations are divided up, and as the International Astronomy Union reorganization in 1928 proved, the boundaries can change. The other problem is whether to take official boundaries or the stars themselves. Almost 100 different dates have been given for the Age's beginning, ranging from 1457 to 3550, a difference of 2,000 years. According to the International Astronomy Union the Sun will rise in the constellation of Aquarius *c*.2600.

'If you would have a man that is pious, pure and good, you will find him born when the first portion of the Waterman rises above the horizon.'

Roman poet Manilius, *Astronomica*, 1st century AD

'If thou can beare
Cherefully the Winters wrathfull cheare:
For age and Winter accord full nie,
This chill, that cold, this crooked, that wrye.
And as the lowering Wether lookes downe,
So seemest thou like good fryday to frown.
But y flowring youth is foe to frost,
My shippe unwont in stormes to be tost.'

'February' from Edmund Spenser's *Shepheardes Calendar*, 1579.
Winter is like old age, but can be defied by a youthful spirit.

THE ASTROLOGICAL AQUARIUS

Aquarius is classified as an extroverted sign, meaning that it is essentially outgoing. This conforms with the Greek astronomers' opinion that it was masculine, although their belief that it was 'fixed' implies stubbornness and a refusal to change. In the Jungian system it is classified as a 'thinking' sign, good with facts, strong on logic and keen on communication.

Aquarius is an air sign, like Gemini and Libra. All three are represented by non-animal figures, signifying their particular connection with civilization and the life of the mind, as opposed to instinct. Aquarians tend to be rational, lucid thinkers. However, they may over-rationalize and be rather uncomfortable with instincts and emotions.

Astrologers see Aquarius as perhaps the most individualistic sign of the zodiac. Aquarians, it is said, need to express themselves as free, creative individuals, yet

they also need to be part of society. Their sense of social responsibility reflects the rulership of the sign by Saturn, the planet of duty and order.

Contradictions and paradoxes are at the heart of the sign's psychology. The typical Aquarian may have wildly radical ideas, but becomes set in highly individualistic ways, failing to shift with the times, change plans, or let go of a conviction in the face of new evidence. Aquarius is often a rebel without a cause, or a revolutionary fighting yesterday's battles.

THE SHADOW

Aquarius elevates ideas and ideals above all other considerations. The aim is not merely to opt out of, or even destroy, the old order, but to replace it with a new and better one. This is fine as far as it goes, until other considerations are completely ignored. Being concerned with

groups rather than individuals, Aquarius is the social reformer who expects everyone to conform to its particular prescription, for their own good; wherever there are people who attempt to force their own ideals on others, there we can identify the Aquarian shadow. Aquarius' worship of the group becomes a fear of the terrible powers the group unleashes. The collaborator becomes an individualist who destroys all attempts at cooperation, and the democrat who becomes a dictator. The Aquarian shadow proclaims, 'Don't do as I do: do as I say'.

> **GANYMEDE, THE LOVER OF ZEUS**
> The Greeks believed that Aquarius was Ganymede, who was said to have been the most beautiful boy alive. He was the son of King Tros, after whom Troy was named. Even Zeus became infatuated with the boy, transformed himself into an eagle and carried him off to Olympus. As with all myths there are other versions. In one, Ganymede was abducted by Eos, the goddess of dawn, who had a passion for young men; he was then stolen from her by Zeus, who appointed him cup-bearer to the gods — the Aquarian water was turned to nectar. The story of Zeus' love for Ganymede was popular in Rome, where it was taken as divine sanction for homosexuality.

> Aquarius was said to rule the legs and ankles. According to 17th-century English astrologer William Ramesey, the Aquarian person was reputed to be 'of a tall wel-set corporature, of a strong body, of a long visage, usually of a fair, flaxen hair, and of a paler whiter countenance'.

> 'If Aquarius is in the ascendant one should do things pertaining to servants, drinks, metals, ceremonies, carriages, blows, feats of battles and swords.'
>
> Indian astrologer Sphujidhvaja, c.AD270

RELATING

The Aquarian may care deeply about society as a whole, and even be part of a wide social network. Yet ironically members of this sign often find it hard to relate closely to individuals. They may have numerous friends but sometimes no one to whom they feel especially close.

Aquarians value their independence and the typical Aquarian may not have the time or the inclination for a conventional relationship. In fact they may be quite happy without a partner for months on end, absorbed in their interests and social commitments. A busy social life becomes a means of avoiding emotional involvement. Even within a relationship, companionship and shared interests may mean more to an Aquarian than sex or sentiment.

IN THE WORLD

Astrologers expect Aquarius to take a special interest in group objectives. The typical Aquarian is often happiest in a career which includes an element of social idealism, or which is at least of benefit to the community or the world as a whole, such as social work, teaching or politics. Aquarians like to be at the cutting edge, tend to embrace new working methods long before they have become popular, and are often attracted to modern technology. However, as workers, they need to be given independence and personal responsibility.

The Abduction of Ganymede by Rubens (1577–1640). In Greek myth, Zeus transformed himself into an eagle in order to abduct the beautiful boy with whom he was infatuated.

PISCES

The Sun enters the tropical zodiac sign of Pisces around 20 February and leaves around 20 March. Its traditional ruler is Jupiter, but modern astrologers regard it as being ruled, either jointly or solely, by Neptune. Mercury is debilitated (weak) in Pisces, and Venus is exalted (strong). It is a cold, wet, mutable, feminine sign and a member of the water element. Its colours are white and glittering, delicate blues; its guardian angel is Barchiel. Its symbol is the Fish or Twin Fish.

Pisces' name in most cultures means 'fish', whether Babylonian Nuni, Nunu, Zib or Zibbati ('[fish]tails'), Syriac Nuno, Indian Meena, Greek Ichtus, Roman Pisces, Persian Mahik or Turkish Balik. This is not surprising for cultures who were in close contact with each other, but even the Aztecs called the constellation Atl, or Fish. The Babylonians are also believed to have shown the northern Fish with the head of a swallow, perhaps because this bird appeared in the spring. In China it corresponds to the months Yu Shui ('rain water') and Ching Chih ('excited insects').

The Greeks and Romans welcomed Pisces as a sign of improving weather. Of the two fish, one sees the end of winter, the other the beginning of spring. 'When the returning Sun courses through the watery stars, then winter's rains mingle with the showers of spring: each sort of moisture belongs in the sign that swims.'

Roman poet Manilius, *Astronomica*, 1st century AD

Some say the Latin word *pisces* shares a root with the Greek *ichtus*. The Romans knew the sign as Imbrifer ('rainy') Duo Pisces, Gemini Pisces and Piscis Gemellus. Some classical writers said that the stars were connected to the rain-bearing northerly wind, Aquilonius or Aquilonaris or even to Eurus or Vulturnus, the south-east wind.

March was Martius, the first month of the Roman year, named after Mars. No doubt the Romans felt that the beginning of the campaigning season should appeal to their god of war. Their astronomers believed that the planet Mars 'ruled' Aries, the sign that the Sun entered near the end of the month. The Anglo-Saxons called March Leneth-monath, or Long month, after the lengthening of the days around the spring equinox. This is the origin of the Christian festival of Lent, the forty-day period during which devout believers renounce worldly pleasures – in earlier times they were probably making a virtue out of the scarcity of food at the end of winter.

'The great ones called the last sign a Pair of Fish, the feet of Time. It dwells in good people, Gods and Brahmins, and in fords, rivers, oceans and streams.'

Indian astrologer Minaraja, 4th century AD

RIGHT **The two Piscean fish represent the sign's dual nature and the divisions it embodies between the spiritual and material, between mind and body, and the Piscean individual's ability to face in contradictory directions.**

THE STARS OF THE FISH

Pisces is hardly a bright constellation. It contains fifty visible stars, but its brightest are relatively faint, and none was given astrological significance. Perhaps the most important is Alpha Piscium, or Alrischa, from the Arabic meaning 'the cord' or 'the knot'. The name may originally have come from the Babylonian Riksu, the Cord. Astrology includes one star in watery Pisces, the malevolent Scheat, said to cause shipwreck and death by drowning, but astronomers locate it in Pegasus.

LOVE AND DESIRE

The Greeks believed that Pisces was linked to the Syrian goddess Astarte, and thus to Aphrodite, the goddess of love. In Greek cosmology, the gods of Olympus fought and defeated their predecessors, the Titans. However, Mother Earth (Gaia) held a shock in store to punish the triumphant gods. After mating

with Tartarus, the lowest region of the underworld, where the god Zeus had imprisoned the Titans, she gave birth to Typhon, the most terrifying monster the world had ever seen. Gaia sent Typhon to attack the gods and goddesses, who fled in terror. Aphrodite and her son Eros leapt into the river, perhaps the Euphrates, and were saved when

A painted wooden cupboard door in the Temple of the Thousand Buddhas, Sha Tin (New Territories, Hong Kong), showing the sacred fish, one of the eight sacred symbols of the Buddhists.

they were transformed into two fish, and later placed in the heavens. In some versions Aphrodite and Eros were merely transported to heaven by the fish rather than themselves turned into fish, but the meaning is the same. The Romans adapted the myth and made the two fish themselves the saviours who rescued Venus and her son (Cupid) and carried them out of danger. The poet Manilius wrote that 'Venus owed her safety to their shape'.

TOTEMS AND TABOOS

Unlike many zodiac myths the Pisces fish connection had a real impact in daily life. The special connection between Pisces, the Fish, Venus, goddess of love, and the Euphrates, archetype of the Great River, may have been the reason for certain taboos against the eating of fish. Some Syrians treated fish as totems, or sacred objects, believing they were divine, and refused to eat them.

'Still larger in front of the Ram and still in the vestibule of the South are the Fishes. Ever one is higher then the other, and louder hears the fresh rush of the North wind. From both there stretch as it were, chains, whereby their tails on either side are joined. The meeting chains are knit by a single beautiful and great star, which is called the Knot of Tails. Let the left shoulder of Andromeda be thy guide to the northern Fish, for it is very near.'

Aratus, *Phaenomena*, 3rd century BC

The Twin Fish of Pisces, from a zodiacal relief by Agostino di Duccio in the Chapel of the Planets, Tempio Malatestiano, Rimini, Italy (*c*.1450). The constellation has been seen as a fish or a pair of fish by many ancient cultures, even those who had no contact with other civilizations, such as the Aztecs.

Some just refused to eat the fish from the river Chalos. As Ovid wrote:

'Hence Syrians hate to eat that kind of fishes;
Nor is it fit to make their gods their dishes.'

The Egyptians are said by some to have found sea-fish odious and to have abstained from eating them out of dread and abhorrence, and when they wished to express anything disgusting, they used the hieroglyphic symbol for a fish. Perhaps this is the tradition Pliny drew on when he said that the appearance of a comet in Pisces indicated great trouble. Later, the Roman Catholic Church, by banning the eating of meat on Friday (the day sacred to Venus), started a custom in which virtually everybody in western Europe ate fish on Friday. Demand for fish became so great that by the 1480s English sailors may have been fishing for cod off the coast of Newfoundland. It is thought that this encouraged Columbus to make his first transatlantic voyage in 1492.

LOAVES AND FISHES

Possibly the most interesting occurrence of Piscean mythology is in early Christianity. To any Jew of the 1st century AD the two stories of the loaves and fishes (first the feeding of the 5,000 and second the feeding of the 4,000) had an immediate zodiacal

The Miracle of the Loaves and Fishes, by Giovanni Lanfranco (1582–1647). The biblical tale contains astrological symbolism that would have been instantly understood by most people in the early days of Christianity.

THE AGE OF THE FISH

Christianity's use of the fish symbol was the subject of a study in the 1950s by the psychologist Carl Jung. He noticed that around the time when Christ was preaching, the spring equinox moved into Pisces – or rather, on the day of the equinox, the Sun rose in the constellation Pisces instead of Aries. He was not the first to point this out, but he was the first to give it a serious psychological meaning. He believed that the fish symbol indicated something real about the first Christians' motives and state of mind, and about Christian culture in general. He compared the symbolic submergence of the fish in the Piscean ocean to the individual's submergence in a sea of faith, the sacrifice of the self to God. In Jung's opinion the gradual shift of the zodiacal constellations represented a sort of timing mechanism, indicating shifts in the collective unconscious, or group mind. He regarded what he saw as the crisis of confidence in the 20th century as an early symptom of the dawning of the Aquarian Age (see p.105).

reference. The loaf would have been instantly connected with Virgo as a symbol of the corn goddess. More than this, in Mark's gospel Christ attaches special significance to the

numbers of baskets of crumbs left over after the two miracles: twelve and seven respectively. Almost nobody at the time could have been unaware that twelve referred to the Sun and the twelve solar months and zodiac constellations, and seven to the seven days of the week, the seven planets and the Moon's quarter period. The message was simple. The faithful should be sustained by universal cosmic truths and could not 'live by bread alone'. The Pisces aspect of the calendar myth was represented in Christ's promise that he would make his disciples 'fishers of men', and can also be seen in the early Christians' use of the fish as their principal symbol before the cross, a solar symbol, was adopted, probably under Roman influence.

Christ's use of the fish as a metaphor would have had another very important reference. In 6BC there had been a particularly important conjunction of Jupiter and Saturn in Pisces and the Jewish astrologers of the time would have made it clear that Pisces symbolized their hope for a messiah.

THE ASTROLOGICAL PISCES

Pisces signifies 'grounds full of water, Springs, Fish-ponds, Rivers, places where Hermitages have been, Water-mils, Moats about houses, Wells, Pumps, Conduits, Cisterns and those places in houses where water is most frequent.'

English astrologer William Ramesey, 1653

Psychologically Pisces is one of the inward-looking 'neurotic' signs. In the Jungian system it is a 'feeling' sign, high on emotion. In the wheel of the zodiac it falls at the end of the cycle of the zodiac, representing the sacrifice of the self, the river merging with the sea.

Adaptable and rather restless, averse to routine and structure, often difficult to pin down, the typical Pisces is easy-going, sensitive, compassionate, emotional, imaginative, intuitive and empathetic.

Pisces was associated with two of the Olympian gods. While the Roman poet and astronomer Manilius linked it to Neptune, most Greek astronomers claimed it was ruled by Neptune's brother Jupiter. Jupiter was a sky god, while Neptune was limited to rulership of the sea. In a sense Neptune, Water, can be read as a symbol of the unconscious while Jupiter, Sky, represents the conscious mind. Both gods in their different ways relate to the transcendence of boundaries and limitations. Jupiter seeks distant goals; Neptune seeks to tran-scend the boundaries of the self by merging with the other. The twin fishes of Pisces bring the two together, and the Piscean personality yearns to transcend the boundaries of life.

RELATING

Pisces is capable of deep feeling and great sensitivity. The Piscean dreams of universal love, of an almost mystical merging with a single partner. The 'urge to merge' can make Pisceans romantic and captivatingly seductive. They will quickly establish shared reference points, and this, combined with their natural empathy, often gives those they meet for the first time the feeling that they have met before.

Piscean men often appeal to women by seeming to need to be looked after, while Piscean women may appear to offer escape from a harsh and unsympathetic world. When relationships go wrong, they may sacrifice themselves to the happiness of their partner or children, even while complaining about their lot.

THE SHADOW

The true Piscean shadow emerges from the sign's submergence in the ocean. Pisces sacrifices itself to the group or to a dream. Piscean martyrs sabotage relationships by sacrificing their own feelings and then blaming partners. Devout Pisceans find solace in the simple rituals of religion. Disillusioned Pisceans escape into the arms of Bacchus or Morpheus, the gods of alcohol and intoxicants. The shadow Pisces is the helpless soul who does more than sacrifice its own interests; it places itself at the mercy of others, of circumstances and of fate.

IN THE WORLD

Pisces takes its creative imagination and compassion into its work, and often finds itself in the 'caring professions', such as medicine and counselling. The typical Piscean is also attracted to design, the arts and entertainment. Flexible and open to new suggestions, they cope with changing demands, and often flow around problems rather than confronting them. They can be very pleasant colleagues, willing to put themselves out for others and to make sacrifices. Some are well-intentioned but actually rather lazy. Relatively few take easily to management and leadership, and most prefer to be told what to do, provided they have scope for imagination within the

given framework. At its worst Pisces lacks ambition, finds it hard to get down to work, cannot stick to a schedule or a brief, and cannot organize its thoughts. However, just as the two fish swim in opposite directions, so Pisces often defies its impractical, inept reputation.

Pisces is lacking in two of Jung's four functions of consciousness, 'thinking' and 'sensation'. This is why some Piscean people are said to place great emphasis on academic success as a means of disciplining their otherwise confused minds, and why they are naturally out of touch with their physical needs. Some deliberately take on intellectual or physical challenges in order to overcome their weaknesses.

The month of March, from the early 15th-century *Très Riches Heures du Duc de Berry* by the Limbourg brothers. Pisces is on the left of the celestial sphere, Aries on the right. The main activity for the month is ploughing the ground in preparation for the sowing of seeds that will take place under Aries.

'The joyous time now nigheth fast,
That shall alegge this bitter blast,
And slake the winters sorrowe…
… And stouping Phebus steepes his face:
Its time to hast us homeward.'

'March' from Edmund Spenser's *The Shepheardes Calendar*, 1579. March brings relief that winter is over and sows the seeds for April — and love. The Sun is moving to its home in Leo.

THE PLANETS

Our solar system consists of nine known planets orbiting a central star (the Sun), with countless smaller satellites and comets. The most numerous objects are the thousands of asteroids in the asteroid belt between Mars and Jupiter; and an estimated 35,000 objects with a diameter of over 100 kilometres (60 miles) exist beyond Neptune and Pluto in the so-called Kuiper belt. There may also be billions of comets in the 'Oort cloud' which surrounds the solar system in a sphere almost 1 light-year in radius.

Most of the bodies in the solar system orbit the Sun on a plane that is almost flat, like a disc, which is roughly the same as the ecliptic (the plane of the Earth's orbit around the Sun). Although all planets deviate from the ecliptic, only Pluto does so to any notable degree.

Astronomers have only a vague understanding of how the Sun and planets came into existence. Mythology relates that a god or gods created the universe out of nothing or chaos. In Judaeo-Christian belief, God created the world in seven days – a notion inspired by the seven known planets, each representing a creative impulse. According to current astronomical theories, the Sun and planets emerged out of a cloud of dust and gas over a period of about 100 million years, 4.55 billion years ago.

Until the 16th century there were thought to be seven planets, including the Sun and Moon. With the revolutionary discoveries of Copernicus, Kepler, Galileo and Newton, the Sun and Moon were excluded and Earth was added; Uranus was discovered in 1781, Neptune in 1848 and Pluto in 1930. No planet has been found beyond Pluto, but other objects have been discovered, including a new class of celestial body: 'Centaurs', which originate in the Kuiper belt beyond Pluto and are pulled into vast, planet-crossing orbits by Neptune's gravity.

In this view from Apollo 11, Earth rises above the lunar horizon, 384,000 km (240,000 miles) away. Photographs such as this, taken in 1969, profoundly affected people's ideas of humanity's place in the universe.

THE SUN

The Sun is the star around which our solar system has grown. Without it there could be no life on Earth; without its heat and light our planet would be a dead lump of freezing rock, with an average temperature of –270° C. The Sun first gives life and then controls it. Our lives are divided into days and years, created respectively by the Earth's rotation and by its orbit around the Sun. Our calendars are regulated according to whether the Sun is visible or not, and its height in the sky.

Although small compared to other stars in the galaxy, the Sun is a giant in relation to the Earth. Its diameter of 1.4 million kilometres (870,000 miles) is 109 times that of the Earth, which could itself fit into the Sun 330,000 times over – roughly equivalent to filling a beach ball with peas. The Sun is about 149 million kilometres (93 million miles) from the Earth, so that its light takes about 8.3 minutes to reach us.

> 'The Sun is God, anybody can see that.'
>
> Hopi Indian to Carl Jung

Its light has been regarded as a symbol of good, of reason, of love and of hope. In most civilizations, the Sun has been revered as a symbol of the universal God or Goddess, and of all that is best in humanity.

In the ancient world the Sun was revered as Shamash (Babylon); Ra and Amun (Egypt); Mithra (Persia); Helios (Greece); and Apollo (Rome). To the Aztecs he was Tonatiuh (He Who Makes the Day); to the Maya he was the cosmic Jaguar. To classical astronomers the Sun was a hot, dry planet. He ruled Leo and was exalted (strong) in Aries and debilitated (weak) in Libra and Aquarius. Medieval astronomers knew the Sun as Sol, Titan, Ilios, Phoebus and Osiris. His special day was Sunday, his angel was Michael and he was friends with all the planets.

To all ancient peoples the alternation of day and night was one of the great mysteries of the world. The setting of the Sun brought fear, even despair; its rising brought joy. In Egyptian religion, for example, the myths of the Sun's daily journey had a central place: following his triumphal journey across the daytime sky the Sun god was

A photograph taken by an orbiting NASA satellite in 1980, showing a solar prominence – a violent eruption on the Sun's surface, arcing at least 40,000 km (25,000 miles) into the sky.

obliged to descend to the underworld to confront the forces of darkness. Victorious, he was reborn at dawn, restoring life to his kingdom. Beliefs such as these formed the prototype of all myths in which a god of light or life is destined to suffer in the underworld before his rebirth. In this way, the simple fact of the Sun's daily appearance and disappearance provides the central theme for many of the world's greatest religions.

RIGHT **The solar centre of the 13th-century zodiac in the Baptistery in Florence, Italy, with its hermetic Latin palindrome around the edge.**

MOTHER SUN

Long before the beginning of recorded history our ancestors knew that without the Sun's light and heat there could be no life on earth. Sunrise and sunset were seen as times of spiritual significance, solar eclipses inspired dread, and solstices and equinoxes were celebrated as important turning points in the calendar. It is not surprising that all mythological systems feature at least one solar divinity. In some cultures, such as the Babylonian, the Sun was represented by a deity of lesser rank. In others, such as the Egyptian or Inca civilizations, the Sun was the representative of the supreme god.

That we tend to think of Sun deities as male rather than female is mainly due to Western culture's inheritance of the Babylonian and Egyptian Sun gods; adopted by the Greeks and Romans, they are familiar to generations of children brought up with the classical myths. However, the Celts, Basques, Lapps and Finns all worshipped solar goddesses. In Teutonic and Scandinavian mythology the Sun is feminine – the goddess Sunna or Sol. Native North Americans and Aboriginal Australians also revered female Sun deities. Amaterasu, the Japanese Sun goddess, is the central deity of Shinto religion.

The Indo-Europeans, who spread across Europe, central Asia and northern India, are responsible for many of the common Sun-goddess myths, which can be traced back to before *c*.2000BC. Ushas, the goddess of dawn in the Hindu sacred texts (the Vedas), is linked to Auzurine, the Baltic daughter of the Sun, to the Greek Eos or Aurora (Dawn, sister of Helios), the German Eostre (Ostara), the Celtic Eriu, and other goddesses of the dawn, spring and morning.

One of the ancient world's greatest Sun goddesses was the Egyptian Hathor (see pp.31–2), who is represented as a cow-headed woman, holding the Sun between her horns. The Bull image connects her to Taurus, the constellation in which the Sun rose at the spring equinox prior to *c*.2000BC, and indicates the antiquity of the image. However, the male pharaohs of Egypt, who identified themselves with the Sun, needed a male Sun god to legitimate their rule, and Hathor was gradually demoted to the lesser position of mother or daughter of the Sun god.

AMUN-RA

One of the most celebrated Sun gods was the Egyptian Ra (or Re or Phra), which it is thought means simply 'creator'. His chief sanctuary was Heliopolis (Greek 'city of the Sun'), near modern Cairo. According to the priests of Heliopolis, in the beginning Ra (as Atum) had reposed in the bosom of the primordial ocean, Nun, enclosed in the bud of a lotus. The creation commenced when, weary of his own impersonality, he made an act of will and rose from the abyss into the sky, appearing in glittering splendour and giving birth to the eight great gods.

Ra's forms and names were innumerable. In the later kingdom (*c*.1st millennium BC) he was known as Amun (Amon or Ammon) or Amun-Ra. As a universal sky god Amun was associated by the Greeks with Zeus. In his form as Aton or Aten, he is thought by many to have inspired the Hebrew devotion to the worship of one god when the pharaoh Akhenaten forbade the worship of all other gods – including Amun.

GREATER AND LESSER GODS

There is a distinction to be made between gods who are closely associated with the Sun, such as Helios, who drove the Sun chariot, and gods such as Apollo, who embodied the Sun's light, but had a much wider role.

'This great deity actually is the Sun in heaven, which even now illuminates the world before our eyes.'

Shinto hymn to the Sun goddess Amaterasu

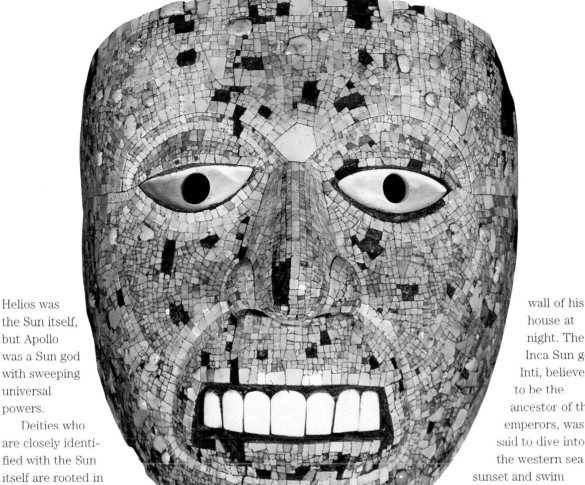

Helios was the Sun itself, but Apollo was a Sun god with sweeping universal powers.

Deities who are closely identified with the Sun itself are rooted in animist religion. A typical example is the Navajo god Tsohanoai, who carries the Sun on his back and hangs it on a peg on the west wall of his house at night. The Inca Sun god Inti, believed to be the ancestor of the emperors, was said to dive into the western sea at sunset and swim beneath the earth to return at dawn; the *intihuatana*, at Machu Picchu in Peru, was his 'hitching post', a ceremonial shadow clock built of stone pillars and used in observance of the Sun's course. Astrologer-priests would gather there to observe and interpret cosmic events. The Aztec Tonatiuh, the last of the series of four Aztec Sun gods, was a more bloodthirsty deity, who required regular human sacrifices and moral asceticism in order to sustain him in his birth, daily journey across the sky and nocturnal struggle for survival.

The Maidu Indians of California believed that the Sun was a fierce woman. At first she lived with her husband, the Moon, in a stone house, and the Earth was in total darkness. Nothing could persuade the couple to come out and light up the world. Eventually the Angle Worm drilled a hole through the wall and the Gopher slipped some fleas through it. Sun and Moon were driven mad by the itching and fled to the sky. Initially the Sun wanted to travel by herself at night, without the Moon. But, harassed by the stars for sex, she changed her mind and travelled by day, leaving the Moon to travel by night.

The Sun Chariot of Apollo (1907–10) by Odilon Redon. The painting captures the force and glory of the Sun god as he drives his chariot in his daily journey across the sky.

Sometimes simple animistic and more universal solar gods existed side by side, one usually being the more important. Inca mythology gradually gave less weight to the universal Sun and storm god Viracocha, who wandered the earth as a beggar, and more to the animistic Inti. Generally, however, animistic gods declined with the development of urban civilization.

A personification of the Sun seated on a lion, from the Doge's Palace, Venice, Italy (probably 15th century). The sign of Leo (the Lion) is ruled by the Sun.

The lowly status given to Helios in the Greek pantheon is illustrated by the story of the allocation of land amongst the gods. When Zeus was apportioning territories, Helios was late and was forgotten. He arrived in time to see some land just rising out of the sea, and persuaded the gods that it would be his. It turned out to be Rhodes – the only place where Helios was given prominence by the ancient Greeks.

HELIOS AND APOLLO

The Greeks allocated the Sun two principal deities, Helios the Sun itself, and Apollo the solar light. Helios' cult flourished throughout Greece and appears to have been very ancient. Myth relates that he was the son of the Titan Hyperion, grandson of Ouranos, brother of Eos (Dawn) and Selene (the Moon). Although Zeus and his brothers vanquished the Titans, Helios retained a place in the Greek pantheon, daily driving his chariot across the heavens, pasturing his four horses in the Isle of the Blessed, and sailing home on the Ocean Stream; like the Babylonian Shamash, he rode a chariot during the day, but as with the Egyptian Ra his night journey was in a boat.

Apollo, the son of Zeus and Leto, was given a much more extensive role, as heroic avenger and patron of the arts. When only four days old, he killed Leto's enemy the dragon Python, and with his sister Artemis he

APOLLO AND ASCLEPIUS

Asclepius, son of Apollo and a lake nymph, learnt the healing arts from the wise Centaur Chiron. His powers were great, and on at least one occasion he resurrected a dead man. Hades, lord of the underworld, protested to Zeus at this theft of one of his rightful subjects, and Zeus duly killed the healer with a thunderbolt. Apollo took revenge by loosing his golden arrows fatally upon Zeus' armourers, the Cyclopes, for which insubordinate act he was obliged to spend a year herding sheep for King Admetus.

killed the giant Tityus, employing as always a shower of golden arrows – symbolizing the Sun's rays. Apollo was a hero, commanding great respect; whenever he entered the assembly at Olympus the other gods and goddesses all stood, as a mark of honour, and Zeus personally welcomed him and gave him nectar in a golden cup.

Apollo's most important practical task – one shared by Shamash in Babylonian mythology – was to dispense answers in response to oracular questions. His most important role, though, was as a future world saviour, the Greek messiah. The Greeks believed that history could be divided into seasons, each one embodying a phase in the life of the Sun. The universe had been ruled first by

Ouranos, followed in the Golden Age by Cronos; then came Zeus, the current lord. It was prophesied that in the not very distant future Apollo would succeed Zeus, and the Golden Age, the primeval paradise, would be restored. This myth was well known to early Christians, who took it as support for their belief in Christ's second coming.

The Roman emperors found that the solar cult was the perfect way to focus religious devotion on themselves. Nero (ruled AD54–68) was the first to compare himself to the Sun, but it was the 3rd-century BC emperor Heliogabalus, who had been a priest of the Sun god in Phoenicia, who established the religion of Sol Invictus (the Unconquered Sun), in which the Sun was worshipped in the form of a large black cone or obelisk.

CHRIST AS THE SUN

Many early Christians found it natural to compare Christ to the Sun god. They understood that the Roman god Apollo was not actually the Sun, but was an aspect of the universal god whose symbol was the Sun. This is clear in the gospels, in which Christ is compared to the Sun. Matthew writes (17.2) that

LEFT Pagan symbolism often survives into modern-day Christian ritual. In this float for an Assumption Day procession in Messina, Sicily, the display is dominated by the golden image of the Sun.

shortly before his ascension to heaven, Jesus' face shone like the Sun; and it was common to quote Malachi 3.20, describing Jesus as the 'Sun of Righteousness'. St Paul advised his congregation to let 'Christ shine on you' (Ephesians 5.14), while in AD200 Clement of Alexandria described Christ as the Sun driving his chariot across the sky. There is even a mosaic of 'Christ-Helios' in the Vatican. As late as the 4th century some Christians in Rome complained that worshippers turned to venerate the Sun before entering St Peter's Basilica. After the emperor Constantine, a supporter of Sol Invictus, legalized Christianity in AD312, Christianity took over many of the rites and rituals of the solar religion, fixing Christmas for 25 December, one of the most important solar festivals.

HERO, CIVILIZER AND SEER

Several themes link the solar gods of different systems. They are active and vigorous, and many are heroes. Animistic solar deities tend to fight their heroic struggles when they sink into the western darkness at dusk, to arise triumphant in the east at dawn; anthropomorphic ones go out and look for trouble, which occasionally involves them in a symbolic descent into the underworld.

In Greek mythology this heroic aspect is found in Apollo, but not in Helios. The Babylonian Shamash is strong and courageous, but is over-taken in heroic stature by Marduk, who slays Tiamat, the symbol of Chaos. Solar heroes usually have great enemies with whom they are locked in perpetual battle: Apollo slays Python; the

THE SOLAR PERSONALITY
'When well: Very faithfull, keeping their promises, a kind of itching desire to Rule: Prudent, and of incomparable Judgment; of great Majesty and Statelinesse, Industrious to acquire Honour and a large Patrimony, yet as willingly departing therewith againe; speaks with gravity and great confidence; full of Thought, Secret, trusty, Affable, and very humane to all people, loving Sumptuousnesse and Magnificence; no sordid thoughts can enter his heart.

'When ill: Arrogant and Proud, disdaining all men, boasting of his Pedigree, blind in Judgment, restlesse, troublesome, domineering, expensive, foolish, endowed with no gravity in words, or sobernesse in Actions, a Spend-thrift, thinks all men are bound to him because he is a Gentleman borne.'

English astrologer William Lilly, 1647

Solar imagery in a 9th-century stone tablet depicting the founding of the temple of Shamash, the Sun god, at Sippar, Babylon.

Egyptian Sun god Ra has as his arch enemy the serpent Apepis.

Solar gods may also be bringers of civilization. The first of the four Aztec Sun gods, Tezcatlipoca, was, like Apollo, a god of music. The Celtic Lugh (Bright One) claimed expertise in all arts and crafts – omnicompetence. The Indian Surya's involvement with craftsmanship was less direct – he was too bright for his wife, and had his brightness shaved down on the lathe of his carpenter father-in-law.

The omniscience of many solar gods provided a good basis for sitting in judgment. Shamash was god of another civilized institution – justice. Zeus himself – dispenser of justice – was associated with the Sun, although he was not actually a Sun god. Even more closely connected with the Sun, and with consciousness and truth, was the Persian Mithra (see pp.32–3), who became Mitra – god of contracts and friendship – to Hindus, and Mithras to the Romans.

THE HERO'S JOURNEY

Some of the great heroic myth-cycles of the ancient world were built around a calendar theme. The Babylonian epic of Gilgamesh is divided into twelve sections, one of which, probably relating to Aquarius, is the prototype for the biblical story of Noah's flood. In Greek myth, Heracles' twelve labours also depict the passage of the Sun through the seasons, facing a different struggle in every month. Some of his 'labours' have obvious links to the constellations – for example, the battle with the Nemean Lion relates to Leo – but others have no apparent direct connection to the stars and their

original meaning is now obscure. The journey of Jason and the Argonauts was another Greek myth based on the Sun's annual cycle (see pp.24–5).

The Sun's courage in battling with the demons of night and restoring his energy every spring was considered a model for the heroic life, and it was common to describe great men as being like the Sun. The Roman emperors borrowed the Egyptian belief that the monarch and the Sun god were one and the same. Originally the royal crown was a solar symbol, made of gold (the Sun's metal), and consisting of a band with rays rising to heaven, an image found on coins dating to the reign of Nero in the 1st century AD. This tradition survived until relatively recently, even if in a watered-down form: Louis XIV of France (1638–1715) was known as the 'Sun King'.

The Babylonians believed that the Lebanon was sacred to the Sun. In the epic of Gilgamesh, written down *c*.2000BC, we read that 'the country where the cedar is cut [Lebanon] belongs to Shamash'.

THE DESCENT

The solar hero's journey through the year was relatively untroubled. Far more threatening was his nightly descent to the underworld to face the demons of darkness. The prototype for Middle Eastern descent myths was the Sumerian legend of Dumuzzi (later known as Tammuz, see p.23). Strictly,

Dumuzzi was a vegetation deity, and lover of Inanna, the Sumerian Venus; but he embodied the qualities of the solar hero, and as a vegetation deity he was an aspect of the Sun as guardian of the seasons. Dumuzzi's sacrificial descent to the underworld is an extension of the myth of the descent of Inanna (see p.153). In the myth, Dumuzzi and Inanna were lovers, but as soon as Inanna embarked on her journey to the underworld, where she became trapped, Dumuzzi forgot her, suppressing his desires and busying himself with affairs of state. In order for Inanna to return to the overworld Dumuzzi was obliged to take her place in the underworld – as the archetypal substitute king.

As Tammuz, Dumuzzi was worshipped throughout the Middle East, and was popular amongst Hebrew women, much to the annoyance of the biblical prophets. The myth of Christ's three-day descent to hell and the attendant Easter rituals are partly based on Tammuz-worship and similar rites based around Marduk in Babylon.

The substitute king is a familiar figure in many folkloric customs. It is believed that in some cultures before *c*.3000BC the king might actually have been sacrificed. However, in

Babylon after *c*.2000BC the king would be ritually replaced by a slave for a set period, and then, spiritually reborn, would ascend the throne again in imitation of the rising Sun.

The mythographer Mircea Eliade believed that traditional descent rituals from different cultures tended to follow a universal pattern of stages: (1) separation from the family; (2) the cosmic night, indicating regression to a pre-natal state; (3) death, dismemberment and suffering; (4) rebirth; and (5) the killing of another person, perhaps representative of an aspect of the self.

In many cultures descent rituals became part of shamanic initiation (in which the shaman, or spirit healer, entered the world of the spirits through a trance state), and the individual who returned from such experiences was endowed with special powers or great wisdom. Similarly, solar gods are often all-seeing, or at least very wise, representing the triumph of individual consciousness over ignorance, chaos and injustice. Sometimes their omniscience is linked with the traditional descent of the Sun god into darkness, and they become associated with divination, mysteries and death. Both Apollo and Shamash were gods of divination, answering questions through dreams, riddles or the entrails of sacrificed animals – symbolically shedding the solar light on the unknown.

THE COSMIC BATTLE

On occasion, the Sun's descent to the underworld was accompanied by a cosmic struggle. This was the case in Egypt in which Ra, the Sun god, was under permanent threat of attack from the forces of darkness. During the twelve hours of darkness the dangers reached a peak and the Sun was temporarily vanquished. Yet he survived and after bringing light, if only temporarily, to the inhabitants of the underworld, he was reborn at dawn. Egyptian astral religion may have long since faded, but the concept of the cosmic battle has proved one of the most enduring and disruptive myths in European history. It became the basis of the belief in a universe in which good and evil were engaged in a perpetual struggle that would climax in a dramatic final battle. It was this hope that drove the vast waves of Christian 'millennarians' who swept Europe in the Middle Ages with the goal of establishing the 'millennium' of Christ's rule, and that eventually gave rise to the modern revolutionary tradition. Similar myths grew up in other cultures. For example, the Aztec Huitzilopochtli, the god of the

LEFT **An Egyptian papyrus, dating from *c.*1150BC, depicting the adoration of the Sun in the form of the falcon Ra-Harakhty. This name was the one most often used for the Sun in his daytime aspect and represents a fusion of Ra and the ancient god Harakhty, or Horus.**

MULTIPLE SUNS

Sometimes, on a bright sunny day, the distortion of light caused by high clouds can cause images of the Sun to appear elsewhere in the sky. The Romans listed occurrences when up to three Suns appeared. In the 17th century the astrologer William Lilly actually issued a series of predictions based on the appearance of a 'mock-Sun'. The appearance of a mock-Sun at the celebrated Glastonbury festival in 1971, one of the great New Age gatherings in England, caused much excitement. The Romans also noted 'night Suns', a rarer occurrence.

---

blue sky and daylight, was engaged in a perpetual struggle with the nocturnal powers, led by the Moon, in an effort to prevent the gods of darkness destroying the Sun, and wiping out humanity.

The myths of the Sun became a vehicle for fears and longing, and while we have lost the myths, the behaviour patterns remain. It seems that human beings long for the light but have a deep-seated need to peer into the darkness.

ECLIPSES

Solar eclipses are the most dramatic celestial events visible from the Earth. They are not rare (in 1996 there were two) but total eclipses are very unusual – even when one occurs it will be visible only from part of the Earth's surface.

To people who believed that the entire universe was alive, and that any dramatic event contained significance for them, solar eclipses were awe-inspiring. We know that one of the principal functions of the stone circle of Stonehenge, England, was to predict eclipses. Some biblical scholars believe that Solomon began construction of the Temple at Jerusalem after an eclipse, which he took to be a message from God.

In many cultures eclipses were explained through the mythical consumption of the Sun by its sworn enemy, a cosmic demon or dragon. To the Egyptians, Ra was assaulted by Apep, the great serpent who lived in the depths of the celestial Nile. During total eclipses Apep succeeded in swallowing the entire Sun-boat, but he was always eventually vanquished by Ra's defenders and cast back into the deep.

The Yucho people of North America believed that the Sun goddess was menaced by a monstrous demon toad who tried to swallow her – when it succeeded the Sun was eclipsed. As soon as the solar disc began to be darkened the Yucho performed special rituals, firing arrows at the Sun to drive off the toad and painting their bodies with red designs. They

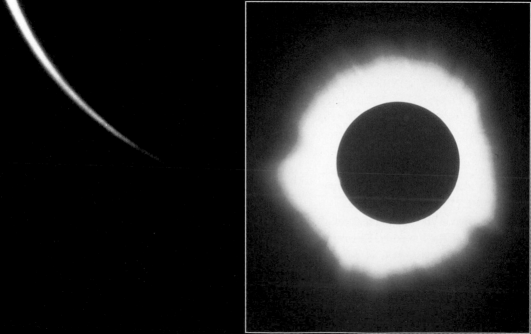

believed, symbolically, that their mother was dying, but as soon as the Sun began to recover, their despair gave way to celebration.

Such myths were not meant to be taken literally, but formed the basis of the rituals by which a universe that was thought to be genuinely threatening might be appeased. They were magical rites intended to have material consequences. Sometimes eclipses were thought themselves to be caused by magic. In classical times it was believed that they could be caused by witches, while some Aboriginal peoples in Australia believed that they indicated that some- one was working black magic on an enemy.

It was through observation of eclipses that the ancient Greeks worked out that the Sun was farther from the Earth than the Moon was. Aristarchus of Samos (320–250BC) calculated the Moon's distance from the Earth by the curvature of the Earth's shadow on the Moon during a lunar eclipse. Using this figure, he was then able to work out the distance of the Earth from the Sun. He did this by measuring the angle between the Moon and the Sun when the Moon was at first quarter. Although he proved

LEFT Two stages of an eclipse of the Sun. A solar eclipse occurs when the Moon passes between the Earth and the Sun. Historically, eclipses have often been believed to be portentous of significant events.

an important point, his figure of 8 million kilo- metres (5 million miles) was not very accurate. With modern radar methods we now know the true average distance to be 149 million kilometres (93 million miles).

Solar eclipses occur when the Sun's declina- tion (its distance north or south of the celestial equator) is within about 5 degrees of the Moon's at the New Moon. They offer a valuable chance to study various solar and celestial effects. In India and South-East Asia, where the gods and goddesses are still believed to 'speak' through natural phenomena, they are thought to be inauspi- cious, and at the total eclipse of 24 October 1995 devout Hindus were warned to stay indoors.

THE GIANT NUCLEAR REACTOR

The Sun provides us with enough heat and light to sustain life. Its temperature is about 5,800° C at the surface, rising as high as 15 million degrees at the core; and the energy it emits would be sufficient to make all the water on the Earth's surface – rivers, lakes, icebergs and oceans – evaporate within 10 seconds. Yet because of its distance the earth captures only one half of one billionth of the total energy given off.

The Sun is composed mainly

According to the Tiwi, an Aboriginal people of Melville Island, Australia, the Sun woman Wuriupanala received her role at the end of the Dreamtime. Every day she powders her body with red ochre and travels across the sky, carrying a torch of blazing bark. At the end of the day she rests for a time in the celestial lagoon, Kumpinulu, before return- ing to her home in the East along an under- ground passage.

of hydrogen and the helium into which it is being constantly converted by the colossal force of nuclear fusion (see below). However, about 1 per cent of it is made up of heavier elements such as sodium, magnesium, iron and calcium, while a very small part of it consists of other substances in gaseous form. We know this from what are called 'Fraunhofer lines' after the German instrument-maker and physicist who discovered them in 1811 using a spectroscope to analyze the sunlight. (In simple terms, the burning of different substances produces light in different areas of the spectrum.)

The Sun is in effect a massive thermonuclear reactor. Its huge size creates an equally huge gravity force; this in turn creates intense pressure at its centre, which although gaseous is twelve times as dense as lead. In these conditions, hydrogen atoms are converted into helium. Four protons (hydrogen atom nuclei) are forced together into one alpha particle (a helium nucleus) and in this process – nuclear fusion – a small amount of mass is converted into energy. Small though this mass is in relative terms, it still adds up to an astonishing 4,600,000 tons of mass per second. This has been going on for 5,000 million years, and it cannot go on for ever; within 8,000 million years the Sun will be exhausted.

DAY AND NIGHT

Of all the astronomical cycles that shape our world the most dramatic is the rapid change between light and dark, night and day. Once a day the Sun rises in the east, bringing light and warmth; once a day it sets in the west, bringing darkness and cold. At night, when the Earth has turned away from the Sun, facing the darkness of space, we dream. And from the realm of dreams there emerged over time the magical rites of ancient shamanism, the complex beliefs of astral religion, and eventually our myths and tales of the stars.

NASA, the US Space Agency, takes account of the disruptive effect of sunspots when planning space flights and satellite launches. During sunspot peaks the terrestrial magnetic field is disturbed, disrupting radio communications and electrical power supplies. There is also a danger for astronauts, while the lifetimes of low orbit satellites are considerably reduced.

Even in the modern world, with electric light and cities that never sleep, to the vast majority of people – especially in rural areas where life revolves around the land – the alternation of day and night is the central fact of life. After the Sun has risen, millions of office workers take to the highways of the world's metropolises. Seen from space their behaviour might be thought to resemble that of inse0e active at dawn or swarm at dusk.

Not only are humans at their most active during the day, but they are virtually blind at night, and unaware of the richness of the night-time existence. As daylight animals go to sleep the night-time animals – such as foxes, badgers, owls and bats – emerge. Even plant life switches to a different gear. Flowers close, and leaves begin to send out carbon dioxide instead of oxygen. The animals that are active during the day are often completely unaware of those that come to life at night. They rely on different senses, and sometimes cannot even see each other. It is almost as if the Earth carries two completely different ecosystems, one diurnal and one nocturnal, like two sets of tenants inhabiting the same house but never meeting.

CIRCADIAN RHYTHMS

Whether they stay up all night or not, human beings, like other animals, are subject to roughly uniform daily cycles known as circadian rhythms. At their most obvious these are the cycles which, according to our internal body clocks, wake us up in the morning – and wake nocturnal animals up at dusk. Body temperature, urine production and metabolic rate all fall at night, while hormone production and susceptibility to drugs also show regular 24-hour cycles. The consequence of this metabolic change is a fall in both physical and mental powers, lower concentration and a reduced ability to use figures or to perform simple repetitive tasks. The lowest point is about 3.00am – which coincides with the time of most industrial accidents involving night-shift workers.

Circadian rhythms have a use in animal survival. For example, without its biological clock a bat in a cave would constantly have to make its way to the entrance to see whether night had fallen.

Some animals are neither diurnal nor nocturnal. They are crepuscular – that is, they thrive in the twilight, when the Sun is on the horizon. Rodents show two peaks of activity, one at dusk and the other at dawn. Many fish are crepuscular, as are birds such as the bittern and the water rail. The dawn chorus marks many bird species' excitement as the Sun rises.

SUNSPOTS

Does the Sun influence the Earth other than by gravity, heat and light? The search for influences is focused on the sunspot cycle. Sunspots are dark, cold areas on the Sun's surface, and although we do not know for certain what causes them, they may be a result of disturbances in the Sun's magnetic field. These in turn could be connected to the movements of other planets, especially Jupiter, the giant of the solar system.

Sunspots have attracted attention because their frequency varies according to a regular cycle in which they reach a peak ('sunspot maxima') roughly every eleven years, although the cycle varies between twelve-and-a-half and nine years. There is also a 22-year cycle caused by the reversal of the Sun's magnetic poles, which happens exactly at the peak. A long-term pattern has been observed in which the number of spots at each successive peak increases or decreases. The most famous example of a long-term cycle was the near-absence of sunspots between 1650 and 1700 (known as the 'Maunder minimum'), which coincided with a colder climate in Europe. The river Thames in London, England, regularly froze in winter, and many traditional romantic images of 'white Christmases' date from this time.

The first astronomer to look for connections between sunspots and terrestrial cycles

In 1896 the Norwegian physicist Olaf Kristian Birkeland confirmed that something other than light and heat was arriving at the Earth from the Sun. This was the solar wind, a cloud consisting of parts of the solar corona rushing into interplanetary space at supersonic speeds. It passes the Earth at 400 kilometres (250 miles) per second, sweeping up gases and dust and carrying them beyond the edge of the solar system.

was William Herschel. In 1801 he spotted a relationship to corn prices. This is quite logical, for if we assume that sunspots influence climate then they will also have an impact on plant growth, which will affect crop prices. Herschel's work was taken up in 1878 by a British economist, W. Stanley Jevons, who advanced the theory that sunspots' impact on agriculture caused 'commercial crises'. In 1934 two Harvard University research workers, Carlos Garcia-Mata and Felix Shaffner, set out to check Jevons' work. They found, contrary to expectation, that peaks in US industrial production preceded sunspot peaks, but that there was no connection with crop production.

Other research links sunspots to the number of rabbit furs collected by Hudson Bay trappers; the rise and fall of the waters in Lake Victoria in central Africa; the number of icebergs; and famines in India. Some evidence suggests that great epidemics of diphtheria, typhus, cholera and smallpox also occur at eleven-year intervals, which may be linked to sunspots.

Perhaps the most revolutionary research to date connects the sunspot cycle to political events. Social anthropology – the study of human beings as groups – deals with the broad trends and changes in human behaviour over which individuals have little or no choice. The Soviet historian A.L. Tchijevsky was the first to notice possible correlations between mass human excitability and the sunspot cycle. For example, he argued that in 19th-century Britain the Liberals were stronger during sunspot peaks, the Conservatives weaker. Tchijevsky was imprisoned by Stalin and, although later released by Khruschev, he died in 1964 without completing his work. Ironically, his theory received further support in 1989 when a sunspot peak coincided with the collapse of Communism in Eastern Europe.

However, despite various evidence apparently connecting the Sun with events on Earth, we still know very little – and even where a correlation can be shown, we still cannot say how the Sun causes events. All we can do with confidence is to list the.correspondences.

THE MOON

The Moon is our closest celestial neighbour, at an average distance from Earth of 380,000 kilometres (238,000 miles) – or 1.3 light-seconds. It has a diameter of 3,475 kilometres (2,160 miles), about a quarter that of Earth, and a density 3.34 times that of water. Whereas in myth the Moon is often the husband, wife or sister of the Sun, it is really 'married' to the Earth, which it orbits in 27 days, 7 hours and 43 minutes, or 27.3217 days (the 'sidereal month'). Because it has to catch up with the Earth in its own orbit, its synodic rotation period – the time between two full moons – is the synodic month of 29 days, 12 hours, 44 minutes, and 3 seconds (29.5306 days).

In traditional astrology the Moon is a moist, wet planet, bringing rain and fertility, exalted (strong) in Cancer and debilitated (weak) in Capricorn. Her day is Monday, her enemies are Mars and Saturn and she is sacred to the archangel Gabriel. In the Middle Ages the Moon went under a variety of names, including Lucina, Cynthia, Diana, Phoebe ('brightness'), Latona, Noctiluca and Proserpina.

FATHER MOON, MOTHER MOON

In classical mythology the Moon was female. From Greece the feminine Moon travelled to Rome and on to medieval Europe. Yet most cultures have pictured the Moon as male, a father rather than a mother.

Lunar gods include the Babylonian Sin, who was worshipped throughout the Middle Eastern world, the Persian Mâh, the Indian Candra, and the Inuit Igaluk. Most pagan peoples in Europe worshipped male Moon gods, as did the

The Australian Aborigines believed that a lunar eclipse was an omen indicating that someone on a journey had met with a serious accident.

Native North Americans and the Australian Aborigines. The Japanese Moon god, Tsuki-yomi, the 'underworld Moon', plays little part in Japanese religion, although he may have been the husband of the Sun goddess in early mythology.

Although the Greeks borrowed most of their astronomy and astral mythology from the Babylonians, one of the few changes they made was to switch the Moon's sex. The Moon god was abandoned in favour of Selene, Hecate and Artemis (and, for the Romans, Diana). Lunar goddesses were often the sisters or wives of Sun gods. Thus Selene and Artemis were the sisters of, respectively, Helios and Apollo. Metzli, the Aztec Moon, was wife of the Sun, and the Inca Moon goddess Mama Quilla was both sister and wife of the Sun god Inti. Similarly, male Moons are often partnered by female Suns, as in many Native American myths.

THE GREAT WOMB

The Greek mystics held that when the soul was incarnated at birth it descended through the planetary spheres, beginning with Saturn. As it did so it gradually acquired its human attributes – pride and wisdom from Jupiter, aggression and martial energy from Mars, beauty and grace from Venus, and learning and logic from Mercury. When it arrived at the Moon it was ready for birth in a physical form. In the ancient mystery teachings the Moon was seen as the great spiritual womb from which all human beings emerged.

The Moon was also seen as the crudest planet. The stars, being close to God, were believed to be almost perfect. The Earth, being farthest from God, was subject to continual change – usually for the worse. It followed that, since the Moon was close to the Earth and far from God, it was the most imperfect planet. Evidence for this was seen in its phases, as the crescent Moon gradually grew, became full, faded and then disappeared, itself seeming subject to the same processes of decay that destroyed life on Earth. Yet, as a mother, the Moon shared the hopes and fears of her children, and could sympathize with the human condition more than any other god or goddess.

The ancient mystery teachings also held that the Moon was the first planet encountered by the initiate on the spiritual path back to heaven. After spiritual cleansing and rebirth in the lunar womb he (in the mysteries of Mithras) or she (in those of Isis) could shed the physical needs and desires of the material world and prepare for salvation.

FAR LEFT **The Full Moon, showing part of the far side that is never visible from the Earth, in a view from Apollo 17 in 1972.** LEFT **The Syrian goddess Astarte is more usually associated with Venus, but in this 3rd–2nd-century BC statue she is portrayed wearing the horns of the Moon on her head. In ancient mythology symbols were very fluid, with imagery being appropriated and re-assigned as necessary.**

ARTEMIS AND HECATE
Warriors and Witches?

Some lunar goddesses had specific roles aside from the Moon's great parental function. In Greece, while Selene was the actual Moon disc, Hecate and Artemis were associated with, but distinct from, the Moon itself. Hecate was an older goddess who allied herself with Zeus against the Titans. She guarded flocks, ruled navigation and conferred wealth, victory and wisdom. She was also associated with magic (especially witchcraft), murder, crossroads, tombs, dogs and Hades. She was used widely by Shakespeare to conjure up the forces of darkness and fate, as when she was invoked by the witches in *Macbeth*.

Artemis, with whom Hecate was sometimes merged, was a wild huntress, goddess of night, nature and fertility. As with her brother Apollo, her weapon was the bow.

Diana the Huntress (*c*.1550) by an unknown artist of the French Fontainebleau School. The Roman Diana, like the Greek Artemis, embodied the feminine principle; she was a protector of innocence and virginity and was herself chaste, yet at the same time she was a fertility goddess and the deity to whom women prayed in childbirth. Unlike Artemis, Diana was the subject of a major cult in ancient Rome, and was worshipped at public festivals and in secret rites, or mysteries, open only to women.

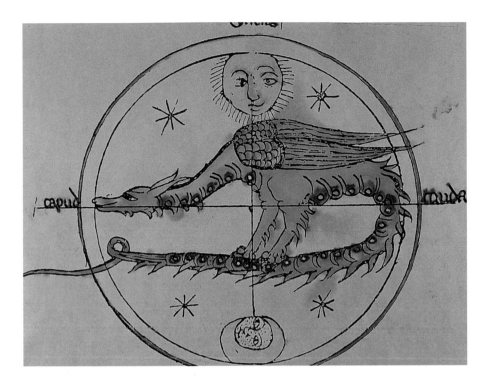

An image of the Sun–Moon Dragon by the 13th-century astrologer Michael Scot. The two points where the Sun's path crossed the Moon's path were of great significance. The northern point was Caput, the Dragon's Head, and the southern was Cauda, the Dragon's Tail.

In one of the most famous tales about her she punished Actaeon for disturbing her bathing in the forest by turning him into a stag, to be devoured by his own dogs. The Romans identified Artemis with Diana, also a huntress, who became a romantic and vigorous figure in the European poetic imagination.

THE CALENDAR

The Sun is the primary basis of our modern system of time-keeping, the 24-hour day, but it is not necessarily the best measure for regulating the agri-cultural year. The Moon, with its rapid changes in size, is a far clearer means of working out how many days have passed or when crops should be harvested.

In many cultures the Moon had a reputation for wisdom, stemming from its mysterious phases and their use in calendar-keeping, which was especially important to agricultural soci-eties. The Moon god Sin arranged the order of the months in Babylon, while many Native North Americans believed that the Moon 'took care of the months'. The Moon's calendrical

On the occasion of her first period a girl of the North American Cahuilla was laid recumbent on a bed of brush and herbs in a heated trench. She remained there for three nights while men and women danced and sang songs alluding to the institution of this custom by the Moon. The first menstruation generally occurred at the New Moon, it is said, and the girl remained under care until that Moon disappeared.

function, together with its association with water, provided an obvious connection with fertility, but also with social organiza-tion; the North American Cahuilla people believe that Menil, the Moon, established their clans, lineages and social hierarchies.

The earliest known attempt to record time seems to have been notches marking lunar phases on animal bones, dating as far back as 35,000BC; and in most cultures the first calendars appear to have been lunar. The calendar was much more than a means of establishing future engage-ments: it was a mathematically ordered reflection of the celestial order which enabled societies to regulate the acts necessary for everyday survival and organize their religious devotions. To the ancient Babylonians and Hebrews the observation of the lunar calendar was a moral duty of the highest order.

Ancient lunar calendars were based on observation of the Moon's position, and in Babylon the month began when the crescent Moon first rose above the horizon at dusk. In many cultures the day begins at dusk; in Europe as late as the 17th century the hours of the day were counted from sunset. The ancient Hebrew calendar was lunar and the most important festivals took place on Full Moons. Passover began with the rising of the first Full Moon after the spring equinox.

To ignore the calendar festivals could result in dire consequences. In Babylon, conquest by the Assyrians was attributed to the failure to observe the Akitu, or New Year festival (see p.23). For a Hebrew to forget the correct observations was to insult God's order and incur divine wrath; in this way the calendar became an instrument of social and religious control.

No calendar can be exclusively lunar, for it is impossible to ignore the Sun completely. Most cultures with complex calendars, including Egypt and China, adopted combined lunar and solar systems. It is only in the modern Western world that we have begun to ignore the Moon.

In the Babylonian creation myth, Marduk's first act following his victory over the forces of chaos was to establish order in the sky, placing the planets and stars in their proper positions. His central act was the instruction to Sin, the Moon god:

'At the month's beginning to shine on Earth
Thou shalt show two horns to mark six days.
On the seventh day divide the crown in two;
On the fourteenth day, turn thy full face.'

The imposing basalt funeral stele of Si Gabbor, 7th-century priest of the Syrian Moon god.

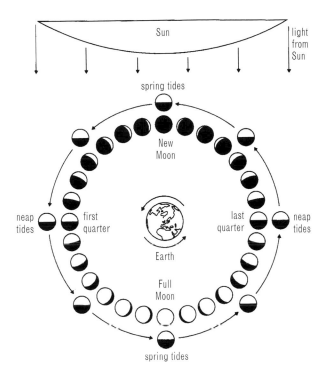

spring tides

New Moon

neap tides

first quarter

Earth

last quarter

neap tides

Full Moon

spring tides

Sun

light from Sun

LEFT Diagram showing the phases of the Moon and the spring and neap tides (tides exhibiting, respectively, the greatest and the smallest changes of level in their rise and fall).

THE MAN IN THE MOON

Ancient peoples were fascinated by the Moon, with its phases, its silvery light, and its markings in which different figures were identified. Now we know that the Moon shines dimly and in phases because it only reflects the light of the Sun, and that its markings are the geographical features of a dry, barren landscape.

In the 3rd century BC, Aristarchus of Samos (see p.131) knew that the Moon's phases depended on its position in its orbit around the Earth. He was also able to work out the Moon's distance from the Earth, but he had no idea of the true nature of the lunar landscape. That, together with more accurate measurements, had to await modern telescopes, satellite photography – and the astronaut.

Many myths explain the Moon's markings, phases and dimness relative to the Sun. Whereas people in the West have traditionally seen a 'man in the Moon', the Chinese, Japanese and Indians see a hare. The hare is thought to make the elixir of immortality in the palace of the Moon, also inhabited by Ch'ang-o, who fled there from her husband, I the Excellent Archer.

Maoris see a woman, Rona, who went to fetch water by moonlight. They believe that when Marama, the

THE TIDES

The tides' connection with the Moon inspired the classical notion that the Moon was a cold, moist planet; even in inland cultures the Moon was often associated with water – particularly with the dew. The Aztec words for Moon (*citatli*) and water (*atl*) were interchangeable. Most cultures have linked the Moon to the tides. According to a Maori myth, the tides grow as the body of Marama, the Moon, swells, receding again as she grows old.

Greek astronomers knew that the Moon pulled the tides, but were not sure how. Many cultures believed that human affairs followed similar tidal patterns. Around 2000BC it was believed that if the Moon pulled the oceans it must also exert a pressure on human bodies. However, according to current knowledge there is no way that the Moon's gravity could influence us individually.

The Moon is responsible for about 69 per cent of the tidal pull; the Sun causes about 31 per cent. The daily cycle of high tides corresponds to the movement of the Moon over the meridian (directly overhead); there is one high tide when it crosses and another 12 hours and 25 minutes later at the opposite point on the Earth. The tidal rise and fall increases at New and Full Moons (spring tides), at those times when the Moon is closest to the Earth (perigee), and at the spring and autumn equinoxes (around 21 March and 21 September). It also depends on local coastal formations and the weather.

Moon, disappeared behind a cloud, Rona stumbled and insulted the Moon, who angrily abducted her. Rona can still be seen on the Moon, with her water gourd and basket, and the tree to which she vainly clung.

The Indian Moon god Candra made the mistake of favouring one of his 27 wives, with tragic consequences. One of his fathers-in-law condemned him to die of consumption. However, all the wives protested and the curse was made periodical instead of permanent, which explains why the Moon disappears once a month.

A typical myth explaining the Moon's dimness is told by the Abaluyia of Kenya, who believe that the Sun and Moon were two brothers who quarrelled. The Sun splashed the Moon with mud, and the supreme being was forced to separate them.

LIFE ON THE MOON?

A hoax took place in August 1835 at the expense of Sir John Herschel, astronomer son of the discoverer of Uranus. A series of articles in the *New York Sun* described how Herschel, using a massive telescope that could magnify objects 42,000 times, had observed animals, plants and buildings, including a sapphire temple and – most astonishingly – winged humanoid bat-beings with faces that were a 'slight improvement upon that of the large orang-outang'. Virtually everybody was taken in, and an enthusiastic American preacher even looked forward to selling his Bibles to the 'lunarians'.

THE ASTROLOGICAL MOON

The Moon occupies a privileged position in astrology alongside the Sun. The Sun has a primary role during the day, but, as in the book of Genesis God made the 'lesser light' to rule the night, so the Moon has special significance during the hours of darkness. Western astrology borrowed the Greek belief that the Moon was female, and used it to represent women in general, the mother in particular.

The Moon was especially important in the Middle Ages – in medicine, in which it was used to regulate treatments such as bleeding and the administration of herbal remedies; and in political forecasting, in which New Moons, Full Moons and eclipses warned of future events. In weather forecasting it signified rain, and in horary astrology, which was used to answer specific questions, it invariably indicated the final outcome of an event. If the Moon were not benevolently placed when launching a new enterprise, disaster would be predicted.

Psychological astrology places great emphasis on the Moon as either the mother or one's maternal needs and desires.

A Jungian astrologer might see the Moon as indicative of the individual's relationship with the archetype of the mother or the universal feminine.

LUNAR MANSIONS

On a clear night the constellations are visible behind the Moon, but it takes a leap of imagination to picture them as an invisible backdrop to the Sun by day. This may be why in many cultures the passage of the Moon through the stars was noted before that of the Sun, and was used as a basis for dividing the sky into sections, known as 'lunar mansions'.

In Indian astrology the lunar mansions (Sanskrit, *nakshatras*) were seen as the Moon god's wives. Each mansion is 'ruled' by an ancient Vedic god. The sky is divided into 27 sections, which were originally unequal in size, but were later mostly replaced by equal sections of 13 degrees, 20 minutes.

The Arabic system used 28 mansions (Arabic, *manazil*), but similarities between the two schemes in other respects suggest cross-influences, perhaps even a common source.

The Chinese also used 28 mansions, or *hsiu*, but there the resemblance ends. The Chinese plotted the positions of the stars and planets according to a system based on the celestial equator, rather than on the ecliptic (the apparent path of the Sun round the Earth). The Chinese constellations were

A miniature from a 15th-century manuscript, *De Sphaera*, showing the Moon (Luna), together with associated images such as the horn of Diana the Huntress, the Crab of Cancer (ruled by the Moon) and ships at sea – ruled by the Moon through its connection with the tides.

mostly very different, too, although the stars themselves do more or less coincide in some cases – the Pleiades (Chinese Hsiu 18, Mao) being one such case. Each *hsiu* is associated with one of the five Chinese elements (see p.13).

Although the passage of the Sun and planets through the lunar mansions plays a part in astrological interpretation, the position of the Moon is more important. In the Indian system, a man born with the Moon in the lunar mansion of Krittika (the Pleiades) would have a large appetite, be energetic and famous, and enjoy other men's wives. To a Chinese astrologer, the Moon's passage through the corresponding *hsiu* (Mao) would be associated with legal matters and untimely death.

THE MOON'S MATTER

There are three main theories about the Moon's origins: it was created in another part of the solar system and 'captured' by the Earth's gravitational pull; it was created nearby; or it was somehow torn from the Earth.

In the 5th century BC Empedocles believed the Moon was made of air mixed with fire.

Nobody could be certain it was solid until Galileo studied it through his telescope. The idea that it was torn from the Earth, perhaps in a primeval cataclysm, was generated in the 17th and 18th centuries; when the Pacific Ocean was mapped it seemed plausible that it occupied a gigantic crater left by the material that had made the Moon.

The idea that the Moon was once part of the Earth has now been discredited by the analysis of Moon rock brought back by space probes. In addition, study of moonquakes – lunar earthquakes – suggest that the Moon's core is made of iron, unlike that of the Earth. Current thinking tends toward the theory that it was created nearby.

The Moon's relatively small size means that its gravity is only 0.165 times that of the Earth, and it has a correspondingly small escape velocity – the speed that any object or gas has to achieve to escape its gravitational pull. To escape the Earth's gravitational pull, a rocket has to achieve a speed of 11.18 kilometres (7 miles) per second. The figure for the Moon is a mere 2.37 kilometres (1.5 miles) per second. Hence any atmospheric gases the Moon once had have long since escaped into space. This lack of atmosphere means that the Moon is exposed to rays that are harmful to humans and that surface temperatures fluctuate between +100° C and –200° C. No real evidence of life has been found, but the likelihood of the Moon sustaining life in the future – such as a manned research station – increased dramatically when water, in the form of a deep frozen lake, was discovered there in 1996.

With the earliest telescopes astronomers began to have some idea of the Moon's surface features. There were craters, which we have named after famous astron-omers, including Kepler and Copernicus; mountain ranges, named after mountain ranges on Earth; and large dark patches that the German astronomer Johannes Hevelius, on his 1647 map of the Moon, referred to as seas – in fact these are plains. The craters are as much as 290 kilometres (180 miles) in diameter; their origin is uncertain, but it is generally agreed that most were formed by meteoric bombardment.

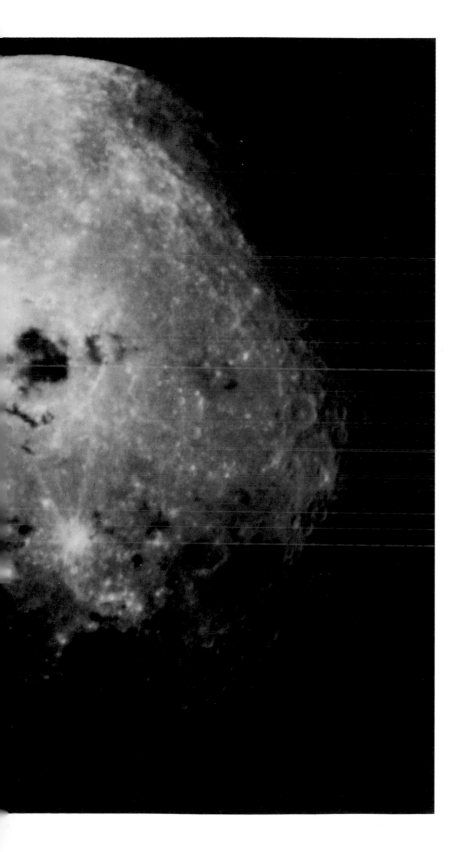

EXPLORING THE MOON

The great period of lunar exploration lasted just eighteen years, from the unsuccessful US probe, Able 1, launched on 17 August 1958, to the last Soviet probe, Luna 24, launched on 9 August 1976. In between came six US manned landings, beginning with Apollo 11 and Neil Armstrong's historic first step on to the Moon's surface on 20 July 1969. The last manned landing was Apollo 17, launched on 6 December 1972, which conducted geological surveys and returned with samples. Between 1976 and 1996 there were only two more probes. One was the Japanese Hagomoro lunar orbiter, launched on 24 January 1990; the other was the US mapping probe Clementine, launched on 24 January 1994. With the coming of the US space shuttle and the Soviet Mir space station, space research shifted to the conducting of experiments in zero gravity conditions and the study of both local and distant space, whether research into the solar wind or the search for the origins of the universe. The Moon has become the poor relation.

The Moon and (inset) the famous footprint that was left there on 21 July 1969. 'That's one small step for man, one giant leap for mankind.' Neil Armstrong meant to say '...for a man', but who can blame him for fluffing his lines a little in leaving the most historic footprint ever?

MERCURY

Mercury is the smallest of the planets, with a diameter of only 4,800 kilometres (3,000 miles) and a mass of 0.05 times that of the Earth. It is also the closest planet to the Sun, averaging a distance of 58 million kilometres (36 million miles), although its orbit is elliptical. Because it is closer to the Sun than the Earth is, it has phases, like Venus and the Moon. These accord with its 88-day orbit of the Sun – its year. Mercury is so close to the Sun (it can never be more than 27 degrees away, as seen from the Earth) that it is rarely visible in the night sky; it can be seen most easily on spring evenings or autumn mornings.

In ancient Sumer, before c.2000BC, Mercury was known as Gud, while in Babylon it was known as Shihtu ('jumping'), and was sacred to the god Nabu. In Persia it was sacred to Tira and in Greece to Hermes. In Rome it was the star of Mercury, and in India it was sacred to the god Vishnu. The planet was often given different names depending on whether it appeared after dusk or before dawn. As an evening star, it has been known as Horus (Egypt), Rauhinya (India) and the Sparkling One (Greece). As a morning star, it was known as Set (Egypt), Budha (India) and the Lovely One (Greece). In China it is Ch'en or Mien, the Water Planet.

Medieval astronomers also knew Mercury as Stilbon, Archas and Cyllenius, and believed that he governed Wednesday, that he was friends with Venus, Jupiter and Saturn, and that his guardian angel was Raphael.

In Latin the fourth day of the week was known as *Mercurii Dies* and in modern French it is *Mercredi*. In English it is Wednesday, after Wotan or Odin, the Norse Mercury.

'When there are errors in judgments, retribution comes from the planet Ch'en.'

Chinese treatise *Ssu Ma Ch'ien*, 2nd century BC

THE MESSENGER

In myth, Mercury's primary role was to communicate, carry messages and impart wisdom. In Babylon the planet was sacred to Nabu, the god of scribes, who replaced the earlier Sumerian goddess of wisdom, Nisaba or Nidaba, c.1800BC. He was also a rain-maker, and in this role had significance for the harvest, and hence for commerce – functions inherited by the Greek Hermes and the Roman Mercury. As a scribe, Nabu oversaw such commercial functions as weighing, measuring, bargaining and keeping records. Nabu's most important ritual function came on the eleventh day of the Akitu, the New Year festival, when he recorded the fates drawn up by the other gods and goddesses for the coming year.

Zeus, in Greek myth, made Hermes messenger of the gods; hence he is a god not only of

The figure of Nabu is carved into the door of the annex to the Library of Congress in Washington DC, USA – an interesting appropriation of an ancient figure to a modern use. The Babylonian god Nabu was associated with the planet Mercury and, like the Roman Mercury and the Greek Hermes, was a god of wisdom and communication. Nabu was also the god of scribes and, as well as recording the harvest, recorded the fates determined for humanity by the gods and goddesses.

words, language and intelligence, but of travel and of crossroads. He even became god of music (like the Indian Budha), having invented the lyre, whose prototype he made from the shell of a tortoise. Hermes displayed ingenuity, daring and love of trickery. He had fewer sexual adventures than his father, Zeus, but nevertheless managed affairs with Persephone, Hecate and Aphrodite, as well as with a number of nymphs and mortals. His children included the goat-footed Pan and the master-thief Autolycus.

The Greeks also identified Hermes with the Egyptian lunar ibis-headed deity Djehuti, whom they called Thoth. This god, who has been associated with the mythical figure of Hermes Trismegistus (see p.147), may be seen as a more scholarly Hermes. He was the scribe, herald and archivist of the gods, and is said to have invented hieroglyphic writing. He was associated with law, learning and magic – especially the magic of words.

The Indian Budha, the son of Candra (the Moon), shared with both Nabu and Hermes an association with knowledge, learning, commerce and music; one of his names, Sutala, means 'keeping good time'. Budha's elusiveness was embodied in his marriage to Ida, who changed sex several times.

Hermes' mischievous nature inspired Carl Jung to associate him with the Trickster, the psychological archetype that represents sudden reversals of fortune and unexpected twists of fate. The Trickster has a darker side, and to medieval astrologers Mercury was the planet of thieves and pickpockets.

MATTERS ASSOCIATED WITH MERCURY

'Contracts, Negotiations, all manner of subtill Arts depending upon a sharp Fancy, or upon speech, invention of new Arts and Devices, Divination, Geometry, Astronomy, Astrologie, Curiosities, the Liberall Sciences.'

English astrologer William Lilly, 1647

THE PSYCHOPOMP

Modern psychotherapy has also made much of Hermes' other significant role, as the only god who could move freely between Earth and Hades, between life and death. His symbol, the caduceus, shows two serpents intertwined around a central pole, symbolizing the reconciliation of opposites. Hermes was the *psychopompos* – the god who guided souls on their way to Hades. Since Hades has been associated symbolically with depression and sleep, as well as with death, the psychopomp is the bridge between different mental states, central to the healing processes of therapy and analysis.

In Egypt the psychopomp was the jackal-headed Anpu, known to the Greeks as Anubis. In the Egyptian funerary texts he presided over funeral rites, such as embalming the corpse, and then introduced the deceased to the panel of judges in whose presence their souls were weighed. The Greeks later cemented Anubis' link to Hermes by calling him Hermanubis.

THE MAGUS

When the English renamed the classical days they selected the Norse–Teutonic god Woden, Wotan or Odin as Mercury's closest equivalent – hence 'Wednesday'. In his principal form Woden actually corresponded to Jupiter and Mars as a violent sky god. However, he had a Hermetic role as 'magician-god of the Other World', presiding like the astrological Mercury over all magical matters. In Scandinavia, Odin was more typically Mercurial; he was a god of intelligence, speaking with such power, often in verse, that it was impossible to disagree with him. Whereas Nabu merely read the fates at the beginning of the year, Odin ordained the laws of fate by which everybody lived, and as psychopomp he presided over the parties of dead heroes who passed their time in his vast glittering palace, Valhalla. Even as god of war he rarely fought in battles himself, preferring to intervene magically. Mercury prefers to consider rather than act.

A jackal-headed Hermes–Anubis, carrying his symbol, the caduceus, in a 2nd-century AD mosaic from Thysdrun, Ed Djem, Tunisia.

THE ASTROLOGICAL MERCURY

The Greeks adapted the planet Mercury's astrological significance directly from the functions adopted by their god Hermes, and it has remained remarkably constant. Mercury symbolized everything that is connected to wisdom, learning and communication, including thoughts, inspiration and the mind's ability to transcend the physical limits of life. Such knowledge could lead to power – often occult power. In China the planet acquired a similar reputation, becoming the governor of divination.

THE HERMETIC TEACHINGS

During the 1st and 2nd centuries BC in Egypt, Greek and Egyptian mysticism fused and gave birth to a revived astral religion in which the soul at birth incarnated through the planets in turn, each one of which gave the soul a different aspect of its destiny. Most of the writings of this mystical movement were ascribed to Hermes in order to give them added authority. This Hermes was Hermes Trismegistus, or Hermes Thrice Great, an amalgam of three separate mythical teachers. When the 'Corpus Hermeticum', the complete collection of these texts, was rediscovered in the 15th century, it was believed that Hermes had actually lived and was a greater philosopher than Plato and as important a

prophet as Moses. The result was an explosion of interest in classical myth, mystical astronomy and ancient astrology which historians call the 'neo-pagan revival', and which provided much of the intellectual fuel for the Renaissance. Once again, it seemed that the stars might provide a path to salvation.

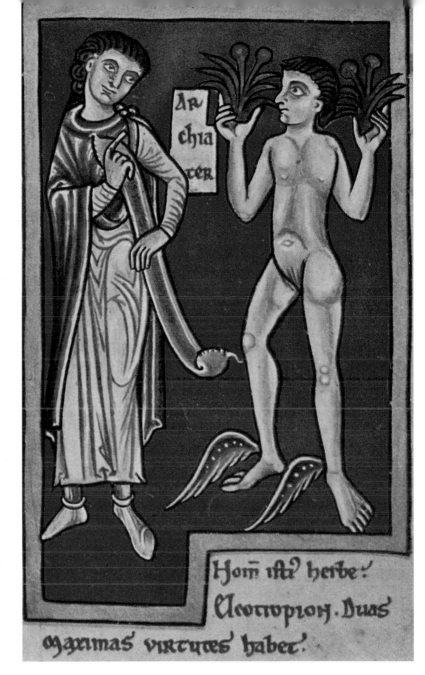

This 13th-century herbal manuscript painting shows Hermes, with winged feet, bearing the herb 'electropion' to the poet Homer. Being connected not only with wisdom and communication but also with inspiration, Hermes was naturally associated with the arts of poetry and literature.

ALCHEMY AND TRANSFORMATION

The Hermetic texts also provided a boost to medieval alchemy. The alchemists believed that mercury, or quick-silver, was the vital ingredient required to transform 'base metals', such as lead, into gold. The physical was thought to be inseparable from the spiritual, so chemical processes were thought to depend on such matters as the positions of the planets and the state of being of the plane-tary angels. These processes also related to individual spiritual evolution. Lead was 'ruled' by Saturn, gold by the Sun: the conversion of the one into the other represented the soul's passage from darkness to light. Philosophically and physically the alchemist believed that Mercury stood at the boundary between two states of being.

RELATIVITY

Whereas the Earth wobbles on its axis, causing the seasons, Mercury is almost perpendicular on its axis, and therefore has no seasons. In 1889 the Italian astronomer G.V. Schiaparelli claimed that Mercury rotated on its axis once in 88 Earth days, a period exactly the same as one orbit around the Sun. Several other astronomers confirmed his findings. Mercury seemed to behave like some carefully calibrated fairground ride, always keeping the same face to the Sun.

This harmonious belief was shattered in 1965 when radar observations showed that the planet rotates on its own axis in 58.65 days, exactly two-thirds of the time it takes to orbit the Sun. Thus the rotation of Mercury, in common with that of Venus and the Moon, is locked into its orbital period in a rather beautiful dance, one of a circle moving within a circle – like a dancer who spins slowly, at the same time tracing a circle around the room and returning to the same point in the room, facing the same way, exactly every two years.

Yet the planet still exhibited awkward behaviour which meant that its elliptical orbit could not be exactly explained by Newton's laws of gravity. Even though the discrepancy between its predicted and its actual motion was slight, adding up to no more than 43 seconds of arc per century, astronomers needed an explanation. Einstein found that this was provided by the warping of space – and therefore of Mercury's orbit – by the Sun's gravitational pull. As a result of this finding, in November 1915 he was able to put the finishing touches to his general theory of relativity, changing our views of the cosmos for ever.

THE MERCURIAL PERSONALITY

'When well: Represents a subtle and diplomatic brain and intellect, excellent with argu-ing, logic, learning and discretion and using much eloquence, a searcher into all kinds of Mysteries, sharp and witty, learning almost anything without a Teacher; desirous natu-rally of travel and seeing foreign parts; able by his or her own Genius to produce won-ders; given to Divination; nobody exceeds him in way of Trade or invention of new wayes to obtain wealth.

'When ill: A troublesome wit, turning his tongue and Pen against every man, uses his time in prating; a great liar, boaster, busybody, false, a tale-carrier given to wicked Acts, as Necromancy, and such like ungodly knowledges; an asse or idiot, cheating and theeving, frothy, or no judgment, constant in nothing but idle words and bragging.'

English astrologer William Lilly, 1647

RIGHT The surface of Mercury is pockmarked by meteor impacts. The debris is far less scattered than similar debris on the Moon, owing to Mercury's stronger gravity field.

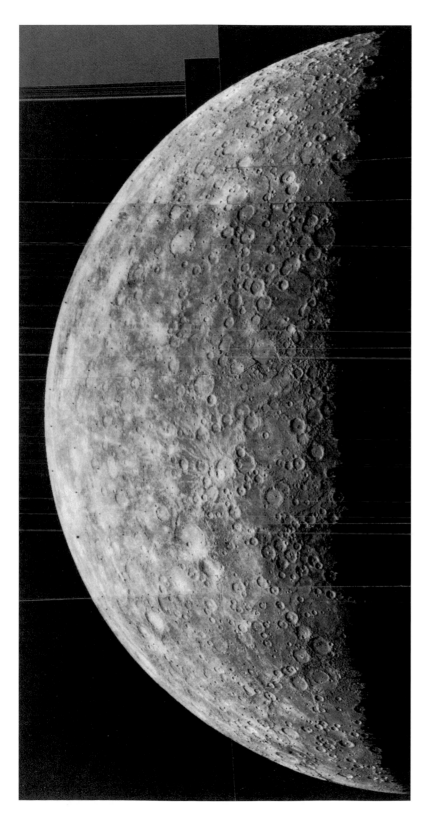

CONDITIONS ON MERCURY

Mercury's proximity to the Sun makes conventional telescopic observation difficult. However, in 1974–5 the Mariner 10 spacecraft bypassed Mercury several times, and sent back some stunning photographs. The pictures show a planet roughly divided into two types of landscape. One part is covered by large areas of smooth plains, which are probably lava flows. The largest of these, the Caloris Basin, is 1,280 kilometres (800 miles) in diameter. The other part has a rugged surface not unlike that of the Moon, pockmarked with craters, but with two major differences. The first is that because Mercury has a greater gravitational pull than the Moon, the debris thrown up and around by a meteor impact cannot travel nearly so far: it is scattered over an area only one-sixth of the size it would be on the Moon. The other is the presence of extensive 'lobate scarps' – shallow scalloped cliffs probably created by the planet's iron core cooling and contracting. In effect these are chains of wrinkles in the planet's crust.

Being so close to the Sun, Mercury has the second hottest surface temperature of all the planets, with daytime temperatures exceeding 400° C. Like the Moon, it has virtually no atmosphere and temperatures can drop to below –200° C, making life as we know it next to impossible.

VENUS

Venus is 107 million kilometres (67 million miles) from the Sun. Thus, like Mercury, it is an 'inferior' planet – meaning that it is closer to the Sun than the Earth is. Venus is bigger than Mercury, but still smaller than the Earth, having a diameter of 12,104 kilometres (7,521 miles). Its calendar is very different from that of the Earth – its year (the time it takes to orbit the Sun), at 225 Earth days, is shorter than its day (its rotational period). Strangely, while its atmosphere rotates every four Earth days, the solid planet takes 243 Earth days, and it does so in a retrograde direction, like Uranus, so that its dawn is in the west.

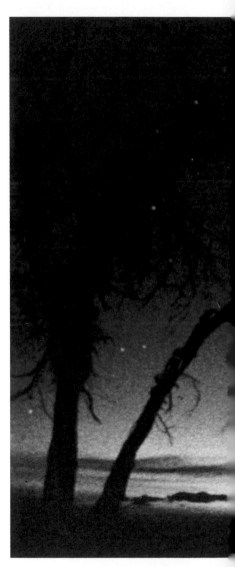

After the Sun and Moon, Venus is the most noticeable celestial body. It appears as a bright and beautiful star, often the first to appear in the evening or the last to disappear in the morning. This no doubt helped it to take a major place in mythology; in the ancient Middle East, as early as *c*.2000BC, Venus deities were as important as those of the Sun and Moon. Such deities went under a variety of names, mainly Inanna, Nanay, Ashtar, Ishtar and Astarte. The planet was even worshipped as the Egyptian goddess Isis. The Babylonians knew it as Dili-pat, while to the Persians it was sacred to the goddess Anâhitâ. To the Greeks it was the 'star of Aphrodite', and to the Romans the 'star of Venus'. In India the planet is Sukra, sacred to Lakshmi. In China it is T'ai Peh, the Great White, or the Metal Planet.

In Central America Venus played a vital role in Mayan worship, its symbol – probably representing Venus' dual aspect as morning and evening star – appearing frequently in Mayan temple reliefs. To the Aztecs Venus as morning star was Tlahuizcalpantecuhtli, the Dawn Lord, son of the maize god and brother of the Sun.

In the Middle Ages Venus was known as Cythera, Aphrodite, Phosphorous, Desperugo and Ericina, as Hesperus in the evening and Lucifer before dawn. Her guardian angel was Aael and she was friends with all the planets except Saturn. In classical astronomy she ruled Taurus and Libra, was exalted (strong) in Pisces and was debilitated (weak) in Aries, Virgo and Scorpio. Venus' day is *Vendredi* in French, Friday in English, after the Norse goddess of love, Freya or Frigg.

> 'It presides over killings; when someone is murdered retribution is wrought by the Great White.'
>
> Chinese treatise *Ssu Ma Chi'en*, 2nd century BC

To the Aborigines of Arnhem Land in northern Australia, Venus as morning star was Bornumbirr, a symbol of eternity, carrying the spirits of the dead along its light to Baralku, the island beyond the sunrise. To the Aboriginal Adnyamathanha people the planet was Warta Vurdli, a male spirit closely involved in the rites by which boys turned into men.

Venus as the evening star. Owing to the proximity of the planet to the Sun, Venus is only seen from the Earth shortly after sunset or before dawn.

'If Venus disappears in the west from the first to the thirtieth day there will be rains; the harvest of the land will prosper.'

Assyrian astrologer Nergal-Atir, c.8th century BC

THE MORNING AND EVENING STAR

It seems that prior to c.2000BC the Middle Eastern Venus deities were part male. There is evidence that some were hermaphrodites, portrayed as bearded women. Elsewhere it seems that the evening star was female and the morning star male. However, by the first Babylonian empire, after c.1800BC, the planet's female attributes took clear precedence.

The goddess Ishtar, associated with Venus, on a Babylonian terracotta jar dating from *c.*1700BC. In the Middle East, Venus deities were as important as Sun gods.

In classical Greece and Rome Venus' male attributes were the preserve of her son, Eros or Cupid. However, purely female Venus deities, even when they had a male consort, possessed a complex nature involving the reconciliation of extremes.

THE SACRED MARRIAGE

Some of the richest Venus myths survive from ancient Sumer and date back to *c.*3000–2000BC. As evening star the planet represented the goddess Inanna in her guise of herald of night, lady of darkness. As morning star it was the face of Inanna as herald of day, lady of light.

Inanna's powers were prodigious. As the bringer of universal love she pre-dated the Christian concept of the God of Love. As a fertility goddess she presided over the cosmic force which stirred desire in humans and ripeness in plants. As the sister of Utu, the Sun, she was one of the creators: without the sexual act there could be no life. And as the ruler of attraction between men and women she was responsible for the uncontrollable desires that sweep people in love, including the dark passions – jealousy, hatred and destructiveness.

One of the central religious rituals in Sumerian civilization prior to c.2000BC was the sacred marriage, in which the priestess symbolically took on the form of Inanna while the king became, in a spiritual sense, her mythical husband, Dumuzzi. The earliest known love poems are the words spoken between the king and priestess during these rites (see box), which usually began on the night of the first crescent Moon after the equinox. By the invocation of Venus' sacred feminine cosmic power and its marriage with Dumuzzi's masculine energy, the priestesses and priests ensured the king's powers of leadership over the coming year and both his and the land's fertility.

> 'My face covers thy face like a mother over the fruit of her womb,
> I will place thee like a graven jewel between my breasts,
> During the night will I give thee covering.
> During the day I shall clothe thee.'
>
> Inanna to Dumuzzi during the marriage of Venus to the king

THE DESCENT TO THE UNDERWORLD

The myth of Inanna's descent to the underworld has given us one of the great mythic motifs of the ancient world. According to ancient tablets, Inanna was queen of heaven and earth, over which she had total power. However, the universe consisted of three parts, one of which – the underworld – was closed to her. Yet she could only be truly complete once she had experienced the underworld.

To prepare for her journey Inanna first abandoned her worldly possessions, her seven cities and temples, each one representing a day of the week and a planet. Thus she withdrew from time and space and entered the unknown. She then gathered seven aspects of her chosen destiny, represented by such objects as a crown, jewellery and a gown. On her journey she passed seven gates, each a mirror of the seven planetary qualities of the overworld, as well as of her destiny. And at each she left one of her possessions, symbolically abandoning a part of her ego.

In the underworld, Inanna's sister Ereshkigal, a less forgiving, darker aspect of the feminine, condemned Inanna to death. She was turned into a corpse, which was hung on a stake. After three days her father, Nanna (the Moon), began to worry and eventually the gods worked out a way to restore her to life. She was resurrected by two little androgynous beings who slipped into the underworld to give her the 'food of life' and the 'water of life', although her husband Dumuzzi had to take her place in the underworld (see p.127).

The tale of Inanna's descent is a time-myth, or perhaps more properly a calendar-myth. Like the myth of Persephone (see p.196) it relates generally to the mystery of death in winter and rebirth in spring. Specifically it refers to the periodic disappearance of Venus when the planet is invisible due to its conjunction with the Sun, between its alternate phases as morning and evening star. Inanna as queen of heaven and earth is the goddess of the morning star, but to become one with herself, healing the divisions between light and darkness, life and death, she must also descend to the underworld, disappear and be reborn as the evening star.

Psychologically the Inanna myths represent the union of the conscious self or ego with the unconscious or the 'shadow' or 'other' (all the characteristics we disown). In order to discover our true selves we have to perform the twin act of releasing ourselves from our everyday existence, and acknowledging our other halves, whether we define this materially (by renouncing our possessions) or psychologically (by giving up negative behaviour patterns). If we fail then, first, we can never be whole; and secondly, sooner or later, our inner demons, like Ereshkigal, will come to get us.

SUKRA AND KACA

In Indian mythology the planet Venus is Sukra ('white', or 'sperm'), the guru of the demons. In one story, Sukra was swallowed and then ejaculated from the penis of Shiva, the great destroyer.

Sukra had a secret mantra (sacred syllables) with which he could restore life to the dead. The guru of the gods, Brhaspati, sent his son Kaca to discover the mantra. Sukra agreed to have Kaca as his student, and Kaca led Sukra's daughter Devayani to think he would marry her.

The demons disapproved of their guru's student and murdered him, but Devayani asked Sukra to restore him with the mantra. This happened several times, until finally the demons killed him again, burnt his body, and put the ashes in wine, which they gave Sukra to drink. When Kaca was nowhere to be found, Sukra once again spoke the mantra. Kaca answered from Sukra's stomach. Since he would not be able to emerge without killing Sukra, the guru had to teach Kaca the mantra, so that he could restore his master to life after tearing his way out.

APHRODITE

The myth of Inanna's descent to the underworld found a place in Greece as the story of Kore, the daughter of Demeter, who was abducted to the underworld; there her name was changed to Persephone and she became the wife of Hades (the Roman Pluto).

The Greeks associated the planet Venus with Aphrodite, their goddess of love. Aphrodite lacked Inanna's over-arching power, but is notable for the myth of her birth, which even today is an icon of feminine mystique. Around 700BC Hesiod recorded the myth that Aphrodite was born from the foaming severed genitals of the sky god, Ouranos, which had been cut off and thrown into the sea by Cronos. To the Greeks the myth suggested the origins of personal love in the sea of primal unity; and there may also be sexual overtones (the independence of the female

According to the Skidi Pawnee people of North America everything was planned in the east, the male direction. One day the Morning Star presided over a great council of all the star gods and planned the creation of people. The Evening Star, guardian of the western, female, direction, opposed the plan, for fertility and creation were her province. Eventually the Morning Star made a perilous journey to the home of the Evening Star, arriving only after encountering many dangers. Eventually the two stars mated and the first human, a baby girl, was placed on the Earth.

form from male sexual potency) or moral ones (feminine harmony surviving male destructiveness).

Aphrodite had love affairs both with gods and with mortals. For example, she disputed possession of the beautiful boy Adonis with Persephone. On another occasion, falling in love with the Trojan herdsman Anchises, she pretended to be mortal and seduced him; his fears on discovering the truth were justified, for in one version he was struck by

lightning, and in another he had his eyes stung out by bees for seeing a goddess naked: love has perils as well as pleasures. The theme of conflict and love is clear in the myth of the Judgment of Paris, in which the Trojan prince, Paris, reluctantly agreed to judge a beauty contest between the goddesses Hera, Athene and Aphrodite. Aphrodite wore only her magic girdle – and promised Paris the beautiful Helen of Troy if he judged her the winner. But Helen was married to Menelaus, King of Mycenae, and the tragic result was the Trojan War.

LEFT *The Birth of Venus* by Sandro Botticelli, *c.*1485. In some versions of the myth Venus is said to have sprung from a cockleshell, which carried her to Cythera.
RIGHT Tlahuizcalpantecuhtli, a destructive deity associated with Venus, in a drawing after the Mayan Codex Cospi from Copan.

THE WARRIOR

The Aztecs placed great importance on Venus, more than on any other planet. Their culture was based around war, death and bloody sacrificial rituals. Venus, usually in combination with Jupiter, was the planet that determined decisions about when and where to do battle. (The Chinese, too, associated the planet with war.)

The Maya – another Central American people who placed great store on military success – aligned some of their great government buildings with Venus, such as the Governor's Palace at Uxmal, Mexico; when the planet rose at its most southerly, its light shone straight in at the palace's east door.

The warrior Venus was also known in the West. Ishtar herself, bow in hand, rode a chariot drawn by lions, and even when amorous she could be wilful and threatening. She was a demanding but fickle lover, and although she could be generous, many men suffered by her attentions. Even her animal lovers grew weak – suggesting the power of sensuality to sap will and aggression. When the Sumerian hero Gilgamesh refused her, Inanna demanded that the sky god Anu make a great bull to attack him. Gilgamesh's friend Enkidu tore it to bits and insulted her – for which she took his life.

Athene Nike, the Greek warrior goddess, preserved Ishtar's combative nature and

> 'Venus causes fame, honour, happiness, abundance, happy marriage, many children, satisfaction in every mutual relationship, the increase of property, a neat and well-conducted manner of life. Further she is the cause of bodily health. She brings nourishing winds, good air, clear weather, success, profit and abundance of the fruits of the Earth.'
>
> Ptolemy, *Tetrabiblos*, 2nd century AD

survives in Britannia, the female personification of the British Empire, while in medieval astrology the planet could be used to indicate victory in war.

THE ASTROLOGICAL VENUS

The earliest collection of Babylonian astrological omens, the Venus Tablets of Amizaduqa, dating from *c.*1700BC, show that the planet's astrological significance was almost invariably beneficial. Greek, Roman, Indian, Islamic and medieval European astronomers stuck to the principle that Venus was a fortunate planet (second only to Jupiter in its benefits), conferring beauty, gracious manners, a love of the arts and a balanced temperament. At its worst it was decadent and indulgent, and from these failings other problems could develop, but it was never as troublesome as the other planets. As the planet of peace it was the antidote to Mars, the planet of war. Western astrology shared some of its

Venus attributes with other cultures. The Chinese made Venus a planet of war, for example, but also made it the governor of the harvest, reflecting its Western image as a bringer of fertility.

In Jungian astrology Venus represents the anima, the archetypal feminine qualities in both men and women. A modern astrological counsellor will look at Venus' traditional astrological connections in a non-traditional way, encouraging the client to explore his or her feelings and emotions, the goal being to enhance Venus' positive qualities and minimize the negative ones.

CONDITIONS ON VENUS

Being closer to the Sun than the Earth is, Venus can only reach a maximum of 48 degrees from the Sun, as seen from Earth. This means that, like Mercury, it has phases: it was these that in 1610 convinced Galileo that the Earth and planets orbited the Sun.

Unlike Mercury, Venus has a dense atmosphere – it owes its brilliance to the reflective nature of the thick white clouds that blanket it. Its atmosphere, which extends between 35 and 65 kilometres (22 and 40 miles) above its surface, is composed largely of carbon dioxide and droplets of sulphuric acid which fall like

rain. High winds in the upper atmosphere cause swirling clouds where temperatures fall to below 50° C.

On the surface of the planet, conditions are very different. The thick, dense atmosphere holds in the Sun's heat, and temperatures approach 500° C. This blisteringly hot dust-desert is scattered with volcanoes, craters and loose rocks, and racked with thunder and lightning, while its atmospheric pressure is ninety times that of the Earth. If Venus ever did sustain life, it seems highly unlikely that it could do so now.

RIGHT Venus appears beautiful from this distance, but surface conditions are inhospitable in the extreme.
BELOW Volcanic lava fields on Venus – not the seas of soda-water that were anticipated by some astronomers before 1962.

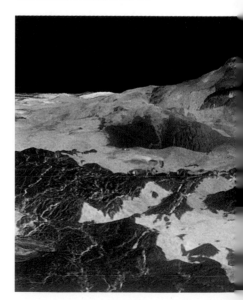

In 1962, the US probe Mariner 2 flew past Venus at a distance of 32,000 kilometres (20,000 miles), the third of 27 probes between 1961 and 1990. Before that date, astronomers had speculated that the planet was covered by soda-water seas, created by the carbon dioxide in the atmosphere penetrating ordinary sea water. This marine image tied in rather nicely with the mythological representation of Venus (Aphrodite) being born from the ocean. Mariner 2 disproved such theories. However, a more recent notion suggests that at one time – perhaps when the Sun was cooler than it is now – there may have been oceans on the planet's surface, and perhaps life. When the Sun heated up, the oceans boiled away, the carbonates were leached out of the rocks, and Venus lost all potential for life.

EARTH

The Earth is our home planet, the third planet from the Sun, and unique in its fluid combination of solid, liquid and gas – rock, water and air. It is this combination that makes life possible. The Earth has a diameter of 12,756 kilometres (7,926 miles) at the equator and orbits the Sun at an average distance of 149.6 million kilometres (93 million miles). It hurtles through space at supersonic speeds, wobbling on its axis and making a corkscrew motion, spinning once a day, orbiting the Sun once a year and following the Sun on its own flight around the galaxy. The atmosphere extends up to 5,000 kilometres (3,100 miles) into space, although at heights above about 700 kilometres (435 miles) particles of gas are so sparse that they are unlikely even to collide with each other. Behind it trails its own magnetic field, which at its broadest is as much as forty times the planet's radius. As it passes through space it collides with the solar wind, and is thus bombarded with the energy that makes life possible – and has the capacity to destroy it.

The Aztec Earth goddess Coatlicue, with skulls and serpents. This statue marked the 'omphalos' – the navel or centre of the Earth – for the Aztecs.

When human beings developed religious consciousness they first focused on the Great Mother Earth as the supreme goddess. In Babylon she was Ninhursaga, in Greece she was Gaia, the 'deep-breasted Earth', and to the Norse people she was Nerthus. She also took on different forms, often doubling as queen of heaven. In Middle Eastern religion she became the partner of the sky god, in which role she was gradually reduced in stature. In Judaism, Islam and Protestant Christianity she has no role. In Roman Catholicism she survives as the Virgin Mother.

Myths often speak of the creation of the world by gods and goddesses, indicating that they were outside it – the God of the Jews and Christians is an obvious example. Yet many early religions in the Middle East, Egypt and Greece believed that the deities were one and the same as the physical universe. If, then, all matter was animated, it was either conscious or the expression of a larger consciousness. Thus

The 'Venus of Willendorf' is one of a number of such figurines dating from *c*.30,000– 25,000BC, that have been discovered across Europe. They may have been representations of the Earth goddess; certainly the shape of the naked female figures, with their large breasts, swollen stomachs and fleshy thighs and buttocks, suggests an association with fecundity.

Gaia was more than the goddess of the Earth. She *was* the Earth.

The Greek poet Hesiod related that Gaia arose by herself from the primeval Chaos. She gave birth to Ouranos, the 'starry heaven', the universal sky god. She and her son then united to produce the twelve Titans, six female and six male. Although one of the Titans, Cronos, was specifically linked to time, the twelve as a whole represented the division of time emerging from matter itself, rather than having an independent existence: time, as Einstein would have said, is a property of matter in motion.

IS THE EARTH ALIVE?

The first philosopher known to have set out the belief that the Earth is 'alive' was Plato. In his treatise the *Timaeus*, he describes the creation of the Earth, the stars and the planets as acts of will by God, emerging from the mind of God. If God is divine, he reasoned, so is the physical universe. He talked of the Earth and planets as 'divinities', seeing them not as gods or goddesses themselves, but as aspects of the one God. The Greek theory that the world is alive is known as 'hylozoism'. The Romans knew the soul of the world as the 'Anima Mundi'.

The idea that the world contains living energies reaches perhaps its highest expression in China, where the ancient discipline of feng shui is used to harmonize buildings with the 'dragon lines' that are believed to flow across the land, much like acupuncture meridians on the body. Dragon lines have influenced the theory of ley lines, which owes its

LEFT A 15th-century stained-glass window, in the church of St Etienne, Mulhouse, France, depicting the globe schematically divided into three continents. RIGHT The Earth seen from space, with South America visible below the centre of the picture.

of the Earth as a mother, supporting all life and deserving of respect. In 1969 the British scientist James Lovelock published *The Gaia Hypothesis*, in which he set out his thesis that the Earth is 'alive', even if not in the same sense that we are (that is, fully conscious, making choices and exercising free will). Lovelock argued that if ecosystems are made up of living creatures, both plants and animals, then each ecosystem is, in a sense, alive. And if we link all ecosystems on the Earth together, and add the geological processes that shape the continents, then we have a single giant living system.

Lovelock added an apocalyptic slant by arguing that this giant system – 'Gaia' – is self-regulating, and will defend itself. He suggested that if human beings pollute their environment beyond tolerable limits then natural processes will be set in train that will curb humanity itself. Human beings might participate in their own destruction

inspiration to Alfred Watkins, a British antiquarian. In 1925 Watkins published *The Old Straight Track*, in which he noted that many archaic sites – especially obvious sacred sites such as pre-Roman mounds and medieval churches, but including ancient wells and pathways – often seem to line up in straight lines. One such line, the St Michael Line, can be traced across Britain from St Michael's Mount in Cornwall through to East Anglia. Watkins speculated that early Britons may have been instinctively aware of lines of energy which are still not understood. His followers believe that many of the astronomically aligned standing stones in the British Isles act to channel both celestial and terrestrial energy.

Contemporary Western theories of the living Earth can be traced back to Plato via the psychologist Carl Jung. In his theory of the 'collective unconscious' Jung asserted that every individual is linked to all others through a shared unconscious mind. Equally influential are the ideas of surviving religious traditions that preserve the concept

The biologist Rupert Sheldrake has tackled the problem of why certain developments in the animal world appear to take place around the same time in separate parts of the world without any obvious connection. To explain this phenomenon he hypothesizes the existence of 'morphic fields', which enable unconscious communication between organisms, even between crystals. As yet, though, we have no idea as to how these fields might actually work.

through global warming or depletion of the ozone layer, through the spreading of new diseases, through pollutants, or through other problems such as a fall in the sperm count. Earth, freed from humanity, will survive.

Such ideas are difficult to test scientifically, but they raise the question, if the Earth is 'alive', then why not the entire universe?

The Romans thought that the Earth lost moisture to the rest of the solar system. This was then soaked up by nearby planets such as Venus. Saturn, which was farthest from Earth, was one of the driest planets, while Mars, being hot and red, was thought to evaporate the oceans.

MARS

Mars is the fourth-largest planet in the solar system, after the Earth, with a diameter of 6,787 kilometres (4,217 miles). Its distance from the Sun varies between 208 million kilometres and 248 million kilometres, averaging 230 million kilometres (129 and 154 million miles, averaging 142 million miles), and it is between 56 million kilometres and 96 million kilometres (35 and 60 million miles) from the Earth. Its year, the time it takes to orbit the Sun, is 687 Earth days, and its day is 24 hours, 37 minutes. Mars' light takes between one and five minutes to reach the Earth, depending on whether the two planets are on the same side of the Sun or on opposite sides.

Medieval astronomers regarded iron as Mars' metal. Recent space probes proved this to be correct when it was shown that the Martian soil has a high iron content, while its core is probably molten iron. True to the furious nature of the mythological Mars, great red dust storms occur when Mars comes closest to the Sun, causing temperatures to soar.

Mars' earliest mythology can be traced back about 4,000 years to Mesopotamia, where the planet was known as Sal-bat-a-ni and was sacred to Nergal. In Egypt it was 'Horus the Red' or 'Horus the Horizon, and in Persia it was sacred to Verethragna or Varhan. The Greeks called it the 'star of Ares' and the Romans the 'star of Mars', from which our modern name is taken. In India the planet is Kuja or Mangala and its god is Kamara. In China it is Ying Huo, the Fire Planet.

In classical astronomy Mars was a hot, dry planet, ruling Aries and Scorpio, exalted (strong) in Capricorn, and debilitated (weak) in Taurus, Cancer and Libra. He governed Tuesday and the third month after conception, his guardian angel was Samael and his only friend Venus. In the Middle East around the time of Christ the planet was held sacred to God.

The Valles Marineris hemisphere of Mars, from 2,500 km (1,550 miles). In the centre can be seen the Valles Marineris canyon system – ancient river channels, now dry.

THE RED PLANET

As a god, Mars' mythical reputation is based entirely on the planet's red appearance. From this have arisen all its associations with heat and anger. In Babylon Mars was sacred to Nergal, an unpleasant deity who was lord both of the fires of hell and of the summer heat which, unchecked, caused drought and starvation. It has never entirely lost this reputation.

When the Greeks named the planets, they made the planet Mars sacred to their god Ares who, legend relates, was born in Thrace to Hera, wife of Zeus. However, although he is sometimes called the son of Zeus, the strange circumstances of his birth contradict this. One version of the story is that Hera was angry when Zeus gave birth unaided to a daughter, Athene, who burst from his forehead fully armed. Hera therefore decided to become pregnant

> 'Of these same countries Britain, Gaul and Germany are in familiar with Aries and Mars. Therefore, for the most part their inhabitants are fiercer, more headstrong and bestial... Yet the Greeks have the qualities of leadership and are noble and independent, because of Mars.'
>
> Ptolemy, *Tetrabiblos*, 2nd century AD

A 15th-century depiction of Mars from the *De Sphaera* manuscript, showing the god's red skin, his warlike attributes (including the martial activities in the lower half of the picture) and the zodiac signs with which he is traditionally associated: Scorpio (the Scorpion) and Aries (the Ram).

without Zeus. She asked the Earth goddess Gaia for help, and was granted this in the form of a herb, or flower, that made her conceive.

Ares was born out of anger, rivalry and revenge, and many of the stories told about him feature the fierce rivalry that later developed between him and his equally warlike but wiser sister, Athene. He was primarily a god of war, pictured as a small, dark, bearded man in heavy bronze armour, carrying a huge spear. He roamed the battlefield in his chariot, spreading death and destruction, accompanied by his terrible companions Deimos (Fear) and Phobos (Fright).

Mars, the Roman god equivalent to Ares, was held in far more respect. He was initially a god of agriculture and fertility, and was associated with sexuality, especially with male potency. He also fathered Romulus and Remus, the legendary founders of Rome. Legend relates that the infant twins were suckled by a she-wolf, a creature sacred to Mars. As

A 5th–4th-century BC bronze statue showing the she-wolf suckling Romulus and Remus, the legendary founders of Rome.

Mars and Venus by Sandro Botticelli (*c.*1444–1510). Greek myth depicted Ares as much more violent, brutal and unrestrained than the Roman god Mars with whom he later became identified. When not on the battlefield, Ares mainly features in myth as the lover of Aphrodite (Venus), and is sometimes said to be the father of her son Eros (Cupid). See also box, below.

Rome's imperial ambitions grew, Mars took on the attributes of a war god. His sacred spears and shields – cult objects – were kept on the Palatine Hill in Rome.

In Hindu mythology, Mars is called Mangala. His other Hindu names mean 'son of the Earth' and 'beloved of farmers', revealing a shared tradition with Ares, who sprang miraculously from his mother alone, and the agricultural Mars of Rome.

THE ASTROLOGICAL MARS

Jungian psychologists connect the mythic Mars to the archetype of the 'animus', the male aspect of the personality, which exists in both sexes. Those Jungian analysts who use astrology will check the location of Mars at their clients' birth to shed light on such questions as their relationship both to other men and to 'male' qualities within themselves.

Mars' astrological attributes were derived from his warlike qualities, and the planet's reputation was one of the few to span different cultures – the Chinese gave it the same significance as it held in

ARES AND APHRODITE

There was at least one Olympian with whom Ares found favour – the beautiful but faithless Aphrodite, who was married to the lame smith-god Hephaistos (Hephaestus). On hearing of his wife's affair with Ares, the furious Hephaistos forged a fine net of invisible but unbreakable chains, hung it over his bed, then let the lovers think he was going away. When informed by the Sun that the pair lay, drowsy with love-making, on his bed, he dropped the net and trapped them – to the guilty couple's dismay and shame. This union produced the beautiful Harmonia, who became queen of Thebes.

Europe, India and the Middle East. They also regarded the planet as the governor of 'growth and development'. In classical and medieval astrology Mars represented people who were strong and assertive or angry and violent. Its professions included any that used knives or fire – smiths, butchers, barbers and surgeons as well as soldiers. It could also bring feverish illnesses, hot and sometimes stormy weather, and drought. Its colours were red and scarlet, its plants covered in thorns and prickles. The practical implications in terms of ancient and medieval society were clear. An astrologer advising a general would have counselled his master to launch an invasion when Mars was favourably placed in Aries, while a physician would treat a feverish patient with soothing herbs symbolized by Venus.

THE MARS EFFECT

The Mars Effect, discovered by French statistician Michel Gauquelin, could turn out to be the one of most revolutionary discoveries in the history of science. It has also proved to be one of the most controversial astronomical discoveries of the 20th century, mainly because Gauquelin was a statistician but also because his work seemed to support astrology. Orthodox astronomers have largely ignored his results.

Gauquelin began his work in 1949, studying the planetary positions at the births of 570 French sportsmen, all taken from standard reference books. By 1955 he had demonstrated that champion athletes are statistically likely to be born with Mars either rising over the eastern horizon or culminating overhead.

The Mars Effect has become a scientific *cause célèbre*, and the argument concerning its significance has now been raging for forty years, mainly focused on how he selected his data. The most substantial review was conducted by Suitbert Ertel, Professor of Psychology at Groningen University in the Netherlands and co-author of the *The Tenacious Mars Effect* (1996). A few of Gauquelin's findings have been rejected, but Ertel and Professor Arno Müller of the University of Saarland in Germany, have refined and clarified the core – the link between Mars and sports champions. Gauquelin's principle academic backer for many years was Hans Eysenck, Professor of Psychology at London's Institute of Psychiatry. All three are convinced that Gauquelin had stumbled upon a new form of scientific astronomy, perhaps one that should legitimately be called 'astro-psychology'.

What possible mechanism could link Mars to athletes? The truth is that we just do not know. The astronomer Percy Seymour suspects that the planets may act via the Sun's magnetic field, and that this may disturb the Earth's field in such a way as to affect personality. However, the astronomers of ancient cultures, who had no knowledge of electromagnetism, connected Mars to soldiers. Gauquelin appears to have done more than demonstrate a planet–profession link. He also seems to have statistically demonstrated that ancient peoples' intuitive approach to

RIGHT **The rocky, iron-rich surface of Mars, with (inset) a highly magnified image of a tubular form less than one-hundredth the width of a human hair – one of many found in a Martian meteorite, and which NASA scientists think may be fossilized bacteria (see pp.169, 274–5).**

knowledge may have produced some genuine discoveries.

Gauquelin's Mars Effect is a statistical truth, which means that although many champion athletes are born with Mars in the favoured positions, others are not. Mohammed Ali was born with Mars culminating, but neither Willie Mays, one of the all-time champion North American baseball stars, nor Jack Nicklaus, one of the century's greatest golfers, were born with the planet in a favoured position. Clearly other factors are involved, but we know so little about the Mars Effect that we are a long way from being able to say what might cause variations in it. The search for a mechanism in the sense that we understand it may be misleading; perhaps the real explanation must await a breakthrough in the study of consciousness.

It might one day be shown that Gauquelin's results were a statistical blip, but so far the most rigorous tests have shown that he was correct. Gauquelin himself, however, pointed out that even his positive results failed to support most astrological claims.

LIFE ON MARS
The Fantasy

There has been more speculation about life on Mars than on any other planet. Martians abound in children's comics, science fiction and popular imagination. David Bowie posed the question in a popular hit song of the 1970s – 'Is there life on Mars?' So, why has interest focused on Mars?

In the medieval mind Mars itself was thought to be a living body in a living universe populated by angels and demons. Galileo, who stood on the boundary between the medieval world of astral deities and the modern world of scientific astronomy, examined Mars through his telescope but was unable to make out much detail.

In 1659 the Dutch physicist and astronomer Christiaan Huygens (1629–95) spotted a large dark area on the planet's surface – Syrtis Major – and over the years speculation grew that the shading of this and similar dark areas was due to vegetation. Other astronomers concluded that they must be vegetated, because otherwise they would soon be covered in red dust.

Belief in intelligent Martians was boosted in 1877 when Giovanni Schiaparelli mistakenly reported observing canali on the planet – channels. This was mistranslated as 'canals'. Then around the turn of the century the respected US astronomer Percival Lowell caused a sensation by suggesting that these 'canals' had been built by Martians.

In the late 1950s Russian astronomer Iosif Shklovsky suggested that Mars' two moons, Phobos (Fear) and Deimos (Terror) were in fact Martian space stations. It was not until 1982 that he announced that this had been a practical joke.

Current fringe theories focus on the so-called 'face' on Mars, a giant geographical feature which appears to have eyes, a nose and mouth, much like the 'man on the Moon', and which believers claim is the legacy of a long-lost civilization. NASA photographs of pyramid-like structures have even encouraged speculation that the ancient Egyptians colonized Mars, reversing the usual fantasy that the Egyptian pyramids were constructed by aliens.

LIFE ON MARS
The Reality

As recently as 1960 it was widely thought that Mars had a smooth surface and a nitrogen-rich atmosphere at about the same pressure as that of Earth, and that its polar ice-caps were only a thin frosting. Some observers reported a darkening around the ice-caps as they melted with the Martian seasons, suggesting the spread of vegetation. Add to this the fact that the Martian day is about the same length as ours, and conditions for life seem quite promising.

In the 1960s astronomer Patrick Moore and microbiologist Dr Francis Jackson collaborated on a combined experiment, constructing a 'Martian laboratory'. They filled it with plants and what they assumed to be the correct atmosphere and regulated its temperature according to the existing

knowledge about Mars. Some of their results were interesting. They reported that 'a cactus fared badly, but more simple organisms did better and we felt quite encouraged'.

There have been successful landings on the planet, and between 1962 and 1993 there were twenty unmanned probes. Of these only seven can

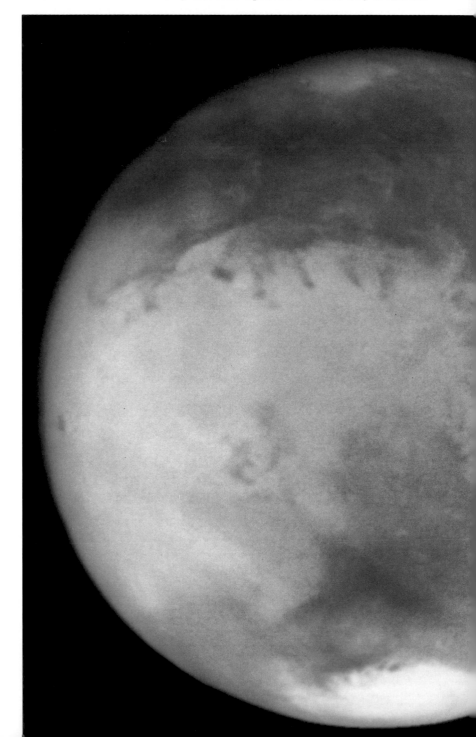

be counted as successes, and at least half were outright failures. The most successful were Viking 1 and Viking 2, which orbited and landed in the summer of 1976, sending back most of our available data. Between 1965 and 1971 four of the Mariner probes flew past, sending back photographs.

Mars was found to be heavily cratered, with giant volcanoes: the largest, Olympus Mons, is 25 kilometres (15 miles) high, with a base 600 kilometres (370 miles) across. As to the dark areas, some were craters, others plateaux. The largest, Syrtis Major, was a high plateau from which the red dust had been scoured by high winds. These winds were caused by the high temperature differential, between −123° C and +20° C, caused in turn by the thinness of the largely carbon dioxide atmosphere, with pressure at just 1 per cent of that on Earth.

In 1990 US president George Bush anounced plans for a human landing on Mars by 2019, although the space exploration budget is focusing on the space station programme rather than planetary landings. The first step, though, is the renewed series of space probes, named Pathfinder. There are plans to despatch these at every available opportunity over a ten-year period beginning in 1997.

THE POTENTIAL

Although there are no artificial canals on Mars, it is now believed that the channels may indeed once have been

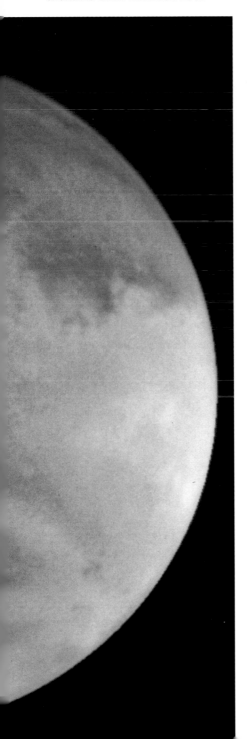

Northern spring time on Mars. The dark regions are coarse sand, not vegetation.

riverbeds. A symposium held in London on 30 January 1996 backed the idea that there might, after all, be life on Mars. Martin Walter of Macquarie University, Australia, suggested that four million years ago Mars could have been a hospitable place, with a climate similar to that of Earth. Could there, he speculates, have been forests, animals and birds?

The sort of life scientists are hoping to find is a world away from 'little green men'. Their interest was attracted by the discovery, announced in 1996, of small worm-like creatures in the 'hot smokers', the plumes of overheated water that shoot up from the Earth's deep-sea beds. Scientists such as Paul Davies of Adelaide University in Australia wonder whether similar life could exist beneath the surface of Mars – especially following the identification of tiny tubes in Mars rock that may be fossilized bacteria (see pp.166–7, 274–5).

Professor Davies even believes that life might have travelled from Mars to Earth. He speculates that life might travel through space cocooned in rocks protecting it from deadly radiation. However, critics such as Professor David Hughes of Sheffield University in England have pointed out that being blasted into space, spending a million years there, and then being subjected to fierce heat on entering the Earth's atmosphere, would almost certainly wipe it out.

JUPITER

Jupiter is the largest planet in the solar system, with an equatorial diameter of 142,800 kilometres (89,000 miles) – eleven times that of the Earth. (If the Earth were a pea, Jupiter would be the size of a cricket ball.) It orbits the Sun at an average distance of 778.3 million kilometres (484 million miles) in 11.86 years. Its rapid (ten-hour) rotation on its own axis makes it bulge into an oblate shape, so that the pole-to-pole distance is 7 per cent less than its equatorial diameter. Due to the length of time it takes Jupiter's light to reach the Earth, we see it in the sky as it was between nine and thirteen minutes earlier.

'If [Jupiter's] rays dart, and it shimmers or it appears small, then large, or its colour changes frequently, it is an indication that the ruler will be afflicted.'

Chinese treatise *Ssu Ma Chi'en*, 2nd century BC. Jupiter's appearance would vary in changing weather conditions.

In Babylon Jupiter was known as Mulu-babbar or Niburu, and was sacred to Marduk, who after *c.*1800BC was recognized as chief of the gods. In Egypt the planet was known as 'Horus who illuminates the Two Lands' or 'Horus who opens the Mystery', and in Persia it was sacred to the supreme god of light, Ahura Mazda. To the Greeks the planet was 'the star of Zeus' and to the Romans it was the 'star of Jupiter' – the origin of its modern name. Jupiter's alternative name was Jove, and people who share his often expansive and optimistic approach to life are known as 'jovial'.

In classical astronomy Jupiter ruled Sagittarius and Pisces, and was strong in Cancer and weak in Gemini, Virgo and Capricorn. He was friendly with all the other planets except Mars, and his angel was Zadkiel. He was also known as Phaethon and in Norse mythology corresponds to the god Thor. In India Jupiter is Guru or Brihaspati, the gods' spiritual teacher, and is engaged in perpetual competition with Sukra, guru of the demons (see p.153). His name means either 'lord of power' or 'lord of sacred speech' and his god is Brahma. In China Jupiter is the Wood Planet, known as the Year Star.

In Latin Jupiter's day was Jovis dies – in French *Jeudi*. In English it is Thursday, after Thor, and in Germany *Donnerstag* after Donar, an alternative name for Thor.

'When the star of Marduk appears at the beginning of the year, in that year corn will be prosperous ... when Jupiter appears in the third month the land will be devastated and the corn will be dear.'

Babylonian omens

bered, and his subsequent resurrection and victory became the model for the other great resurrection stories and provided the focal point of the Babylonian religious year. As soon as the other gods acknowledged his power he established peace and order, placing the stars in their correct places and creating the calendar, measuring the correct order of time and space.

Marduk's festival, the Akitu, was celebrated all over the region, as far north as Harran, on what is now the border with Turkey, and as far west as Jerusalem. Since Marduk was the universal saviour of humanity, the appearance of his planet, Jupiter, was generally associated with prosperity and plenty.

ABOVE A portion of a Babylonian cuneiform tablet (2000–1500BC), relating the legend of the fight between the goddess Tiamat and Marduk, the Babylonian equivalent of Jupiter or Zeus.

OPPOSITE LEFT A view of the planet Jupiter, in an image taken from three separate exposures in red, blue and green light. The dark spot on Jupiter's disc is the shadow of Io, one of Jupiter's moons.

MARDUK, THE PATRIARCH

Marduk, perhaps the most important of all the planet's gods, grew in stature from a lowly fertility god to chief of the Babylonian pantheon, consolidating his supreme position by vanquishing the all-destroying monster Tiamat. Marduk's triumph came only after he had been first killed and dismem-

ZEUS, KING OF OLYMPUS

The classical Greeks borrowed their planetary deities direct from the Babylonians, and to them the planet Jupiter was the star of Zeus, their closest equivalent to Marduk.

Zeus represented a new generation of gods. The son of the Titans Cronos and Rhea, he usurped his father, forcing him to yield up all the offspring –

Zeus' brothers and sisters – that he had swallowed, and leading the gods in the battle against their predecessors, the Titans, which resulted in the Titans' banishment.

Zeus was worshipped on mountains – especially Olympus, the abode of the gods. He was omnipotent, yet compassionate and just. Above all, he dispensed law and order – which might be seen in the relatively lawless ancient world as conferring freedom.

Despite his responsibilities, there is something in Zeus' character that embodies the spirit of adventure and exploration. This emerges in his exuberant and untiring (though sometimes unsuccessful) pursuit of the opposite sex – both mortal and

otherwise. His first three wives suggested attributes of his own deity: Metis (Wisdom), Themis (Law) and the Titaness Mnemosyne (Memory). The wife with whom he is most associated, however, is Hera, who may have been his sister. He is said to have seduced her by changing himself into a shivering, storm-

bedraggled cuckoo, on whom the goddess took pity.

Thus, although Zeus often embodied some of the cruder aspects of human nature, he had a dual role, combining his more unruly attributes with those of a wise, just, all-seeing, all-encompassing sky god. When St Paul was preaching the gospel to the

Jupiter and Thetis **by Jean-Auguste-Dominique Ingres (1780–1867). Zeus (Jupiter) generally got his own way in his amours, but not always. In this painting, he is admired by Thetis, whom he was forced to give up, for fear of begetting by her a son who would dethrone him, as the Fates had prophesied.**

Athenians he compared God to Zeus by using a well-known phrase from the 3rd-century BC Greek court astrologer Aratus. Well educated in Greek mysticism, which, like Christianity, held that there was one supreme God, Paul knew that Zeus was no more than a Greek name for the supreme male God of the Jews and Christians – there could be only one God, even if he was known by different names in different cultures.

ZEUS AND IO

One of many mortal women to be loved by Zeus was Io, priestess of his wife Hera. To keep the affair from Hera, Zeus transformed himself into a cloud. When Hera still became suspicious, he turned Io into a white heifer. Hera pretended to fall for this, and asked for the beautiful animal as a gift. Her wish granted, she immediately put the animal under the guard of the hundred-eyed giant Argos. Hermes lulled Argos to sleep with his flute and Io escaped, only to be pursued across the world by a stinging gadfly sent by Hera. Eventually Zeus turned his lover back into human shape and she bore him a son, after which she married King Telegonus of Egypt.

THOR, GOD OF THUNDER

It was the Romans themselves who first made the connection between Jupiter and Thor, the mighty Teutonic sky god. When the thunder roared people said that this was Thor's chariot rolling across the heavens. When lightning struck they believed he was wielding his battle-axe. As a fearless warrior Thor became the favourite god of the Norse and German tribes in the early Christian centuries, attracting the most lavish shrines and greatest devotion, displacing the storm god Odin in some areas. Thor had other functions, including presiding over contracts, and hence over marriages, which were, it was believed, made in heaven.

RIGHT Thor riding in his sky chariot, pulled by two rams or goats, called Toothgrinder and Toothgnasher. In his right hand he holds aloft his hammer, while lightning flies from his other hand.

THE ASTROLOGICAL JUPITER

The astrological Jupiter is pre-eminently the planet of good fortune. As the ruler of adventurers and philosophers, the classical astrologers knew Jupiter as the 'Great Benefic' and whenever it was powerfully placed they would forecast wealth, power and happiness.

However, in the world of the astrologers nothing is as it seems, and everything contains its opposite. And in the moral universe of ancient astral religion the good are always rewarded and the wicked punished. So, Jupiterian fortune often brings twists of fate or unexpected consequences. The greatest of these is preserved in the tale of King Midas, who wished that everything he touched would turn to gold, only to be faced with the problem that as soon as he came into direct contact with anything living, it died.

Hindu astrologers characterize the Jupiterian individual as rich, powerful, fat and contented. Yet what pitfalls await such persons? They may become ill from overweight. Worse, they may become greedy and forget their duty to the poor. That is when spiritual punishment steps in, for it is believed that the rich person who abuses his or her position is likely to be reincarnated as a beggar.

Jupiter, as the planet of expansion, exists in an uneasy partnership with Saturn, the planet of limitation. The two are dependent on each other, and for Jupiterian good fortune to be of any benefit it must be perfectly balanced with the discipline and devotion to duty that are symbolized by Saturn. In astral mythology only those deserving of Jupiter's benefits will receive them.

JUPITER, THE ACTOR

As part of his research into planetary connections with careers, in the 1950s, the statistician Michel Gauquelin (see p.166) conducted studies into samples of actors and politicians. He discovered that those who reach the top in both professions tend to be born when Jupiter had either just risen over the eastern horizon or had culminated overhead. The opposite points showed slight peaks. Unlike the Mars Effect, the Jupiter Effect has not been thoroughly tested, and further studies are awaited.

'Jupiter has a temperate, active force, because his movement takes place between the cooling influence of Saturn and the burning power of Mars. He both heats and humidifies – and he produces fertilizing winds.'

Ptolemy, *Tetrabiblos*, 2nd century AD

However, it is an ironic comment on our leading politicians that they share a planetary eminence effect with our best actors.

Gauquelin also noted that certain character traits were connected with powerful Jupiter

---

Islamic astrologers believed that the twenty-year periods between conjunctions of Jupiter and Saturn, when they occupied the same zodiac degree, were the building blocks of history. As Jupiter was connected to religious belief they even thought it had a role in the rise of Islam. The 9th-century astronomer Abu Ma'shar linked Jupiter with the other six planets, arranged in their distance from Earth, so that each combination 'matched' one of the world's great religions.

Jupiter–Saturn = JUDAISM
Jupiter–Mars = CHALDEAN RELIGION
Jupiter–Sun = EGYPTIAN RELIGION
Jupiter–Venus = ISLAM
Jupiter–Mercury = CHRISTIANITY
Jupiter–Moon = ANTICHRIST: GOD VANQUISHED
End of the world = KINGDOM OF GOD: GOD VICTORIOUS

An 18th-century Persian manuscript painting showing a personification of the planet Jupiter (on the left), with the fish of Pisces, which is ruled by Jupiter in astrology.

positions. The British astrologer John Addey conducted further studies with these and concluded that characteristics ascribed to people born at different phases of Jupiter's daily cycle (rising, culminating and setting) changed. When rising, Jupiter tended to be connected to wisdom, and when culminating, to power. When setting, it tended to indicate impulsiveness, and when on the lower culmination, it was associated with arrogance. Addey believed that he had found the different faces of the mythical Jupiter, whether as god of justice and king of Olympus, or as impulsive, capricious rapist.

> **MATTERS ASSOCIATED WITH JUPITER**
>
> 'Dignities ecclesiastical, Religion, Government, Justice, by Commendations from persons of quality, Benefices or Church-livings, natural Honesty or Morality.'
>
> English astrologer William Lilly, 1647

JUPITER AND HISTORY

Astronomers have always respected Jupiter's power. In China its twelve-year cycle determined the calendar and it was said to govern birth and death. In the medieval Islamic world astronomers believed that, together with Saturn, Jupiter regulated major historical cycles.

Schemes linking Jupiter with religion (see box opposite) were common in European astronomy until the 17th century. Increasingly elaborate versions were expounded by Christian theologians, especially during the long period of religious war following the Reformation, from *c.*1517 to 1650, when pious people, both Catholic and Protestant, looked to the heavens for signs of the coming of the Kingdom of God. One of the last astronomers to consider seriously Jupiter's role in history was Johannes Kepler, and in 1601 he made some experimental political forecasts for 1602, based partly on Jupiter's movements for the year. On the conjunction between Jupiter and Mars he wrote that 'souls are generally stunned and frightened, or aroused in the expectation of revolts'. In fact, 1602 was not a particularly violent or revolutionary year in European history.

AN INSUBSTANTIAL WORLD

For all its size, we could never land on Jupiter, because it has no crust. Its beautiful banded cloud system, visible through a telescope, is composed of frozen ammonia, ammonia hydrosulphide, water droplets and ice. The different gases produce white, yellow, grey and blue clouds, as well as the famous Great Red Spot. This was first observed in 1664 and is in fact a giant atmospheric storm, 30,000 kilometres (19,000 miles) long and 14,000 kilometres (9,000 miles) wide. There are also a number of smaller white spots.

Beneath the surface atmosphere lie layers of hydrogen and helium gas; beneath that probably liquid hydrogen; and finally a very dense form of

hydrogen called liquid metallic hydrogen. If the planet has a solid core, it is relatively small, so that the average density is little more than that of water.

Chemically, Jupiter resembles the Sun more than it does the Earth, and if it were eighty times as big it would be a star, because gravitational pressure at its core would cause a perpetual thermonuclear reaction. Yet Jupiter must create its own energy in some way, since although atmospheric temperatures are low, varying between –120° C and –170° C, the planet gives out more heat than it receives from the Sun.

Jupiter also has other powers. Its strong magnetic field traps ions and electrons to form large, intense radiation belts. In 1955 it was discovered that Jupiter emits bursts of radio waves.

JUPITER'S MOONS

Jupiter has at least sixteen satellites, or moons, the four largest of which (Io, Ganymede, Callisto and Europa) created something of a sensation when they were discovered by Marius and Galileo in 1610. At the time, many people believed that the Earth was the centre of the universe; it was argued that if the Earth orbited the Sun, the Moon would be left behind. However, Galileo realized that his observation of Jupiter's moons proved otherwise. It also proved that the

LEFT A photograph of Jupiter showing the Great Red Spot, a giant atmospheric storm 30,000 km (19,000 miles) long.
BELOW Jupiter with some of its sixteen moons. In the 17th century, Galileo's observations of the largest four helped to prove that the Earth was not the centre of the universe.

Earth was not the centre of all orbital movement. Not surprisingly, his announcements failed to win instant popularity with the Church. It was reported that one leading cleric refused to look through the telescope, claiming that it was bewitched! Nevertheless, while Copernicus (in 1513) had only proved mathematically that the Earth orbited the Sun, Galileo had proved for anyone with the eyes to see that not everything in the universe travelled around the Earth. Finally, nobody could argue that the Earth was at the centre of the universe.

The moons played another important role fifty years later, when Ole Roemer found that the times between their mutual eclipses were greater when Jupiter was moving away from the Earth than when it was approaching. He deduced from this that light moved at a finite speed.

Io's surface is coloured by active volcanoes; it also has white spots of sulphur dioxide frost. Ganymede and Callisto contain large amounts of ice and frozen ammonia

Jupiter has been described as a giant vacuum-cleaner, protecting the Earth from disaster. According to some astronomers its gravitational effect is so great that as it sweeps through the solar system it mops up hundreds of meteorites that might otherwise pose a danger to the Earth.

and methane. In July 1996 the Galileo space probe photographed signs of 'ice-quakes' on Ganymede, suggesting that its crust is unstable. Callisto is heavily cratered, whereas Europa is smooth except for shallow depressions, and either never had craters, or has them but hidden by water or soft ice which has welled up through the crust. This implies internal heating, which, together with the presence of water, makes Europa a relatively likely candidate for signs of life.

SPACE PROBES

Until 1996 there were a total of six probes sent to Jupiter, beginning with Pioneer 10, launched on 2 March 1972. The most dramatic was Galileo, which reached the planet in December 1995. Among our discoveries has been the extent of the radiation the planet emits. We already knew Jupiter was particularly active, as bursts of radio waves were detected in 1955, but as it flew past in 1973 Pioneer 10 was saturated with 500 times the lethal dose of radiation.

SATURN

Saturn is the second largest planet, after Jupiter, with an equatorial diameter of 143,000 kilometres (88,730 miles), nine times that of the Earth, and a mass 95 times that of the Earth. It is on average 1,427 million kilometres (886 million miles) from the Sun, and takes 29.46 years to complete one orbit. It has a magnetic field 1,000 times stronger than the Earth's but twenty times weaker than Jupiter's. Like Jupiter, it rotates rapidly on its own axis: its 'day' is a mere 10.7 hours. This has forced it into a slightly flattened oblate shape: its polar diameter is 10 per cent less than its equatorial diameter. Saturn is far enough away for us to 'see into the past' – we see it as it was more than an hour previously, owing to the time its light takes to reach us.

'He is a Diurnal Planet, Cold and Dry (being farre removed from the heat of the Sun) and moyst Vapours, Melancholick, Earthly, Masculine, the greater Infortune, author of Solitarinesse.'

English astrologer
William Lilly, 1647

To the Babylonians the planet was Sagush or Kaimânu, the 'star of the Sun', sacred to the god Ninurta. In Egypt it was known as Horus the Bull, or Horus, Bull of the Sky, while the Persians knew it as Mithras Helios, a form of the Sun. The Hebrews worshipped it as Kiyyun, Kaiwan or Sakkuth, and their reverence for the planet was such that they fixed their sabbath for the day held sacred to Saturn, which was subsequently named after it, Saturday.

Some historians have argued that Saturn is one of the root words of Satan, and that the Christian devil's portrayal as a goat is taken from Pan, the Greek deity associated with Capricorn, Saturn's sign. To the Greeks the planet was the 'star of Cronos', the lord of the Golden Age, and to the Romans it was the 'star of Saturn'. To the Indians Saturn is Sani and its god is Yama. In China it is Chen, the Regulator Planet.

In the Middle Ages, Saturn was also known as Chronos, Phoenon and Falciser. Medieval astronomers believed that it ruled Capricorn and Aquarius, and was exalted (strong) in Libra and debilitated (weak) in Aries, Cancer and Leo, and that it was linked to the angel Zaphiel.

THE GOD OF ORDER AND JUSTICE

In Babylon Saturn was the planet sacred to the warrior god Ninurta, also known as Ningirsu, Ninib or Ninurash, a heroic god not unlike his brother Nergal (equivalent to the Roman Mars) and Shamash, the Sun. His greatest triumph, during the primeval cosmic battle, was to rescue, on Marduk's (Jupiter's) behalf the 'tablets of fate' upon which were inscribed the gods' eternal laws (which later occur in the Hebrew Scriptures as the stones of the Ten Commandments). These had been stolen on behalf of Tiamat, the female monster of the deep. Ninurta's victory is seen by some historians as a semi-mythical account of the period c.3000–2000BC when male gods replaced female goddesses as the supreme deities. This myth also provides a basis for Ninurta's role as a god of truth, justice, and law and order.

Cronos, as a former king of the Greek pantheon, was a more important deity than Ninurta, occupying a similar status to Assur, his Assyrian equivalent. He was revered by the Greeks as the ruler of the Golden Age, when human beings lived in a state of complete peace, harmony and justice.

THE ASTROLOGICAL SATURN

This glorious past gave classical astronomers the key to the dire warnings they issued when Saturn was poorly positioned. Cronos represented unattainable ideals, the lost state of perfection that could never be restored. Thus he signified rejection, loss and even despair.

Saturn's astrological role was contradictory and only makes sense in the context of ancient religion. Classical and medieval astrologers knew the planet

Saturn Devouring a Son by Peter-Paul Rubens (1577–1640). Cronos (Saturn) swallowed each of his children in turn, apart from Zeus, whom Zeus' mother, Rhea, replaced with a stone. Note the 'ears' on the planet Saturn: these were in fact its ring system.

In Greek myth Cronos was the son of Ouranos, whom he deposed by castrating him with a sickle, and the father of Zeus, by whom he was in turn deposed and exiled. On one level the myth suggests a rejection of cannibalism and fetishism (Cronos devoured all his children but Zeus); it also represents the triumph of life and youth over death and old age, and the ascendancy of wisdom and justice over instinct.

as the 'Greater Malefic' or 'Greater Infortune'; astrological texts list its dire consequences – short lives for the young, loss of money for the rich, disgrace for the powerful. However, such forecasts assumed a certain way of life. Early astral religion was based on the premise that if one changed one's way of life, the future changed, and for the

person whose character was truly Saturnine – sensible, sober, hard-working, honest and upright, the planet Saturn would bring only benefits. Complacency, ignorance and arrogance would incite Saturn's wrath. This reputation spread to other cultures and even in Chinese astrology the planet governed the growth of virtue.

THE SENEX

A number of Jungian astrologers have made a direct connection between Saturn and the Jungian archetype, the Senex. Jung defined the Senex as that part of the personality characterized by the wisdom of old age, embodied in cultures in which the 'elders' are the source of knowledge and justice. Usually represented as a man, the Senex takes, among others, the mythical form of Merlin, the holder of age-old learning and power. Psychotherapists see Saturn as representing our capacity to sell ourselves short, but also the self-discipline that can

Odin, the Norse storm god, was often, like Saturn, identified with Father Time, and eventually with Father Christmas. This painting shows him flying down to earth to distribute money.

> 'When it is in its proper place, and all five planets are gathered in the same Hsiu [month], the pertaining realm can gain the empire by strength. If the rites, virtue, justice, death sentences and punishments are lacking, Saturn wavers.'
>
> Chinese treatise *Ssu Ma Ch'ien*, 2nd century BC

overcome inadequacy. It indicates the need to develop self-reliance and self-responsibility.

CRONOS, LORD OF TIME

Greek astronomers believed that Saturn's most significant feature was its slow movement. It took twice as long as Jupiter, the next slowest, to make one complete journey through the zodiac, and its ponderousness led it to be considered a planet of old age. In the Middle Ages Cronos, the god, was widely linked to Chronos, Greek for 'time'. Some scholars disagree that there is a genuine link between the two words, but none the less medieval astronomers represented Saturn as 'Old Father Time', the imaginary figure who sweeps away the old year and welcomes the new; or as the Grim Reaper, herald of death.

The Greeks also assumed, correctly, that it was the farthest of the then known planets from the Earth, the stepping-off point to the stars. This was crucial to their religion, in which it was believed that before birth the soul descended from heaven via the stars and planets, beginning with Saturn. The astral mystery cults involved initiations which went symbolically through the planets; Saturn was the last gateway before the soul reached the stars – enlightenment – and therefore represented the greatest spiritual tests of all, including renunciation of all physical possessions.

The Romans linked the Greek Cronos to an ancient agricultural god, Saturn. He was said to have taught agriculture, especially vine-growing, to the Romans, and in their depictions the sickle of the Grim Reaper becomes the means of bringing in the harvest. His festival, Saturnalia (see p. 97), was a time of feasting, when roles were reversed and servants were served by their masters; Saturn's role as god of order was reversed in an orgy of liberation, defying the natural order of death and inevitable decay.

SANI

In Indian mythology the planet Saturn was represented by Sani, son of the Sun god and half-brother of Yama, the god of death. Sani ('slow'), is depicted as small and limping, or as crossing the sky in his iron chariot pulled by eight horses. He is associated with time, death and the earth. (To the Chinese, too, Saturn is the Earth Planet.) The 4th-century Indian astrologer Minaraja associated him with the holy man Utanka, perhaps because of his association with the earth and with age.

The story is told that at one time Utanka was the student of the guru Gautama, the future Buddha. He served his master so well that Gautama kept him on until the youthful student had become an old man. When Utanka finally requested his freedom, Gautama rewarded him by restoring his youth and giving him his daughter in marriage; he also declined to accept the customary offering made by a departing student to a guru Gautama's wife Ahalya, however, asked Utanka for the earrings of the fierce Queen Madayanti. Contrary to expectations, the queen willingly gave Utanka the earrings, wrapped in a deerskin. But on his way back, Utanka climbed a tree to pick fruit, tying his precious burden to a branch for safe-keeping. It fell to the ground and a snake carried off the earrings to an anthill. Utanka used his psychic powers to pierce the anthill, and the Earth itself, until the worried Earth goddess begged Indra to make the snake return the earrings, and Utanka was able to present them to his master's wife.

> 'Saturn stands together with the Moon. This is good for the king, my lord.'
>
> Assyrian astrologer Nabu-Iqisa, *c*.8th century BC

MAIN PICTURE **A close-up of the rings of Saturn. The broad bands are composed of numerous finer rings, made of a range of material from dust to icy boulders.**
INSET **Saturn with six of its moons. The one in the foreground is Dione. In the top left is Rhea, named after the mythological Saturn's mother.**

SATURN'S MOONS

Saturn has at least eighteen moons. Titan, by far the largest, is bigger than the planet Mercury. Its atmosphere is mostly nitrogen, with hydrocarbons such as methane. The possibility that it has methane lakes has encouraged some scientists to speculate that it could be home to 'prebiotic processes', necessary to the formation of life. Saturn's other moons, in order of size, include Rhea, Iapetus, Dione, Tethys, Enceladus and Mimas; these all appear to consist mostly of water ice.

THE RINGED PLANET

Saturn's rings were discovered when Galileo first viewed Saturn through his telescope in 1610. At first he thought he had spotted a triple planet, a large body flanked by two smaller ones. We can imagine his consternation when in 1612 the two smaller bodies appeared to have taken flight. He wrote: 'Have they vanished or suddenly fled? Has Saturn, perhaps, devoured his own children? ... The shortness of the time, the unexpected nature of the event, the weakness of my understanding, and fear of being mistaken, have greatly confounded me.'

Christiaan Huygens (1629–95), with an improved telescope, concluded that the planet was surrounded by a flat, detached ring. It was later believed that there were two rings. Improved telescopes gradually raised this number, but since the observations made by Voyager 1 in 1980 we have known that the broad bands are in fact made up of hundreds, even thousands, of finer rings.

Saturn's rings seem to be made of dust and icy rocks of anything up to boulder size. Saturn must have a solid core, and, like Jupiter, must generate some of its own heat, since it gives out more than it receives from the Sun. One theory is that much of this is generated from the energy that is released as helium sinks through liquid hydrogen toward the core.

Why did the rings disappear in 1612? The answer lies in Saturn's axis of rotation, which tilts 26 degrees to its orbit. Saturn's position relative to the Earth determines our view of the rings. In 1612, as in 1995, they were sideways-on. Because they are only about 5 kilometres (3 miles) thick, when viewed from this angle they are almost invisible from the Earth. They will be much easier to see in 2003.

Saturn is similar to Jupiter in other respects. Despite its astrological association with boundaries and down-to-earth reality, if astronauts tried to land on it they would simply drift through layers of gas: it has no crust. And although ancient astronomers associated it with lead, it is composed largely of hydrogen and helium, in a dynamic atmosphere boasting huge thunderstorms and 900 kph (560 mph) winds – gusting up to 1,400 kph (870 mph).

It also has the distinction of being the least dense of the planets – only 70 per cent as dense as water. If it were placed in a giant bath it would float! Human landings on Saturn are obviously ruled out, but there have been three successful space probes: Pioneer 11 in 1979, and Voyagers 1 and 2 in 1980 and 1981 (see box above).

URANUS

Uranus, named after the Greek god Ouranos, was the first planet to be discovered since ancient times, having remained unknown until 1781. It orbits the Sun once every 84 years at an average distance of 2,870 million kilometres (1,784 million miles), and its diam-eter at the equator is about 52,400 kilometres (32,560 miles), which makes it just over four times larger than the Earth.

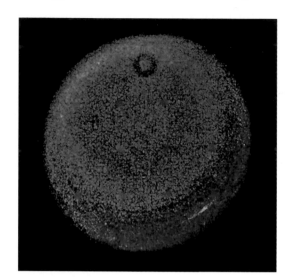

It has the same density as the gaseous giant Jupiter, 1.3 times that of the Earth, and average temperatures of –210° C, making it pretty unin-habitable. Uranus' most unusual feature is the extreme tilt of its axis – 98 degrees, compared to 23 degrees for the Earth.

In Greek myth Ouranos was the son and husband of the Earth goddess Gaia, and the father of Cronos. His name is connected to that of the Indian Varuna, who began as a ruler of the night sky and became a sea/lunar god. Ouranos was a sky god, especially associated with the night sky, as it was at night that he lay with Gaia. Some English translations of the Greek myths give 'Ouranos' as 'Heaven', indicating his all-encompassing power.

Such sky gods occur in almost every culture, and in the Indo-European societies of Europe and Asia they tend to be male. The Babylonian god was An, meaning 'sky', or Anu; the Norse/German sky god was Woden or Tiw; in Greece and Rome Zeus and Jupiter were sky gods of a later generation than Ouranos. The Hebrew equivalent was Yahweh, and, similarly, the Christian God is also visualized as living in the sky, removed from the earth.

MOTHER SKY

The Egyptian Sun gods Amun, Aten and Ra (the names varied according to the time, place and context) shared the omnipotent qualities of other sky gods, but Egypt was unusual in the Middle East in that its sky was feminine – the goddess Nut. Nut is sometimes depicted as a woman arched over the earth, touching its extremes with her feet and toes, and supporting the stars with her body. She is also sometimes depicted as a cow. The story relates that she was ordered to turn into a cow by Nun or Nu (equivalent to the Greek Chaos), the primordial Ocean, after she carried Ra, the Sun, into the sky when he abandoned his rebellious subjects. She rose to heaven, where she was held aloft by Shu, the air, or void, and supported by four pillars (which were either the equinoxes and solstices or the extreme points of the Sun's setting and rising in winter and summer).

The cow symbol may be a deliberate association with the constellation Taurus. Perhaps both were derived from the cow's importance as the primary domesticated animal and sustainer of life. There is, however, a definite connection with the cow-goddess Hathor (see pp.31–2). Hathor was the Greek name for the Egyptian Het-hert, which is translated variously as 'Sky-house', 'House of the Sky' or 'My House is the Sky'.

OPPOSITE LEFT The planet Uranus – the oddball of the solar system. **BELOW** An Egyptian papyrus dating from *c.*1000BC, depicting the sky goddess Nut arched over the earth. Unusually, the sky deity is female in Egyptian myth, while the Earth god, Geb, is male – here represented lying on his back facing Nut.

FATHER SKY

Ouranos had many children, and hated them all. First came the Titans: six brothers – Oceanus, Coeus, Hyperion, Crius, Iapetus and Cronos; and six sisters – Theia, Rhea, Mnemosyne, Phoebe, Tethys and Themis. Then came the Cyclopes: Brontes, Steropes and Arges. Finally came three monsters: Cottus, Briareus and Gyges.

As soon as they were born, Ouranos stuffed his children back into the earth – into the womb of Gaia – by his nightly coupling with her. Gaia groaned with this burden, and determined to put an end to his tyranny. She conspired with her youngest son, Cronos, whom she presented with an iron sickle. When next Ouranos lay with her, Cronos swung the sickle and castrated his father in the act, thus severing the sky from the earth – symbolically male from female, conscious from unconscious, and intellect from instinct.

Cronos slung the severed genitals into the sea, where they foamed, producing the goddess of love, Aphrodite. The black blood from the terrible wound fell on the earth, producing the Furies, Giants and Ash Nymphs.

Sky deities can be seen as both givers and takers of life, protectors and destroyers. They are either nurturers such as Nut or harsh father figures such as Ouranos and Yahweh. Some,

POLIDORO DA CARAVAGGIO INVENTORE

Gio. Bat. Galestruzzi fece   1

such as Yahweh, are perpetually involved in the dramas of human life; others, such as Anu, are more remote. With the exception of Nut, they were increasingly identified as patriarchal father figures, and psychologists influenced by Freud have placed great emphasis on Ouranos' castration by his son Cronos as a sign of the male child's universal need to displace his father. To a Freudian this urge is one of the great motors of human society, climaxing in the revolutionary movements that destroy entire political orders.

THE DISCOVERY

Uranus was discovered by William Herschel, a German from Hanover who had taken up residence in Bath, England. Herschel was a professional musician who had become interested in astronomy, and had even made his own telescopes. It was through one of these that he saw Uranus, in March 1781, while conducting a star-count in one part of the sky. The planet had been recorded as many as 22 times on previous occasions, which is quite likely considering that Galileo had sighted Neptune in 1612, but it seems always to have been

LEFT A 16th-century engraving, after Caravaggio, depicting Cronos castrating his father Ouranos with a sickle provided by Gaia. From Ouranos' spilt blood sprang the Furies, from his cast-off genitals, the goddess Aphrodite.

RANGI AND PAPA
In Maori mythology, Rangi is the sky god and Papa the earth goddess. In the time of primordial darkness, Rangi lay in union with Papa. However, their passionate embrace crushed their divine offspring. Creativity itself was strangled, so that the god and goddess had to separate in order for the light of consciousness to illuminate the world, and so that it could evolve.

This myth has close parallels with that of Ouranos and Gaia, whose separation, brought about by the sickle of Cronos, freed their offspring from Gaia's womb.

recorded as a fixed star.

Herschel made his critical observations of the new planet between 10.00 and 11.00pm on Tuesday 13 March 1781 in Bath. Initially he thought it was a comet, and he told the Royal Astronomical Society as much on 26 April. Other astronomers suspected it was a planet and in 1782 its real nature was announced by Lexell in St Petersburg and La Place in France. Herschel then published the news in England on 7 November 1782, and in honour of the English king, George III, he named the new body Georgium Sidus, Latin for 'George Star'. He was following in a noble tradition in which astronomers named their discoveries after their patrons. In return the king made Herschel his private astronomer at a salary of £200 a year, later

adding £50 a year for his sister and fellow astronomer, Caroline. Herschel was a loyal subject and relates how one night he and his dinner guests went and stood inside the 40-foot telescope and sang 'God save the King' with accompaniment on the oboe and other instruments.

Non-British astronomers, who had no particular loyalty to the British crown, preferred to call the planet Herschel, a name that persisted in some old-fashioned texts until relatively recently. However, even in Britain it came to be felt somewhat demeaning for a planet to be called George, and so Uranus, the alternative name suggested by the German astronomer Johann Bode, was adopted during the 1790s.

THE ASTROLOGICAL URANUS

Astrological meanings are built up partly by the often seemingly random association of words, events and phenomena which might not otherwise seem to be linked. This is not as unusual as it sounds and Ludwig Wittgenstein, one of the 20th century's greatest philosophers, argued that we can draw connections between, say, card games and emotional games. The two might be very different, but they are both games. Astrologers

RIGHT Uranus photographed through ultraviolet, violet and orange filters to bring out subtle details, such as the cloud visible as a bright streak near the rim of the planet (top right of the picture). BELOW Uranus in true colour – blue-green because of the absorption of red light by methane gas in the planet's deep, cold and very clear atmosphere.

describe this lateral way of thinking as Uranian. The connections they make are all quite simple: Uranus has an eccentric orbit, so they link it to eccentric, independent-minded people; the planet was discovered during the opening stages of the Industrial Revolution, fifteen years after the American Declaration of Independence and eight years before the French Revolution, suggesting links with new technology, idealism and political upheaval. The Uranian personality is obstinate, radical, idealistic, antisocial, self-willed, often intellectual, both anarchic and authoritarian; and, to a Jungian, fearful of chaos and disorder yet, ironically, inclined to bring it about. Modern astrologers and psychologists have produced a strange reversal in Ouranos' myth, turning him from castrated father into castrating son.

THE ECCENTRIC WORLD

Uranus has been visited by only one space probe, Voyager 2, which passed by at a distance of 5,000 km (3,000 miles) on 26 August 1989, en route from Saturn to Neptune. In spite of all the information Voyager 2 sent back, Uranus is still shrouded in mystery. Its surface is almost without distinguishing features, beyond its beautiful electric green-blue colour.

The planet's most remarkable feature is its tilt. Most planets rotate roughly parallel to their orbit around the Sun. Uranus appears to have been knocked sideways, perhaps by a massive collision, so that it rotates at 98 degrees, almost a right angle, to its plane of orbit. In other words, as we look at the planet its equator appears vertical, and when it faces us side on it looks as if its moons are moving around it in an up-and-down motion.

This tilt in turn produces extreme seasons, and the planet's polar regions remain alternately in sunlight or darkness for decades at a time. In addition its magnetic field, comparable to the Earth's in intensity, is off-centre and therefore very variable, while the 9.6 million-kilometre (6 million-mile)

RIGHT **A close-up of Miranda, Uranus' nearest and smallest moon.**
BELOW **Titania, unlike its unblemished namesake, bears heavy impact scars. Its neutral grey colour is typical of all the Uranian moons.**

ABOVE **A composite colour picture of Umbriel, one of Uranus' five major moons, which orbits Uranus at a radius of 267,000 km (166,000 miles). The surface is covered by impact craters.**

BELOW **Oberon, the second-largest of Uranus' moons, featuring several impact craters, including a large crater with a bright central peak (centre of photograph), and a mountain about 6 km (4 miles) high (bottom left).**

magnetically charged 'tail', which trails behind it, is twisted into a rotating cylindrical corkscrew.

Uranus' density and gravity are fairly close to the Earth's. However, other factors besides its extreme and protracted seasons make human colonization extremely unlikely. The planet is very cold, especially during a protracted sunless polar winter.

RINGS AND MOONS

Voyager 2 revealed what astronomers had suspected for some time – that Uranus has rings like Saturn's. It has eleven rings in all, ten very narrow and one slightly broader, some tilted at angles to the equator and

others elliptical rather than circular. Like Saturn's they are made up of lumps of matter several metres across, but they lack the clouds of smaller particles that Saturn's include and are less bright, containing much less ice.

Uranus also has at least fifteen moons, five large and ten smaller – although even the largest two, Titania and Oberon, are only about half the size of the Earth's moon. Titania and Oberon were the first to be discovered – by Herschel – but Miranda was seen only in 1948.

Voyager 2 found that the moons were composed of 50 per cent water ice, 20 per cent materials based on carbon and nitrogen, and 30 per cent rock. Miranda is interesting geologically and has fault canyons 19 kilometres (12 miles) deep, terraces, mountains, ridges and plains.

NEPTUNE

Neptune was discovered in 1846 and is the eighth in order of the planets from the Sun. It orbits the Sun in 165 Earth years at an average distance of 4,497 million kilometres (2,793 million miles). It has an equatorial diameter of 43,000 kilometres (27,000 miles), similar to that of Uranus, a density 1.8 times that of the Earth, a surface gravity 1.2 times that of the Earth, and an 18-hour day. Neptune only receives 3 per cent of the amount of Sunlight received by Jupiter, but it has a very dynamic atmosphere. Its Great Dark Spot is a giant storm the size of the Earth which moves around the planet in 18.3 hours.

GODS OF THE SEA

The Roman god Neptune had his realm on the earth – in the oceans – rather than in the sky. He never had his own planet but was connected to the constellation Pisces by the 1st-century AD poet Manilius, who reasoned that as god of the oceans Neptune must have a bond with Pisces, the sign of the Fish. This connection has been restored by modern astrologers, many of whom say Neptune 'rules' Pisces.

Many early creation myths record the primeval role of water. In the book of Genesis the creation begins as God's face moves over the water. In Sumerian myth the twin creators were Tiamat, the female salt water, and Apsu, the male fresh water. In later myth Tiamat was banished as a demon while Apsu's role was taken over by Ea, or Enki, lord of both the water and the underworld. After c.2000BC Ea was one of a male trinity with Anu, the sky god, and Enlil, the god of the air. Over the years he gradually encroached on the earth, the territory formerly sacred to the female Ninhursaga. Enki literally means 'lord (en) of the earth (ki)', even though he was also regarded as a god of fresh water. The flexibility of such mythic images is a warning against expecting tight correspondences. Such male trinities existed throughout early religion, and the watery element frequently represented an element of primeval mystery.

POSEIDON AND AMPHITRITE

Poseidon's marriages to sea goddesses gave him rulership of the sea. His marriage to Halia produced a daughter, Rhodos, who gave her name to the island. Less happily it produced six headstrong sons who offended Aphrodite, so that she drove them to sleep with their mother – for which they were exiled by Poseidon. His marriage to Amphitrite was more lasting.

Amphitrite was the beautiful daughter of the sea god Nereus. One day Poseidon saw her dancing happily with her sisters on the island of Naxos. Full of desire, he seized and ravished her. Freeing herself, she fled to Atlas in the western Aegean. Poseidon discovered her whereabouts from a school of dolphins, and sent one to woo her on his behalf and deliver her to him. The successful dolphin's reward was to be placed among the constellations.

POSEIDON

The Greeks inherited the Babylonian trinity, and their ocean god, Poseidon, was partnered by Hades and Zeus. The sea was a threatening place, and to seafarers Poseidon was more savage and unpredictable than his brother Zeus. He possessed some of Zeus' shape-shifting ability but none of his sense of justice. Like Ea, Poseidon had a

The Triumph of Neptune, an early 3rd-century AD marble Roman mosaic pavement, from ancient Hadrumetum, Tunisia.

role on dry land as well as water. He may even have originally been solely an earth god who displaced an earlier water deity. At any rate, he came to rule not only the sea – which laps at the shore – but also rivers, which irrigate and fertilize the earth.

THE SAVAGE UNIVERSE

The sea's threatening role surfaced in Poseidon myths in the roles given to animals. After his birth, we are told, Poseidon's mother, Rhea, prevented her husband Cronos from devouring her son by hiding him in a flock of sheep and giving Cronos a foal to swallow in place of the infant. The sheep may represent Aries, signifying the start of the year, but the swallowing of the foal is the key to the god's nature. The

horse connection suggests ships 'riding' the waves, or surf resembling white horses. Psychologically the horse has often been seen as a symbol of the animal passions that must be tamed by the conscious mind. Poseidon was also worshipped as a bull.

Poseidon possessed a voracious appetite and had several marriages, as well as relationships with nymphs and mortals. When his own sister, the fertility goddess Demeter turned herself

ABOVE The ancient temple of Poseidon at Cape Sounion, Akra, south of Athens, Greece. Although revered and feared, Poseidon always lived in the shadow of his brother Zeus – a fact that he bitterly resented.

into a mare to resist him, he took the form of a stallion – a form in which he also seduced Medusa in the temple of Athene. When he turned Theophane into a sheep to disguise her from her suitors, and himself into a ram, he sired the ram whose golden fleece was to feature in the Jason myths.

Poseidon's greed and his resentment of Zeus led him to contend for dominion over several territories – perhaps symbolizing the threat of the sea inundating the land, or of passion overcoming judgment, or simply the changing loyalties of worshippers.

According to one story, in an unsuccessful contest with Athene over Attica he created the first horse by striking a rock with his trident. He also had territorial disputes with Hera, Helios, Zeus and Dionysus, and even staged a full-scale rebellion against Zeus. Embittered by failure, he brought either floods or droughts.

Sea and river deities are common worldwide, many sharing Poseidon's attributes, some overlapping with other deities. The Hindu Varuna, for example, was particularly associated with the Moon, a planet which through its link to the

The Roman poet Manilius connected each one of the twelve Olympian deities to a sign of the zodiac, linking Neptune to Pisces. He explained that 'this scheme will provide you with important means of determining the future … when your mind speeds among the planets and stars, so that a divine power may arise in your spirit'.

BELOW *Neptune Resigning to Britannia the Empire of the Sea* by William Dyce (1806–64). Neptune, flanked by other gods, including Mercury and Venus (with shell), is used here to legitimate British colonial rule.

tides was widely thought to have control over the waters as a whole. Varuna began life as a sky god like Ouranos or Anu, but became a relatively benign sea and river god. Most sea deities, however, retained a threatening as well as a nourishing character; water is both giver and taker of life. The Peruvian water goddess Mama Chocha was seen as a nourishing provider; conversely, the Inuit sea goddess Sedna was a sinister figure prone to fits of fury, with such a voracious appetite that she even began to devour her parents' limbs.

THE ASTROLOGICAL NEPTUNE

With a recently discovered planet such as Neptune, it is sometimes questioned whether such a modern addition can be made to such an antique art. However, astrology is nothing if not flexible. Astrologers took their cue from the ancient Neptune's role as god of the sea and connected the planet to all maritime matters, many of which had previously been linked to the Moon. Thus boats, sailing, fish and the oceans are all said to be Neptunian. By analogy Neptune's significance is extended first to all liquids, including alcohol, then to other intoxicants, including hallucino-

genic drugs. It is also connected to all activities in which image is often more important than substance. Anything glamorous, deceptive or imaginative is classed under Neptune, including the arts, film and photography, the fashion industry, criminal fraud and espionage. Dreams, visions and ideals are also said to be Neptunian.

It has been argued that Neptune's archetype is revealed by the symbolic nature of the ocean. To those psychologists for whom everything has a symbolic meaning, the sea represents the unconscious: Neptune's myths therefore indicate individuals' willingness to submerge themselves in the group, to sacrifice their own interests for some collective belief, such as a religious or political movement.

Because Neptune's movement is so slow, its significance is sometimes considered to be primarily generational, describing long-term shifts in fashion and ideology. There have been some notable predictive successes following this theory. In the 1940s the French writer André Barbault combined traditional and modern planetary symbolism when he suggested that if Neptune represents ideals and Saturn authority then the combination of the two symbolizes authoritarian ideals – or idealistic authoritarianism. Barbault then argued that the time between Saturn–Neptune conjunctions matched certain periods in the history of socialism. For example, Stalin's death coincided with the Saturn–Neptune conjunction in 1953, exactly 36 years after the Communists seized power in 1917. On this basis both Barbault and a number of other forecasters predicted that the Saturn–Neptune conjunction of 1989 would bring a crisis in socialism – which duly happened with the fall of the Berlin Wall and the Iron Curtain.

RIGHT **The two hemispheres of Neptune. Astrologers say that the astrological Neptune has two sides: on the one hand spirituality, on the other intoxication.**
BELOW **Neptune's Dark Spot, a giant storm the size of the Earth. The planet has a thick hydrogen, helium and methane atmosphere and violent winds.**

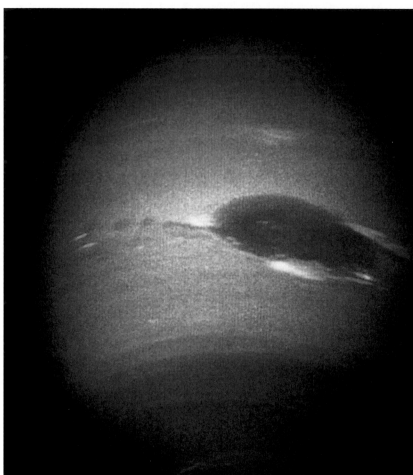

THE ELUSIVE PLANET

Confusion surrounds the discovery of this very distant planet. The usual discovery date is given as 1846, but in fact it was sighted by Galileo on 28 December 1612. He noted that it changed position from one night to the next, yet failed to suspect that it was a planet rather than a star, probably because he did not even consider the possibility that other planets might exist. Rather, he thought that it was a moon of Jupiter.

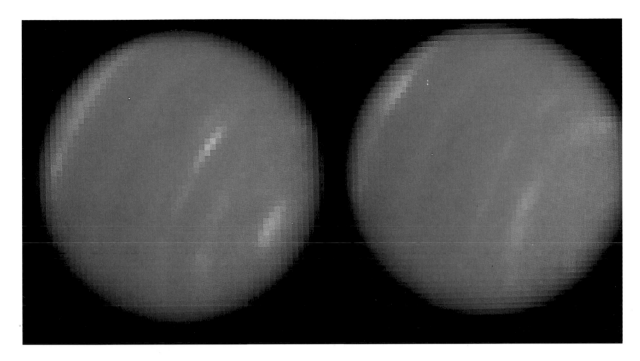

Two centuries later in England, John Couch Adams analyzed the deviations in the orbit of Uranus, suspecting they were caused by another planet. In 1845 he predicted this hypothetical planet's position. However, the Professor of Astronomy at Cambridge did not consider it worth checking the theories of so recent a graduate. Adams went to London to meet the Astronomer Royal, but the illustrious gentleman's butler would not allow his master's dinner to be interrupted, and Adams departed, leaving a copy of his calculations. The Astronomer Royal requested further information, but Adams failed to provide it and all communication ceased.

Meanwhile, in France, Urbain Leverrier had been independently conducting his own analysis. Reports of his progress aroused half-hearted nationalistic interest among the astronomical establishment in England. However, Leverrier sent his findings to an acquaintance in Berlin, Johann Galle. Within hours, probably at about 14 minutes after midnight on 23–24 September 1846, he and Heinrich d'Arrest found Neptune in the predicted position. Leverrier and Adams subsequently became friends, leaving others to argue over which country could claim credit for the discovery.

CONDITIONS ON NEPTUNE

By 1996 there had been only one probe to Neptune, Voyager 2. This had been launched from Cape Canaveral in 1977 and had previously passed Jupiter, Saturn and Uranus, using the gravity of each in turn to set itself on a course for the next. In 1989, twelve years after its launch, the probe flew past Neptune and set a course for the edge of the solar system and interstellar space.

Voyager 2 found a bright blue planet with a thick hydrogen, helium and methane atmosphere, and winds as violent as those on Jupiter, blowing at up to 1,120 kph (700 mph). These are coupled with some of the lowest temperatures in the solar system, as low as –220° C.

Neptune has eight confirmed moons, the largest of which, Triton, is named after a son of the mythological god. Triton is a violent, inhospitable place which has an atmosphere composed of carbon monoxide, carbon dioxide and methane, with geysers shooting nitrogen and dust high into the atmosphere.

PLUTO

Pluto is the farthest known planet from the Sun, although no longer the most distant known object in the solar system. Its average distance from the Sun is 5,900 million kilometres (3,625 million miles) but its orbit is so eccentric that at its farthest it is 8,250 million kilometres (5,100 million miles) away, at its nearest only 4,979 million kilometres (3,100 million miles) – closer than Neptune.

Pluto is much smaller than the Earth; its diameter is just 2,324 kilometres (1,444 miles), half that of Mercury, the next smallest planet, and its mass is 2 per cent that of the Earth. Its axis is tilted by about 65 degrees. Pluto's year is 247.7 years long, while its day is six Earth days and nine hours. Light from Pluto takes seven hours to reach Earth, which means that we see it as it was seven hours previously. When an astronomer looks through a telescope and sees Pluto overhead, it is in reality setting over the western horizon.

PERSEPHONE

One day Persephone, daughter of the goddess Demeter, was picking flowers with her friends. Just as she was about to pick a narcissus, a flower created for the god Hades by Gaia, a chasm opened at her feet to reveal Hades himself. Quickly, he pulled her on to his chariot and carried her to the underworld to be his wife.

When Demeter discovered what had happened, she wandered grief-stricken, and then afflicted the Earth with famine. Zeus eventually ordered Hades to release Persephone. However, Hades slipped a pomegranate seed into her mouth as she left. Having eaten this underworld food, she was thereafter obliged to spend a third of the year with Hades.

This myth tells of the origins of the seasons, for during the time that Persephone is in the underworld, it is winter – the earth is cold and barren; when she is released, spring begins and the earth can grow and flower once more.

THE UNDERWORLD

Pluto was the Roman god of the underworld, and inherited all the attributes of Hades, his Greek equivalent. Hades and his brothers Zeus (the Roman Jupiter) and Poseidon (Neptune) constituted a trinity of masculine gods. Hades was omnipotent in his domain and rarely left it, being revered as Zeus Chthonios (Earthly Zeus). The number of his subjects – and therefore his wealth – could only ever increase, and he was frequently worshipped as a god of wealth (Plouton), especially in Rome.

'Hades' means 'invisible', and when the god moved about the overworld he hid himself with his helmet of invisibility. He was a dark counterpart not only of Zeus, but of Helios, the Sun god. His role relates to the unconscious and to death itself: his retinue included the brothers Thanatos (Death), whose name Freud applied to the 'death instinct', and Hypnos (Sleep).

THE LAND OF SHADES

Hades' kingdom became synonymous with its ruler. Early myths placed it where the sun set, but later it was located beneath the earth, accessible via rivers and caves. The river Styx looped nine times around it, reflecting the nine levels of the skies – seven planets plus the stars and heaven. Belief in reincarnation was widespread in ancient Greece, so death was rarely considered an end to existence; however, it was almost impossible to enter Hades and return to the same life.

The classical belief that the soul had to cross a deep river to reach the underworld was shared by the Aztecs and the North American Hurons, Iroquois, Chippewa, Algonquians and Dakotas. Another belief, held by the Chinooks and echoed in the Greek tale of

A Tang Dynasty (AD618–907) depiction of the Chinese equivalent of Hades, showing miscreants punished by the presiding deity.

Persephone (see box opposite), is that those who take anything to eat or drink in the underworld can never return to the land of the living.

PUNISHMENT AND REWARD

In early myths, Hades' realm was largely undifferentiated, but gradually the idea of judgment arose, with its associated punishments and rewards. Ordinary souls passed a shadowy half-life in the bleak Meadows of Asphodel. Serious transgressors joined the Titans in Tartarus, to be tortured for eternity. Heroes went to a more pleasant life in Elysium – reminiscent of the

Norse Valhalla or the Celtic Tir-nan-og – where they spent eternity in feasting and games.

Pluto obviously influenced the development of the Christian Satan as Lord of the Underworld, as did Saturn. As a god of evil, Satan also owes a vast debt to the Egyptian god Set, the eternal opponent of light and good. Above all, gods of the underworld are considered a profound threat to stability, order and peace. The underworld is the 'other' world, in which the values of the overworld are reversed, and its eruption into the overworld is accompanied by terrible consequences.

THE ASTROLOGICAL PLUTO

Although Pluto was discovered in 1930, its modern astrological image is based almost entirely on its classical mythical associations. It represents any individual, idea, mood or object that is deep, dark, mysterious and intense. The Plutonic person is secretive; Plutonic professions include espionage; Plutonic places are caves and cellars; and black is the ideal Plutonic colour.

This sort of lateral association of images takes astrology well away from scientific astronomy into the realm of symbolic language, but has been

the trigger for some remarkable forecasts. For example, in 1980 the writer Michael Baigent forecast a power struggle in the Soviet Union in 1984–5 and the collapse of the Union between January 1989 and November 1991. As history went on to show, these predictions proved correct. Baigent's reasoning was simple. In classical astronomy the Sun was the embodiment of the emperor, while in mythology Pluto was the god of death. Baigent looked at the position of the Sun on 7 November 1917 – when Lenin became 'emperor' of the new Communist state – and noted that in 1989–91 Pluto

ABOVE *Psyche and Charon* by John Roddam (1829–1908). The ferry-man takes a coin from Psyche's mouth as payment for his services. **RIGHT** An artist's view of Pluto and its moon, Charon, first seen as a bump on the side of the planet in photographic plates.

would be moving through the same zodiacal degrees, leading him to predict the death not only of the emperor but also of the empire.

Such forecasting is based on an astronomy of great simplicity, relying on only one way of measuring planetary position as seen from the Earth. The skill lies in the use of mythological symbolism to make a leap of imagination.

THE LAST OUTPOST?

The most commonly used symbol for this remote and diminutive world is a composite of the letters P and L. This could be taken as the first two letters of the name 'Pluto', or as the initials of Percival Lowell, the great US astronomer. When Lowell died in 1916 he had worked out the approximate position of a 'Planet X' which was thought to exist because of the recorded perturbations in the orbits of Uranus and Neptune. However, Lowell never set eyes on Pluto. The first person to do so was Clyde Tombaugh, who on 18 February 1930 found Pluto,

dimmer than expected, but only about 5 degrees from the position that had been predicted.

It now seems that Pluto is too small to cause the apparent deviations in the orbits of Uranus and Neptune, and many astronomers think it likely that an as yet undiscovered planet is responsible. Lowell's reasoning has turned out to be wrong – yet without it Pluto might never have been discovered.

A PLANETOID?

Pluto is smaller than Lowell expected, and its remoteness has made its size difficult to

ascertain. But in 1978 another US astronomer, James Christy, discovered that Pluto had a moon – now named Charon, after the mythological ferryman of Hades. This enabled scientists to work out Pluto's size – a mere 2,430 kilometres (1,510 miles) in diameter, smaller than our own moon. Charon has a diameter of 1,200 kilometres (750 miles), half the size of its host planet.

Surprisingly, Pluto, despite its small size and correspondingly low gravity, has an atmosphere. This seems to be composed largely of methane. Since the planet must be very cold, there must also be methane ice, and the atmosphere may be sustained by the continual evaporation of this ice. Unlike Jupiter, Saturn, Uranus and Neptune, Pluto is believed to have a solid core with a hard surface, probably comprising rock with frozen water, ammonia and methane.

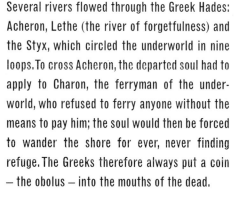

Several rivers flowed through the Greek Hades: Acheron, Lethe (the river of forgetfulness) and the Styx, which circled the underworld in nine loops. To cross Acheron, the departed soul had to apply to Charon, the ferryman of the underworld, who refused to ferry anyone without the means to pay him; the soul would then be forced to wander the shore for ever, never finding refuge. The Greeks therefore always put a coin – the obolus – into the mouths of the dead.

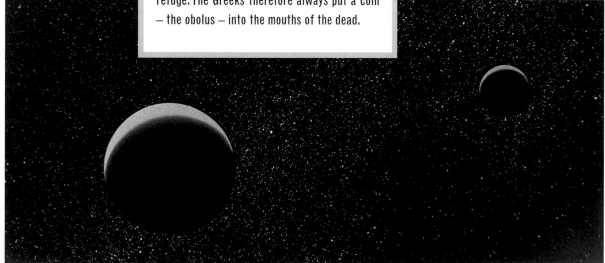

THE HEAVENS

Humanity has always looked for explanations of its own origins and of the existence of the universe. Yet our explanations inevitably give rise to more questions, and to unfathomable paradoxes. How can space be infinite – or have boundaries? Did time begin, or could it be circular? Was the universe ever empty?

The world's religions and mythologies have attempted to explain questions such as these, and creation myths from diverse cultures show remarkable similarities, usually involving gods creating the earth and humans from a primal void or chaos. In 1658 James Ussher, Bishop of Armagh and Primate of Ireland, confidently announced that God created the universe on the evening of 22 October 4004BC. By 1859, when Darwin published *On the Origin of Species*, setting out his theories of evolution, in which the natural world evolved without any need for a creator, it seemed that religious and scientific cosmogonies (theories on the birth of the universe) were moving ever farther apart. However, a major development of the late 20th century has been the recognition of parallels between the two.

The contemporary debate on the origins of the cosmos dwells on the notion of purpose and design: does the universe have a goal? Most religious believers would say that it does – the fulfilment of the divine plan. Most atheists would say that it does not. Scientists tend to divide between the two – many are themselves believers in God, while many of those who once discounted design are now so impressed by the universe's complexity that they are coming back to some idea of purpose.

Part of the Milky Way, showing the Southern Cross bottom left and Canopus, second brightest star in our heavens, centre right. Bottom right is the Large Magellanic Cloud, a satellite galaxy of the Milky Way.

IN THE BEGINNING

Some of the most primitive creation myths are really about re-creation. They take it for granted that the universe exists, and seek only to explain how it developed, and how humanity arose. Most begin with a creator god who has human attributes. In Mali, for example, the Dogon creator god Amma is believed to have created the Sun and Moon as clay pots, firing the Sun to white heat and winding it in red copper, then making black people out of sunlight and white people out of moonlight.

One common figure is the divine potter. The Egyptian god Ptah is described variously as kneading the world into shape or throwing a 'cosmic egg' on his wheel. This is reminiscent of the actual shaping of the Earth and planets by rotation – a feature of which early peoples would have been unaware.

Sometimes the creator god makes the Sun out of one of his eyes and the Moon out of the other, as did the Egyptian god Khepra and the Chinese creator Pan Gu. This notion that the creator god sacrificed himself, or part of himself, by becoming, or entering, the physical world, may be extended. The universe often arises from a divine corpse. For example, Pan Gu dies from the exertion of separating earth from sky, and his flesh becomes the earth, his hair plants, his sweat the rain, his breath the wind; worms from his rotting corpse become the human race. In Norse myth the corpse is that of the first being, the giant Ymir, who was slain by the three gods that he spawned. In Persian myth much of the world springs from the decaying corpse of an ox created by the supreme god Ahura Mazda, which dies of diseases created by the god of dark forces, Ahriman.

'How can you deny God? Did he not give you life when you were dead, and will he not cause you to die and then restore you to life? Will you not return to him at last? He created for you all that the Earth contains; then, ascending to the sky, he fashioned it into seven heavens. He has knowledge of all things.'

The Koran 2:29

Papa (Mother Earth) and Rangi (Father Sky), the creator gods in Maori religion, carved on the base of an 18th-century wooden treasure box.

Another relatively primitive concept – although one that often has more sophisticated undertones – is that of primal parents. Often the father is the sky and the mother is the earth, as with the Maori god Rangi and his wife Papa, who were prized apart by the children (the gods) that they engendered; and the Greek Ouranos and Gaia, whose coupling created all the animate and inanimate elements of the world (see p.186).

THE PRIMAL WATERS

A more sophisticated concept is that of a primordial ocean. The symbolic appeal is obvious: the sea was of inestimable depth and extent, and seemed to embody limitless potential. There may also have been a folk memory of an actual deluge – an occurrence for which there is some historical evidence, and which occurs in some form in myths of cultures as far apart as the Polynesian, Aztec and Sumerian.

The primal waters appear at the beginning of Genesis, the Hebrew creation myth. They also feature in the Egyptian story of

'Verily at the first Chaos came to be, but next wide-bosomed Earth, the ever sure foundation of all, and Eros, fairest among the gods. And Earth first bore starry Heaven, equal to herself, to cover her on every side.'

Greek poet Hesiod, *Theogony*, c.700BC

the creator god Khepra, who performs his act of creation in the watery abyss of Nun, with no solid surface on which to stand. The ancestress of the North American Iroquois fell from heaven into the primeval waters.

To the Babylonians the universe began with the divine couple Apsu (fresh water) and Tiamat (salt water); the inter-

A Tibetan Buddhist *mandala* from the 19th–20th century, symbolically representing the structure of the cosmos. By meditating on such an image the Buddhist monk becomes intuitively aware of the true nature of the universe.

mingling of these two halves of the primordial ocean produced the gods. In Hindu myth, the primordial waters exist – shapeless and formless – before the universe has been created. In Greece, Thales (born *c*.624BC), who is often described as the first classical astronomer, thought water was the *arche*, or first substance, out of which the universe was made.

Psychologically, the primal waters found in so many of the world's mythologies suggest the unconscious, as well as the undifferentiated ego, still at one with the mother. On the physical level, they are analogous to the state of the universe immediately after the Big Bang (see p.207) – when the just-created universe would have been com-posed largely of hydrogen (the 'H' in 'H$_2$O', or water) in a vast ocean of unformed potential.

THE PLATONIC CREATION MYTH

Plato's creation myth, set out in his great work the *Timaeus*, has strong similarities with Eastern accounts, such as those found in Buddhism, and has become the model for all mystical European cosmogonies. Plato describes how all creation arises out of movement. In the beginning only God, the First Mover, existed. As soon as God had a thought, his mind began to move, and the whole of creation kaleidoscoped out of his consciousness. First the world soul was made and out of this were fashioned the dimensions of the universe, the stars, planets and the Earth. Whereas God is eternal and unchanging, everything that he created is marked by change. Change is regulated by time, and time is 'kept' or 'marked' by the planets. For this reason Plato insisted that the study of astronomy and astrology were the highest studies, for they could lead humanity back to God. The Platonic myth took on a new lease of life in the Middle Ages in the Jewish mystical system, Kabbala, and is influential in the modern systems espoused by the mystics Rudolf Steiner, P.D. Ouspensky and George Gurdjieff. The key to such systems is that, even though the individual must live in the changing, decaying, physical world, it is possible through philosophical and spiritual disciplines, to make contact with the eternal, divine, creative principles.

And God said, 'Let there be lights to separate the day from the night;
And let them be for signs and for seasons and for days and years,
and let them be lights in the firmament of the heavens to give light upon the Earth.'

Genesis 1.24–15

THE COSMIC EGG

The Big Bang theory, in its proposition of a single point of origin for the cosmos, is also reminiscent of another widespread mythological image, that of the primeval cosmic egg cracking open to reveal the universe. The shape of the egg brings to mind Einstein's concept of curved space.

One of the earliest Greek myths states that in the beginning there was only the goddess Night, a bird with black wings. In the words of the scholar Professor C. Kerényi: 'Ancient Night conceived of the Wind and laid her silver Egg in the gigantic lap of Darkness. From the Egg sprang the son of the rushing Wind, a god with golden wings. He is called Eros, the god of love.' Eros brings into the light everything previously hidden in the egg. In later myth Eros came to represent desire – which in some sophisticated cosmogonies, such as the Hindu and Buddhist, is the prime motivating factor behind creation.

In Finno-Ugric myth a goddess falls from heaven into the primal sea and a bird lays its eggs on her knee; when she bends, the eggs roll into the Abyss and the universe springs from them. In some Oceanic myths the world hatches from an egg picked up from or dropped into a primal sea.

Perhaps the closest analogy

from this class of myth to contemporary scientific accounts is the Japanese myth in which in the beginning an original pair of principles, male and female, formed a single chaotic mass in an ill-defined cosmic egg, from which heaven and earth eventually separated out.

The more sophisticated cosmogonies go back a step beyond a creator god or divine couple. The godhead is not humanoid, but mysterious, and often conceived of as pure spirit, as in the Hebrew account in Genesis. In some accounts an ineffable, eternal being or spirit creates a creator god to bring the universe into being, as in the Hopi Indian myth (see box on p.209), and in Hinduism, in which the abstract force *brahman* brings into being the creator god Brahma. Here, as elsewhere, there is the idea that in a sense these beings are one and the same, but in different stages of manifestation. Similarly, the Gnostic Christians believed that God was himself a lesser deity born out of the original Creator.

A similar idea is found in Egyptian myths. In one, Neb-er-tcher (a form of Ra) takes upon himself the shape of Khepra, the creator god, who then creates a divine couple, Shu and Tefnut, to continue the creation process. In another, the god Osiris comes into existence by uttering his own name. This

In biblical myth the creation of the universe was a dramatic affair, captured here in Gustave Doré's 1865 print 'The Creation of Light'. Doré was illustrating Genesis 1.2: 'And the earth was without form and void.'

self-naming is another sophisticated feature, seeming to suggest that self-definition is a necessary stage in the manifestation or creation of the universe.

THE EXPANDING UNIVERSE

Strictly speaking science deals only with the origins of the universe, not with its creation. It was in the 19th century that astronomers seriously began to contemplate a universe without God and to recommence the search, begun in ancient Greece, for natural causes.

Essential to our modern understanding of creation is the key discovery, by the astronomer Edwin Hubble, that the universe is expanding. It

THE DREAMTIME

The Dreamtime, the time of creation, symbolizes to the Australian Aboriginal people the belief that all life is part of one vast interconnected web of relationships which came into existence with the stirring of the spirit ancestors. In the beginning, when the Earth was a featureless plain or, in some accounts, covered with water, the spirits began to stir, waking up, and as they moved they began to form the landscape, turning the void into hills and valleys, rivers and seas. The Dreamtime is perpetually present, and through ritual and ceremony individuals can make contact with its spiritual power, energizing and refreshing themselves.

seems that, viewed from any point in the universe, galaxies are rapidly separating from each other. This can be seen from a phenomenon called 'red shift': a receding light source changes in character, shifting toward the red (longer wavelength) end of the spectrum as the lightwaves become farther apart.

In 1929 Hubble proved that a galaxy's velocity of recession was proportional to its distance from Earth. In simple terms, the universe is expanding rapidly, and the farther out we look, the faster it is doing so. When we look into space we are seeing into the past, because of the time that light from distant sources takes to reach us. Thus it seems that the universe was once expanding more rapidly.

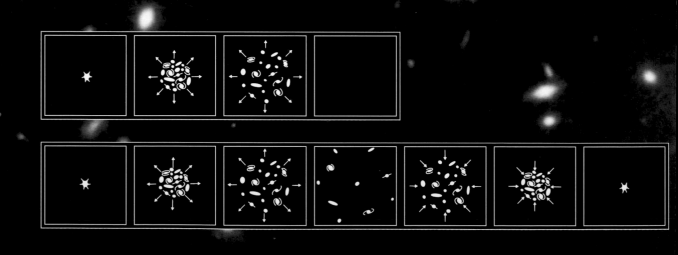

THE BIG BANG

In one Chinese myth an original 'nothing' condenses into unity, which becomes a single point, a 'Mighty Atom', which then itself divides into male (yang or positive) and female (yin or negative). Astrophysics now holds that something rather like this actually happened, with the universe, and its physical laws, evolving from a single point.

The implication of all ancient myths was that the physical and spiritual realms were interdependent. Perhaps the most radical proposition of modern science is that matter and energy are interchangeable, and that the physical world is therefore not quite what it seems. In 1907 Einstein showed that matter was in fact a very condensed form of energy, setting out the now famous formula $E = mc^2$ (E = energy; m = mass difference; c = speed of light). The conclusion is that vast amounts of nuclear energy are locked up in a single atom.

In 1927 the Belgian astronomer G.E. Lemaître suggested that at the beginning of the universe, matter and energy were squashed together into a 'cosmic egg' which then began to grow with extraordinary rapidity to generate the expanding universe. The idea began to achieve considerable support, until one day Fred Hoyle, one of its critics, labelled it the 'Big Bang'. This image of a gigantic primeval explosion of unimaginable power has caught the popular imagination in a way that Hoyle never intended.

While the Big Bang itself, and the idea that the entire universe might be compressed into a single point, is impossible to imagine, the mechanics can be explained. The most basic atom, hydrogen (H), consists of two particles: a central positively charged proton, and an outer negatively charged electron. So long as they exist separately, there is a limit to how far the atom can be compressed. However, past a certain point they fuse to form a mass of electrically uncharged particles, or neutrons. A mass of ultimately

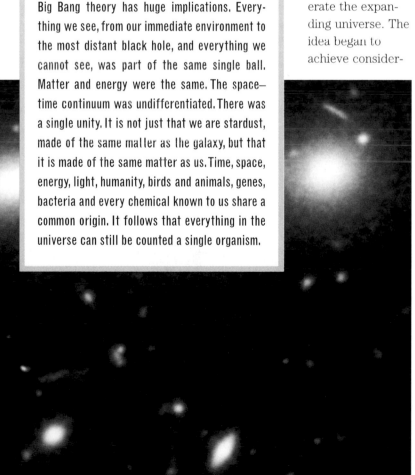

Big Bang theory has huge implications. Everything we see, from our immediate environment to the most distant black hole, and everything we cannot see, was part of the same single ball. Matter and energy were the same. The space–time continuum was undifferentiated. There was a single unity. It is not just that we are stardust, made of the same matter as the galaxy, but that it is made of the same matter as us. Time, space, energy, light, humanity, birds and animals, genes, bacteria and every chemical known to us share a common origin. It follows that everything in the universe can still be counted a single organism.

DIAGRAM, INSET LEFT There are two versions of Big Bang theory. The open universe (top) assumes that the universe was created from nothing and that it will expand for ever. A variation, the closed universe, assumes that the universe will eventually run out of energy and contract to nothing. This echoes the Judaeo-Christian belief in which a once-only creation leads to a once-only end. The oscillating universe (bottom) echoes classical ideas of ever-repeating ages: as soon as the universe has contracted to nothing a new Big Bang begins the process all over again.
MAIN PICTURE Remote galaxies, which existed when the universe was two-thirds of its present age.

compressed neutrons, 'neutronium', would have a density of 1 billion tonnes per cubic centimetre (16 billion tons per cubic inch). Such compression would generate enormous heat.

According to Big Bang theory, all matter was originally compressed by gravity into an incredibly dense, volatile single point. A reaction then took place in which neutronium broke into separate neutrons, which in turn became protons and electrons. Subsequent combinations of atomic particles then led to the creation of all 92 known elements, with stars and planets forming out of clouds of gas. Observation of the expansion rate of the universe enables us to calculate that the Big Bang occurred between ten and twenty billion years ago.

THE STEADY STATE

During the 1940s and 1950s, Steady State theory, championed by the astrophysicists Fred Hoyle, Thomas Gold and Hermann Bondi, vied with the Big Bang as a plausible explanation for the origin of the universe, at least in the popular imagination. The theory proposes that the universe has always existed more or less as it is now, and explains its expansion by suggesting that new hydrogen could be constantly created out of nothing in empty space.

This contradicts the conservation of energy law, which states that the total energy in a system stays the same, even if there are transformations of matter into energy or energy into matter. However, field theory undermines this argument, suggesting that energy, and therefore matter, can emerge out of something as insubstantial as a 'field' of potential.

The discovery of quasars – huge starlike objects which occur more often far out in space, and which therefore must have been more common in the early universe – raised further objections to Steady State theory, because they imply that the universe has evolved. However, the death-blow came in 1965 when US physicists Arno Penzias and Robert Wilson accidentally discovered uniform cosmic background radiation, almost certainly originating from the Big Bang – although actually dating from about a million years after with the first hydrogen atoms.

THE PULSATING UNIVERSE

A fundamental belief in Hinduism and Buddhism, shared by the ancient Greeks, is that everything, from the atom to the universe, is in a state of flux. This is known in Buddhism as *anicca*, impermanence. *Samsara*, the totality of phenomenal existence, may be imagined as a boundless ocean of waters. Incessantly rising and falling upon its surface are an infinite number of waves. Each wave represents a *cakkavala* or system of 10,000 worlds. The rising of the wave corresponds to the period of growth; its falling, to the period of contraction.

On the cosmic scale, both Hinduism and Buddhism conceive of the universe as passing through cycles of expansion and contraction. One such cycle, from birth to destruction, is termed a *kalpa*.

The Hindu trinity, Brahma, Vishnu and Shiva, representing generation, order and destruction (a 12th-century Indian carving).

Hindu texts claim that one *kalpa* is a life of the creator god Brahma, each of which lasts for 4,320 million years. The physicist Fritjof Capra wrote in 1975 that 'the scale of this ancient myth is indeed staggering; it has taken the human mind more than 2,000 years to come up again with a similar concept'.

Capra was referring to a very compelling extension of the Big Bang theory: the oscillating, or pulsating, universe. This pictures the expansion of the universe slowing down – as it seems to be doing – to the point where gravity overwhelms it and forces it to collapse, until eventually there is another Big Bang, and the process starts all over again. This is one variant of the 'closed' version of Big Bang theory. In the 'open' version, the universe expands indefinitely, although it may do so ever more slowly (see diagram on pp.206–7).

BEFORE THE BIG BANG

The 'cosmic egg' must have been unstable – otherwise there would have been no Big Bang. So what came before the Big Bang? Some physicists dismiss the question, saying that space and time began with the Big Bang, much as religious fundamentalists claim that nothing existed before God. Current physics cannot explain the beginning of universe. It begins its search for origins a fraction of a fraction of a second after the Big Bang.

The idea of the pulsating universe may go some way toward envisaging what happened before the Big Bang, but it does not explain the origin of matter. In myth, matter is created out of emptiness, or out of the mind of God, but is there a scientific parallel?

Modern physics no longer distinguishes absolutely between material particles and nothingness. Quantum mechanics (see pp.230–5) has shown that particles are inseparable from the space around them: they determine its structure. In Capra's words, particles are 'condensations of a continuous field which is present throughout space', which 'can come into being spontaneously out of the void, and vanish again into the void'.

Perhaps, then, what existed before the Big Bang was a limitless, formless, omnipresent field of potential, like the mythical primal waters, waiting to be activated by divine will or some unseen force.

THE HOPI CREATION MYTH

The first world was Tokpela [Endless Space].

But first, they say, there was only the Creator, Taiowa. All else was endless space. There was no beginning and no end, no time, no shape, no life. Just an immeasurable void that had its beginning and end, time, shape and life in the mind of Taiowa the Creator.

Then he, the infinite, conceived the finite. First he created Sótuknang to make it manifest, saying to him, 'I have created you, the first power and instrument as a person, to carry out my plan for life in endless space.' ...

Sótuknang did as he was commanded. From endless space he gathered that which was to be manifest as solid substance, moulded it into forms, and arranged them into nine universal kingdoms: one for Taiowa the Creator, one for himself, and seven universes for the life to come.

IN THE END

Even without cataclysm or disaster, the Earth is bound to die: this will happen when the Sun cools down. The Sun is estimated to be about five billion years old, with another five billion years to go in its current state, after which it will evolve into a 'red giant', becoming much bigger and cooler than it is now. Mercury and Venus will be swallowed up, while the surface of the Earth will be scorched and burnt to a cinder. If there are any humans left on the Earth – an unlikely chance – they will have to find somewhere else to live. From its red giant state, the Sun will begin to contract, becoming smaller, hotter and denser, until it turns into a 'white dwarf', about the size of the Earth. The Earth itself, with its barren, desertified surface, will be no more than a dead planet in orbit around its former Sun.

In the Hebrew Scriptures (Old Testament) the prophets searched for celestial portents to warn of the Last Judgment.

'And on that day,' says the Lord God, 'I will make the Sun go down at noon, and darken the Earth in broad daylight.'

Amos 8.9

The fear – and prophecy – of the end of the world has always balanced the quest for its origins. Such prophecies come in different forms. Some anticipate the destruction of the entire universe, others of the Earth alone. Some predict a total destruction, others forecast a renewal and rebirth – the 'new Heaven and new Earth' as envisaged in the Bible.

The Hebrew prophets believed that global destruction would be heralded by celestial portents, such as comets, eclipses and meteors. (The words 'disaster' and 'catastrophe' are derived from the Latin *astrum*, star.) By *c*.400BC it was believed that certain planetary alignments – conjunctions of all seven known planets in Aries, Cancer or Capricorn – could signify the end of time, and therefore of the universe (see pp.22–3, 46, 96). As soon as it had come to an end, however, it would begin again, and the cycle would endlessly repeat. This pattern of creation, destruction and re-creation resembles the current scientific theory of the 'pulsating universe' (see pp.208–9).

Ideas of cosmic destruction can be traced back to ancient Sumer, over 4,000 years ago. The epic 'Lamentation on the Destruction of Ur' records that the great city of Ur was destroyed 'after Utu (the Sun) had cast his curse on the roads and highways' and and after 'Nanna (the Moon) traded away his people'.

Similar ideas are found in India. In Hindu mythology time is conceived of as a wheel, turning through vast cycles of creation and destruction, each cycle regulated by the creator god Brahma. As Brahma breathes out, the universe expands, and peace and harmony reign; as he breathes in the universe contracts, and destruction takes over. The great ages of history are known as *yuga*s, and are connected to Hindu astrology. The current age is the Kali Yuga, which is considered to be the most degenerate before the Earth is reborn. A Western version of the myth is the belief that the Earth is soon to enter a new age of peace and equality – the Age of Aquarius (see p.105).

Some modern theories focus less on a supernatural cataclysm than on the gradual dissolution of nature, or on cyclical disasters, as in the periodic extinction of species. Modern cyclical theories of mass destruction were first worked out in the ancient world. Egyptian priests told the Greek Herodotus in the 5th century BC that the Sun had changed its position four times, 'twice rising where he normally sets, and twice setting where he normally rises', causing global cataclysm. Herodotus reckoned that the last cataclysm must have taken place about 11,340 years earlier, c.12,000BC.

A recent theory attributes cycles of extinction, as revealed in the fossil record, to vast increases in solar radiation, which in turn correlate with the 26-million-year cycle of the Sun across the galactic plane.

Scientific explanations for the end of the world date back to the Stoics, the philosophers who flourished in the classical world after the 3rd century BC. They believed that the Sun and the stars needed fuel, which was provided by

the evaporation of water from the Earth. Gradually, over time, they believed, the world would dry up, becoming one vast desert. The Roman philosopher Seneca (c.4BC–AD65) followed Stoic ideas, and described the end of the world in terms that parallel the worst present-day forecasts both of global warming, including melting ice and rising sea levels, and of the nuclear winter.

'The first angel blew his trumpet, and there followed hail and fire, mixed with blood, which fell on the Earth; and a third of the Earth was burnt up, and a third of the trees were burnt up, and all green grass was burnt up.'

The Revelation of St John, 8.7

'The Last Judgment' (1865) by Gustave Doré – a vision of the world inspired by Revelation 12.12. In Christian mythology the Last Judgment follows Christ's final defeat of Satan and the physical resurrection of all sinners.

COSMIC COLLISIONS

The dramatic collision in 1994 between the comet Shoemaker-Levy and Jupiter was a reminder of just how vulnerable the Earth is to such dangers. In the 1970s and 1980s many scientists concluded that the dinosaurs had died out as a result of climate changes following such a collision about 65 million years ago. There may even have already been one such collision this century – the great Tunguska explosion in Siberia on the morning of 30 June 1908, which caused destruction over an area 40 kilometres (25 miles) in diameter. The evidence is consistent with a ball of ice, 40 metres (132 feet) in diameter and weighing 30,000 tonnes, having exploded at an altitude of several kilometres with the force of a 12-megaton nuclear bomb.

Certain myths may embody a folk memory of an actual comet collision. For example, the Greek myth of Phaeton relates that one day Helios, the Sun, allowed his son Phaeton to drive the Sun chariot, but the horses galloped out of control, and the boy scorched the Earth; eventually he was struck dead with a thunderbolt hurled by the angry Zeus.

The dinosaur extinction theory is supported by the fact that geologists have discovered layers of iridium, a metal commonly found in meteorites but not on the Earth, together with deposits of soot in places as far apart as Denmark, Spain and New Zealand, suggesting forest and prairie fires on a worldwide scale. Such extensive fires are perfectly plausible. The impact of a meteorite a few kilometres in diameter, travelling at a typical speed, would release thousands of times more energy than a nuclear war and could start fires hundreds of kilometres away. The fires themselves would be devastating, but the clouds of dust released into the atmosphere would shroud the Earth, shielding it from the Sun's light and heat and creating a 'nuclear winter' effect of darkness and cold.

The Roman poet Ovid (43BC–*c.*AD17) described what some scholars think may have been a collision between a meteorite and the Earth in his *Metamorphoses*:

'Phaethon, fire ravaging his ruddy hair, is hurled headlong and falls with a long trail through the air, as sometimes does a star from the clear heaven.'

Some astronomers have argued that events in more recent history, such as those related in Exodus – the plagues, the parting of the Red Sea and the other miracles that accompanied the departure of the Hebrews from Egypt – could have been caused by a smaller meteorite collision.

The odds of the Earth's being hit by an asteroid large enough to create such havoc are impossible to calculate with any accuracy because of the number of variables, although Professor Paul Davies of Adelaide University has estimated that every million years the Earth is hit by a body large enough to destroy entire species, while a city such as London or New York has a one-in-three chance of being wiped out by a cosmic collision in the next 200 years. Such forecasts may be poetic speculation, but emphasize the point that as the Earth travels through space we are exposed to dangers over which we have no control.

THE END OF THE UNIVERSE

The Earth may come to an end, while the universe will carry on – but for how long? According to Steady State theory (see p.208) the universe will go on indefinitely, as new matter is created. According to the currently fashionable Big Bang theory the universe will gradually reach a limit in its expansion and will then very slowly begin to contract; eventually everything, every single particle and wave, will be compressed into a microscopic nothingness. However – assuming that the Big Bang happened about ten to twenty billion years ago and that the universe is still expanding – there are still about fifteen to thirty billion years to go before it comes to an end.

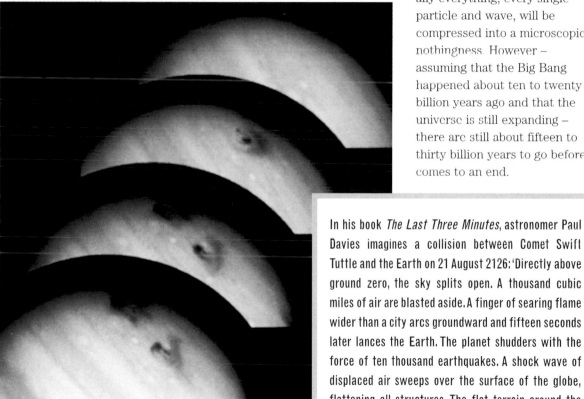

ABOVE **A mosaic of images of the impact of comet Shoemaker-Levy on Jupiter, 18–23 July 1994. A collision of such magnitude on Earth would probably wipe out all life.**
LEFT **An optical image of the comet Hale-Bopp, photographed in Finland in April 1997.**

In his book *The Last Three Minutes*, astronomer Paul Davies imagines a collision between Comet Swift Tuttle and the Earth on 21 August 2126: 'Directly above ground zero, the sky splits open. A thousand cubic miles of air are blasted aside. A finger of searing flame wider than a city arcs groundward and fifteen seconds later lances the Earth. The planet shudders with the force of ten thousand earthquakes. A shock wave of displaced air sweeps over the surface of the globe, flattening all structures. The flat terrain around the impact site rises in a ring of liquid mountains several miles high, exposing the bowels of the Earth in a crater several hundred miles across.' Fortunately, since Swift Tuttle last visited in 1993, revised calculations suggest that it will miss the Earth by two weeks.

TIME

Time can be seen as a river, as a succession of moments, and as rhythm. St Augustine said that he knew what it was until asked to describe it. Popularly it is both healer and destroyer, and that which 'waits for no man': we can choose to stay in one place (relative to Earth), but not in one time. In business, time is money. Time can be on our side; more often it is against us.

In the Orphic tales of ancient Greece, time was personified as Chronos, who produced the egg from which the universe hatched. Thus the world of matter sprang out of time, yet time was only manifest through matter – a view echoed in relativity (see p.217). Chronos is etymologically related to, yet separate from, the god Cronos (the Roman Saturn), whose castration of Ouranos separated sky from earth, conscious from unconscious. Subjectively there is no time without consciousness, because there is no memory.

> 'The Sun, the Moon and five other stars, which are called planets, came into existence for the determining and preserving of the numbers of Time.'
>
> Plato, *Timaeus*, 4th century BC

MEASURING TIME

Our ancestors perceived time in terms of the seasons, the passage of the Sun and Moon, the rising and setting of stars, and bodily rhythms. Time was reflected in music – a means of escaping from time through time. Time was also seen in terms of process; in India, for example, one simple unit was the time rice took to cook – about thirteen minutes. Time was also linked to space – as in 'about three days' ride'.

Little by little, practical necessity replaced the flowing time of the Sun and the Moon with the rigid time of the clock. In the Middle Ages monks began to use clocks so that they could be ready for early morning prayers before the rising of the Sun. In the 18th and 19th centuries, with the Industrial Revolution, came the economic necessity for workers to 'clock on' and 'clock off' at the same time; during the same period the advent of the railways meant that timetables needed to be standardized. Finally, the invention of electric light freed us for ever from the perils of darkness. Now we are prisoners of machine time – a time that has nothing to do with the seasons, the cycles of nature or our own physical needs.

As life became more complicated, ways of measuring time became necessary. Sundials were probably the most ancient time-measuring instruments, the most primitive consisting of a stick throwing its shadow on the ground. Stars or graduated candles marked the passage of the night. Sand 'hourglasses' survive today as egg-timers. Water-clocks, which measured time by the flow of water, were used in various ancient cultures, including Egypt, Greece and China, and Galileo used one to time his experiments.

Clocks became more accurate with the use of the pendulum mechanism, which was first applied by Christiaan Huygens in 1657. Like sand- and water-clocks, pendulum clocks depend on the constant force of gravity; a mechanical clock substitutes a spring for gravity,

RIGHT **The signs of the zodiac provide rich images for the Sun's passage through the seasons. Their function is often purely decorative, as in this medieval German sundial.**

but still works like a pendulum. Even a quartz watch mechanism simulates a pendulum by vibrating at a regular wavelength. The latest atomic clocks are based on radiation waves emitted by caesium-133, and are accurate to 1 second in 1,000

'Tomorrow, and tomorrow, and tomorrow,
Creeps in this petty pace from day to day,
To the last syllable of recorded time.'

William Shakespeare, *Macbeth*, *c*.1606

years; yet even these are actually measuring intervals between events – the wave crests.

Finding an absolute has always been a problem in timekeeping. There is even some evidence that the so-called 'gravitational constant' is changing. If so, gravity-driven clocks would run at different speeds from atomic clocks. Some scientists suggest that we should take the speed of light as our absolute.

TIME'S ARROW, TIME'S CYCLE

Time is often seen as an arrow, always moving in the same direction from the past to the future, through an endless chain of cause and effect. Yet there are other views. Many cultures have believed that time moves in waves or cycles, much like the seasons, in which general conditions are repeated but the details are different each time. Ancient Greek and Roman

The astrolabe was more than a clock. It could be used for determining stellar, zodiacal and planetary positions, in addition to telling the time. As well as being used by astronomers, it was, for mariners, an essential aid to navigation, being a means of calculating latitude. This 14th-century Arabic astrolabe could also be used to locate the position of Mecca.

mystics believed that conditions were repeated in each cycle down to the smallest detail. The Roman emperor Marcus Aurelius believed he had sat on the imperial throne an infinite number of times in the past and would do so an infinite number of times in the future, each time going through identical experiences.

RELATIVITY

To ancient cultures time was essentially relative, and in those that had highly developed mathematical systems, such as India, Egypt and Babylon, time and space were interdependent. The space–time of the here and now existed alongside a transcendent eternal time, which was perfect and unchanging, such as the Platonic world of Being, or the Aboriginal Dreamtime.

Gradually Western societies developed the belief that time is a fixed measure, independent of all other variables. In the 17th century Isaac Newton established the view of time as a mathematically fixed constant, asserting that 'absolute, true and mathematical Time, of itself, and from its own nature, flows equably without relation to anything external, and by

'But all the clocks in the city
Began to whirr and chime:
"O let not Time deceive you,
You cannot conquer Time."'

W. H. Auden (1907–73), from
'As I Walked Out One Evening'

another name is called duration'.

Even as he spoke, Newton's contemporary Gottfried Leibniz (1646–1716) was beginning the march back to relativism. He wrote: 'I hold space to be merely relative, as time is. I hold it to be an order of co-existences, as time is an order of successions. Instants, considered without the things, are nothing at all. They consist only in the successive order of things.'

In Newtonian physics there is no limit to the speed to which a body can be accelerated – be it a particle or a planet. However, Albert Einstein postulated in his special theory of relativity (1905) that nothing can exceed the speed of light (299,792 kilometres/186,287 miles per second). Einstein also held that all motion was relative: a body only moves in relation to other bodies. Since time is measured by movement, time is also relative: one Einsteinian definition holds that 'time is a property of matter in motion'. More significant is Einstein's general theory of relativity (1915), which explains how gravity creates a space–time continuum by warping space itself, thereby altering the course of objects, and even of light, through space. Since we can only measure time in terms of movement, time itself is susceptible to gravity.

This has some strange consequences. Mass increases in proportion to velocity – which is why it would be better to be nudged by an ambling elephant

than hit by a feather travelling at half the speed of light. A body travelling at the speed of light would reach infinite mass; therefore nothing can reach this speed. But if we could travel at the speed of light, time would stand still, because a body at infinite mass would warp the space around it infinitely. At speeds approaching that of light, time dilates: an astronaut embarking on a twenty-year space journey at 99.9 per cent of the speed of light would return to find that 10,000 years had passed on Earth.

This phenomenon has been demonstrated on a small scale with twin atomic clocks. If one is flown round the world at high speed, it falls fractionally behind its twin. The 1969 lunar astronauts returned home having aged 0.005 of a second less than their wives.

TIME TRAVEL

Around 750BC the Greek poet Hesiod suggested that it might be possible for time to flow backward, and that in the Golden Age people would grow younger with time. Experience tells us that the 'arrow of time' points only in one direction – forward. None the less, time travel captures the imagination and has inspired science fiction writers from H.G. Wells onward.

One logical defect of backward time travel is that it would be possible to meet oneself at a younger age, or to prevent one's parents from meeting, unless this happened in a parallel universe. This is often referred to as the 'grandmother paradox', because one could also make one's present existence an impossibility by travelling back in time and murdering one's grandmother. To be able to visit 'the future', on the other hand, implies that events are completely predetermined. The writer Colin Wilson comments that the notion of time travel implies the existence of thousands of parallel universes. In fact there would have to be an infinite number – an idea now seriously considered by some physicists (see p.234).

Travel into the future would theoretically be possible if one travelled at speeds approaching that of light. A form of time travel might also be possible due to the dragging effect that gravity exerts on time, slowing it down; a clock on the Sun would run slower than on Earth, because the Sun has more mass and thus a greater gravitational pull. Gravity increases on approaching the core of a mass, so time runs more slowly at sea level than on a mountain. In a black hole (see p.235), the intense gravitational pull would make light curve round on itself and disappear back into the hole. Intrepid travellers might be able to enter the hole and time-travel within it, but they could never return to their own time, because they would be trapped by gravity.

Such time travel can only take us forward. In a sense it is not proper time travel at all; all that is happening is that the amount of time registered by one person is changing. It would, however, theoretically be possible to construct a gravity machine so powerful that it distorted space–time, allowing the construction of a 'wormhole' through which one could travel as far back as

star
(apparent position)

star
(real position)

light ray from star distorted by Sun

orbit of Mercury

Mercury

Earth

Sun

Space–time is warped by the Sun's mass so that light reaching the Earth is bent, making stars appear to be in different locations (see also p.148).

TIME SCALES

The physicist David Finklestein coined the word 'chronon' for a particle of time – which to date remains in the realm of theory. The shortest observable times in physics are those of short-lived elementary particles, determined by measuring their tracks on a photographic plate. This is about 10^{-14} of a second (less than a billionth of a second), though even shorter lifetimes have been deduced. Another particle, the muon (mu-meson), lives to the ripe old age of 10^{-5} of a second. But this is a mere blink of an eye compared to the average human reaction time of one second.

At the other end of the scale are mythical eras such as the 360,000-year 'Great Year'. In some Hindu traditions one universe lasts for 8,600 million years, a *kalpa*, and 100 of these are a *para*. The universe's actual age, according to Big Bang theorists, is between 10 and 20 billion years.

Our system of counting time in sixes – 60 seconds in a minute, 60 minutes in an hour, 24 hours in a day and twelve months in a year, can be traced back to ancient Sumer, 5,000 years ago. The only attempt to decimalize the measurement of time occurred during the French Revolution – and failed disastrously.

one's own birth, effectively opening up a parallel universe.

Another, physical, objection to time travel was initially put forward by the English theoretical physicist Stephen Hawking. According to the theory of entropy, the universe inevitably becomes less ordered and more chaotic; this makes it physically impossible to travel back to a time when the structure of the universe was fundamentally different, even if only the previous few seconds.

However, in 1995 Hawking, encouraged by other developments in theoretical physics, came out in favour of the possibility of backward time travel, agreeing that, if parallel universes do exist, it might be possible to travel back in one and forward in another. At present the empirical support for such propositions is nil – like the mysticism of old they rely entirely on the manipulation of abstract numbers.

'Probably most of the historical speculations about time and the division of time were influenced by astrological ideas.'

C.G. Jung (1875–1961)

An Allegory of Time (1769) by Martin Josef Geeraerts. Our traditional personification of time as an old man, Old Father Time, is derived from the ancient Greeks' association of their god Cronos (the Roman Saturn) with Chronos, or Time. The scythe that he carries was originally a sickle, which came to be used less for the gathering of crops than for the gathering of souls.

MAPPING THE HEAVENS

Do models of the universe actually tell us about the truth of the universe, or just about the way we perceive it? Most cultures have two views of the universe. One, which is physical, depends on as precise an understanding as possible of the laws governing physical motion and the material nature of the planets and stars. The other, which is symbolic, tries to distil the underlying truths in an attempt to make sense of our place in the cosmos.

Often the two co-exist. For example, Indian astronomers have long known that solar eclipses are caused by the Earth's shadow passing across the face of the Sun. Yet poetic cosmology talks of a great sky dragon consuming the Sun. Nobody really believes that this happens, yet to a Hindu it embodies a truth about the universe which cannot be expressed by science or mathematics.

The Greek mystic Pythagoras (6th century BC) believed that the universe could only be understood through mathematical formulae. Aristotle described his beliefs: 'It is just as the Pythagoreans say, the whole world and all things in it are summed up by the number 3... Hence it is that we have taken this number from nature, as it were one of her laws, and make use of it even for the worship of the gods.'

The Arabs were aware of the Sun-centred system proposed by the Greek astronomer Aristarchus (born 310BC). But they preferred to ignore the evidence of their own eyes and calculations. Why? The answer to this is at the root of early cosmological thinking.

The 12th-century Islamic philosopher Averroës faced up to the problem when he compared the known fact that the Sun was the centre of the solar system with the common-sense proposition, embodied in most classical astronomy, that the Earth was the centre. He said that both were true; although the Sun is the centre, our earthly perspective is equally valid. Averroës'

perception that there need be no one centre was echoed centuries later by Einstein's realization that there need be no centre at all. Ironically Big Bang theory (see p.207) has restored the concept of a single centre.

Even in the modern age, the microscopic accuracy of scientific astronomy, which enables us to send probes to other planets, co-exists with the mystical systems of, say, Rudolf Steiner, Alice Bailey and P.D. Ouspensky, as well as more orthodox religious traditions of East and West, in which the universe is seen as a spiritual entity.

The question of God's role in the universe strikes at the heart of modern astronomy. Most mainstream Christians now accept that having created the laws of physics which control the planetary orbits, God will not intervene. Yet fundamentalists who take the Bible literally insist that at any moment God has the power to interfere and change the nature of the universe, just as when, according to the Bible, he stopped the Sun in order to help Joshua. Fundamentalist adherents of other faiths follow similar beliefs.

Most early societies believed that the stars and planets were moved by God, or individual gods and goddesses. The Greek philosophers Plato and Aristotle saw the entire universe as divine and alive, and believed that the planets were set in order by God and channelled his thoughts and intentions to the Earth. In the Middle Ages many astronomers believed that the planets were moved by angels, and even when in the 15th–17th centuries Copernicus, Kepler and Newton calculated the mathematical principles that kept planetary orbits regular, they still believed that the laws of the universe had been created by God.

The Origins of the Milky Way by **Tintoretto (1518–94). The Milky Way is the dense band of stars running across the sky. It is our galaxy, and because it is shaped as a flat disc we see it head-on as a narrow band. We still do not know how galaxies are formed or how they evolve into different shapes – Tintoretto preferred mythological explanations.**

THE ROUND UNIVERSE

We do not know exactly when people realized the Earth was a sphere. Circumstantial evidence from both Egypt and the mysterious megalithic culture of France and the British Isles suggests it may have been before *c.*3000BC. The first Greek philosopher to argue that the Earth was spherical was Parmenides, *c.*500BC. His ideas were reinforced *c.*400BC by Plato, who argued not only that the planets and stars moved in exactly circular orbits around the Earth but that the entire universe was spherical.

After Plato all classical astronomers accepted that the Earth was a sphere. While it was often portrayed as flat in medieval images (just as it is in modern maps), in the 15th century all educated people knew that it was round. The myth that Columbus and his sailors thought that they might sail off the edge of the world was created by the writer Irving Washington in the 19th century; in order to exaggerate the heroic feat of discovering North America, he had to show that Columbus stood alone against the ignorance of his age.

Plato's notion that the entire universe was spherical finds a curious echo in Einstein's theory that space–time is curved. In the 1970s it was even suggested that it might be possible to travel vast distances by moving instantaneously from one part of a 'space–time curve' to another.

> 'One principle must make the universe a single creature, one from all.'
>
> Roman philosopher Plotinus, *On Whether the Stars are Causes*, 3rd century AD

CRYSTALLINE SPHERES

The quest for natural, as opposed to supernatural, causes in the universe began *c.*600BC in ancient Greece. The Greek philosopher Anaximander (born *c.*610BC) believed that the universe was bordered by a huge wheel filled with fire. The holes in the wheel's rim, through which the fire could be seen, were the planets and stars. His student Anaximenes believed that the stars and planets were like nails

attached to transparent, rotating, concentric crystalline spheres, with the Earth at the centre.

Plato regarded the observed physical universe as a corrupt, illusory version of an ideal one that could only be perceived intuitively. He insisted that the planets moved in perfect circles and at constant speeds, in defiance of astronomical observation, which reveals that the planets wobble from side to side and even seem to move backward. Plato's pupil Eudoxus, anxious to reconcile observation with theory, claimed that 26 concentric spheres were required to move the planets, and one to move the stars. The system still would not work, and so

another of Plato's pupils, Aristotle, proposed a system of 55 spheres, whose interaction would produce such observed phenomena as backward (retrograde) motion. The outermost sphere carried the fixed stars, and beyond that lay the *primum mobile*, the first mover, or God.

Claudius Ptolemy, a Greek astrologer born in Egypt *c.*AD70, built on Aristotle's ideas. Still committed to the belief that the planets moved in perfect circles, he devised a complicated system of 'epicycles' – smaller circles within the greater circle of a planet's orbit – to explain retrograde planetary motion and other apparent inconsistencies in the observed cycles of the planets.

This theory persisted until the early 17th century, when Kepler proved that the planets move in ellipses and Galileo used his telescope to demonstrate that they move freely through space.

THE SUN-CENTRED UNIVERSE

The earliest astronomers followed their everyday experience and, even though they began to devise elaborate models to describe planetary orbits, they assumed that the Earth was fixed at the centre of the universe – it appeared to be perfectly motionless and every day the Sun rose in the east and set in the west. The geocentric solar system was accepted without question by most astronomers until the 17th century, largely because of the enormous combined influence of Plato, Aristotle and Ptolemy.

ABOVE **A 17th-century map of the constellations, with diagrams of the universe according to Ptolemy (top centre) and Copernicus (bottom centre); the seasons (bottom left) and the phases of the Moon (bottom left).**
RIGHT **Planetary *mandalas*, created by plotting the planets' orbits, illustrate the geometrical beauty of the solar system.**

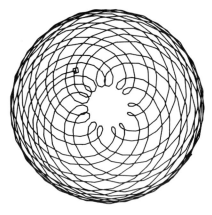

Mars' orbit, plotted 1931–64.

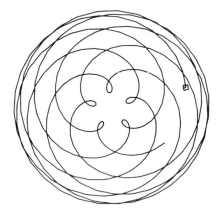

Venus' orbit, plotted 1931–39

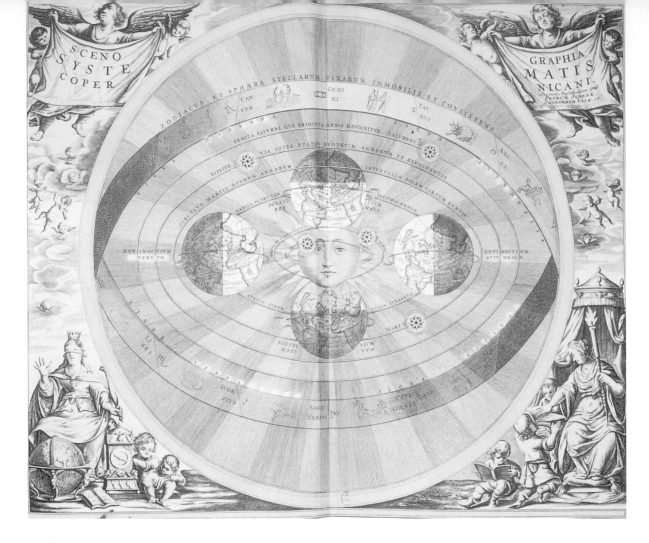

The realization that the Sun was the centre of the solar system was one of the most important conceptual advances that has ever been made. It was Aristarchus (born 310BC) who made the final breakthrough, and his treatise on the Sun and Moon argued on mathematical and geometrical grounds that the Sun must be the centre of the solar system. It is not entirely clear why his system failed to shake the prevailing belief that the Earth was the centre. In an age in which the Sun god, Apollo, was assuming ever greater importance, we

ABOVE Copernicus' discovery that the Earth orbited the Sun revolutionized astronomy in the 16th century. This engraving by Andreas Cellarius of the new solar system dates from 1660.

BELOW Diagram of the apparent path of the Sun as seen from the Earth, showing how the seasons are created by the tilt of the Earth's axis as it rotates around the Sun.

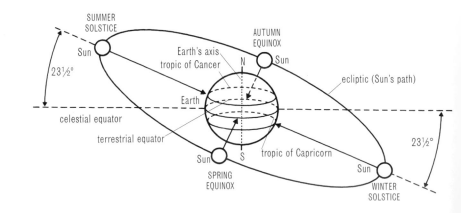

might have expected religious forces to seize on his work; and it would surely have suited those Roman emperors who identified themselves with the Sun, between the 2nd and 4th centuries AD, to have exploited Aristarchus' theories in their support.

It was not until 1513 that Nicholas Copernicus began the astronomical observations that eventually led him to support Aristarchus' ideas and prove mathematically that the Earth does orbit the Sun. Although his *De Revolutionibus Orbium Coelestum* was published in 1543, it was early in the next century before Copernicus' theories were widely accepted.

However, since Albert Einstein developed his theory of relativity (1905–15) it has become clear that, while there are still basic laws of physics, time and space are relative. The Einsteinian universe therefore no longer has a single centre. Instead each individual stands at the centre of his or her own universe.

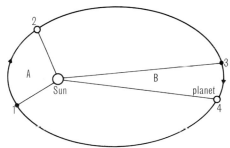

Law 1. Planetary orbits are ellipses with the sun at one focus

Law 2. Planets sweep equal areas in equal times (area A = area B)

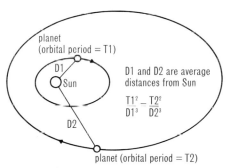

D1 and D2 are average distances from Sun

$$\frac{T1^2}{D1^3} = \frac{T2^2}{D2^3}$$

Law 3. $\frac{T^2}{D^3}$ = constant for any planet

KEPLER'S LAWS

1. Each planet moves round the Sun in an orbit that is an ellipse with the Sun at one focus. (An ellipse is a curve with two focal points, or foci. The sum of the distances from any point on the curve to the foci is constant.)

2. Each planet moves so that a line joining it to the Sun would sweep out equal areas in equal times. In other words, planets move fastest when they are at the 'perihelion' (closest point to the Sun) and slowest when at the 'aphelion' (farthest away).

3. The squares of the orbital periods of any two planets have the same ratio as the cubes of their average distance from the Sun.

PLANETARY MOTION
Kepler and Newton

Pythagoras (*c*.560–480BC) saw the universe in terms of numerical relationships and believed that the planets were spaced at distances analogous to the musical scale (see box on p.262). As they rushed through space they produced a celestial harmony – the 'music of the spheres'. One of the most important people influenced by his views, 2,000 years later, was the German astronomer and astrologer Johannes Kepler (1571–1630). Kepler was convinced that by discovering how the planets moved he could get closer to understanding God's creation – and hence God himself. Among his

three laws, the most revolutionary was the first, which proved that planets moved in ellipses, breaking for ever the old belief that their orbits were circles. It was up to Isaac Newton (1642–1727) to explain the planets' elliptical orbits in his three laws of motion. Together Kepler and Newton provided the formulae that have enabled us to measure planetary motions so precisely that planetary probes can be dispatched with total confidence. Einstein clarified certain minor anomalies, for example the measurements of Mercury's orbit, in his general theory of relativity (1915).

PLANETARY ORBITS
Bode's Law

Bode's Law, publicized by Johann Bode in 1772 but first set out by Johann Titius in 1756, takes the principle of the harmony of the spheres one step farther. Bode showed that Plato's belief that the planets were spaced in harmonious ratios was correct. The law works like this. Take the sequence of numbers 0, 3, 6, 12…, in which each number (from 3) is double the previous one. Add 4 to each, to get 4, 7, 10, 16, 28, 52, 100, 196. If 10 in this sequence is the distance from the Sun to the Earth, then the rest of the sequence approximates to the relative distances of the planets from the Sun:

Mercury 3.9
Venus 7.2
Earth 10
Mars 15.2
Jupiter 52
Saturn 95.4
Uranus 192

Uranus was not discovered until 1781, but it fits the sequence. There still seemed to be a planet missing at 28 in the sequence, and a number of astronomers set themselves to find it. In 1801 Giuseppe Piazzi discovered the planetoid Ceres at this distance, followed by the asteroid belt (see p.117). Bode's Law is not a law in the same sense as Kepler's or Newton's laws, in that it does not explain planetary motions. Yet it is an indication of the geometrical patterns that Kepler believed underpinned planetary motion. Although Neptune and Pluto do not fit the sequence, they are linked by other patterns: Uranus takes half the time taken by Neptune and a third that taken by Pluto to orbit the Sun.

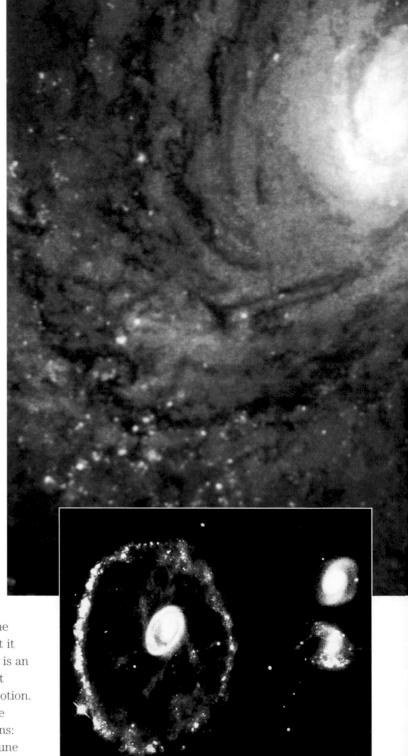

Does God play dice? In the ancient world the gods could interfere in human life. Then Newton proved that the universe was regulated by immutable physical laws. Einstein believed that Newton was right and insisted that 'God does not play dice with the universe'. Since Einstein published his theories all that has changed. With the arrival of quantum physics and the 'uncertainty principle' God does not only play dice, he cheats!

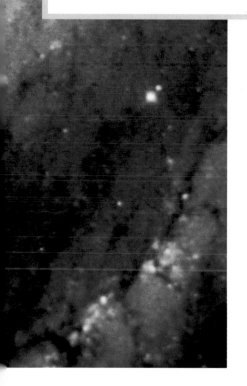

ABOVE **M100, a spiral galaxy in the constellation of Virgo.**
LEFT **The Cartwheel galaxy, created by the collision of two galaxies 500 million miles away in the constellation Sculptor. The ringlike feature is the result of a smaller galaxy careering through the larger galaxy.**

GALAXIES AND CLUSTERS

Stars and solar systems are separated by distances so great that with our current technology it is impossible to travel from one to another. Yet on the large scale they are gathered together in tight groups called galaxies. Our solar system is situated on the edge of a galaxy known as the Milky Way, which contains about 100 billion stars. It was not until the 1920s that the astronomer Harlow Shapley sketched a map of the Milky Way and located the Sun in its outer parts.

Galaxies may be elliptical in shape (like American footballs or rugby balls), spiral (like Catherine wheels), or irregular. Many galaxies appear to lie on the surface of bubble- or sponge-like structures, which may be 100 million light-years in diameter.

Like stars, galaxies are grouped in clusters. The Milky Way belongs to a group called the Local Group, about 3 million light-years across, with at least 25 members. The galaxies in each cluster appear to move around a central point, like stars in a galaxy. The nearest big cluster is the Virgo cluster, about 50–70 million light-years away in the constellation of Virgo.

The Local Group and the Virgo cluster belong to the Local Supercluster, which contains about 100 member clusters. It is pancake-shaped, about 100 million light-years in diameter and 10 million light-years thick. One other strange formation, the 'Great Wall', includes thousands of galaxies spread out in an immense crumpled sheet.

In 1996 astronomers announced the existence of a gigantic concentration of mass, the 'Great Attractor', about 300 million light-years away, toward the southern Milky Way. For reasons not yet understood, the Attractor seems to be pulling nearby galaxies toward it. At its heart lies a cluster known as Abell 3627, containing more than 600 galaxies. Abell 3627 might itself be embedded in a much larger supercluster which may be part of another 'great wall'.

CHAOS AND COSMOS

Modern cosmologists generally assume that at the time of the Big Bang (see p.207), matter was compressed to the point where atomic patterns were broken down into a uniform mass of white-hot neutronium. When the Big Bang occurred, this expanded – probably at an almost unimaginable velocity. Cosmologists comment on the remarkable uniformity of the universe: it looks much the same in all directions ('isotropy'). This would have been even more pronounced in its early days.

Although it is possible that such isotropy does not necessarily reflect the initial state of the universe, since it might have

MEASURING DISTANCES

Distances in space are measured in miles, kilometres, Astronomical Units (AU), light-years and parsecs. An AU is the mean distance between the Sun and the Earth – approximately 150 million kilometres (93 million miles).

A light-year is the distance travelled by light in one year. Light waves travel at 299,792 kilometres (186,287 miles) per second, and distant objects are usually defined by the length of time it would take their light to reach the Earth. For example, the Moon is 1.25 light-seconds away, Venus 2.3 light-minutes, the Sun 8.3 light-minutes and Neptune an average of 4.15 light-hours.

These distances are nothing compared to some.
* Light from the nearest star takes 4.3 years to reach Earth.
* Light takes up to 130,000 years to travel the length of our galaxy, but only 2,000 years to travel across it.
* The Sun lies about 26,000 light-years from the centre of the galaxy.
* Light from the Andromeda galaxy, the most distant object visible with the naked eye, takes about two million years to reach us.
* Light from the most distant star system yet recorded would take about 10 billion years to reach Earth.

Many astronomers measure such distances in parsecs. One parsec is 3.26 light-years.

CHAOS AND ANTI-CHAOS

'Chaos theory' was developed in the 1970s when it became apparent that linear mathematics was inadequate when dealing with systems such as meteorology, where tiny changes could lead to much bigger ones. US meteorologist Edward Lorenz, studying weather patterns, identified the phenomenon of 'sensitive dependence on initial condition'. This is summed up in the famous 'butterfly phenomenon', whereby the cumulative effects of a butterfly flapping its wings may eventually cause a hurricane on the other side of the world.

ORDER AND PURPOSE
The Anthropic Principle

Some astronomers argue that if there is an inherent tendency for chaos in the universe to resolve itself into the complex order of galaxies, solar systems and life-forms, there must be a purpose behind it all. This is where religion and astrophysics meet.

This tendency towards order is remarkable in itself, but some scientists say that even more remarkable is the fact that the kind of order which has developed in the universe is precisely that required for the evolution of life. The odds against the laws of physics being exactly right for this to happen are huge. If any of the forces involved in the Big Bang – notably the nuclear force or gravity – had been fractionally different, the universe could never have evolved so as to support human life.

The idea that the universe has somehow evolved in order to allow human beings to exist is gaining

been highly chaotic but smoothed itself out through frictional processes, the more traditional – and now more credible – view is that small variations developed over time. It seems that total physical uniformity is impossible in the universe: there is always a slight imbalance, leading to movement and evolution.

These slight variations in the density of gases in the early universe were exaggerated by gravity, forming galaxies – at first composed of swirling gas and then of stars – and then solar systems like ours, which display complex internal order. It seems that wherever there is chaos, there is a tendency for it to form into patterns; order is a fundamental tendency in the universe, as well as in the human mind.

RIGHT *Isaac Newton* **(1795) by William Blake. In 1794 Blake had pictured God also holding a pair of compasses. By illustrating Newton in similar style, he reflected the almost godlike status accorded to Newton in the 18th century.**

increasing popularity amongst astronomers. This line of thought has led to the formulation of the 'anthropic principle', which has four main variants:

WEAK: For us to exist, the universe must be such as to have allowed our evolution. So, for example, the Big Bang must have been at least ten billion years ago; otherwise there would not have been time for the universe, and life, to evolve as it has.

STRONG: There are other universes where the laws of physics are different and would not lead to the evolution of life. Inevitably we are in the one that has allowed us to exist. Our universe is as it is because we are as we are.

PARTICIPATORY: Without intelligent life to observe it, the universe would not exist.

FINAL: Intelligent life is an inevitable consequence of the universe's evolution, and once it has come into existence, it can never die out.

The anthropic principle perhaps represents the most radical statement of modern astronomical theory. In its extreme form it restores humanity to the absolute centre of the universe, so much so that the universe becomes almost a product of human imagination. Modern cosmology has returned to the land of ancient myth.

> 'God constructed the Cosmos as a Living Creature, one and visible, containing within itself all the living creatures which are, by nature, akin to itself.'
>
> Plato, *Timaeus*, 4th century BC

THE QUANTUM UNIVERSE

Throughout history human beings seem to have gained a curious satisfaction from thinking in fours. The Babylonians divided the sky and the earth into four quarters and the year into four seasons; the Egyptians believed the sky was supported by four pillars, the arms and legs of the sky goddess Nut; and the North American Lakota people divided time into four – the day, the night, the month and the year. The world was often divided into four sections, according to the directions of the compass or to the four extremes of the Sun's rising and setting. Aristotle, the first philosopher to analyze the mechanism of planetary motion, ruled that it had four 'causes', while modern astronomers list four fundamental forces (see box). In both ancient and modern cosmology the number four thus represents the coming into being of material order, binding together time and space.

The Greek philosopher Empedocles (*c*.493–433BC) suggested that all matter was composed of four elements – fire, earth, air and water – a conception of the world that was integral to astrology, science and medicine until the 17th century. Heraclitus, his contemporary, believed that the four elements were constantly mixed together by the 'upward and downward path' – fire moved up, earth down, and water and air found their respective places between the two.

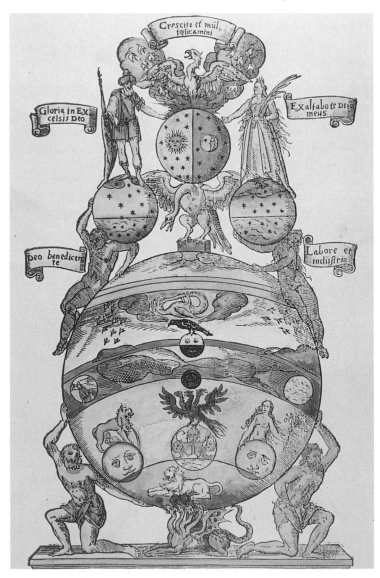

Whereas in the Western system there were four elements (with ether a possible fifth), in China the entire structure of science and cosmology rested on five, each of which corresponded to a planet: wood (Jupiter), fire (Mars), earth (Saturn), metal (Venus) and water (Mercury).

Fire was the prime substance, the one responsible for physical existence as it moved through the other three. The great modern physicist Werner Heisenberg (1901–76) commented: 'If we replace the word "fire" by "energy" we can almost repeat Heraclitus' statements word for word … Energy is the substance from which all things are made and energy is that which moves.' The idea that motion was essential to the universe was taken up by Plato, who was fascinated by the fact that while the Sun, Moon and planets rise in the east and set in the west, their movement through the zodiac is in the opposite direction. It was this motion, Plato believed, that made life possible – an idea later reflected in Einstein's argument that time only occurs when matter moves (see p.217).

Symbolic divisions of the world into four occur elsewhere, as in Buddhism, which sees the universe as being composed of particles, or 'indivisible units', which exhibit four basic qualities of matter: mass, cohesion, temperature and movement. These could be linked to, respectively, earth, water, fire and air.

However, in 1661 Robert Boyle published *The Skeptical Chemist*, redefining an element as a substance that could not be decomposed into simpler constituents. His work showed that the old 'elements' – fire, earth, air and water – could in fact be broken down into their component parts.

The attack on conventional belief was taken a step farther in 1787 when the French chemist

LEFT An allegorical model of the universe from Andras Libavicus' *Alchymia* **(1606). The symbols include, from top: the Phoenix, a symbol of rebirth; the Philosopher's Stone; the Swan (Mercury); and the four elements and cosmic dualities.**

UNIVERSAL FORCES
Modern science postulates four known forces that underpin our universe.
1. The strong or nuclear force, which binds particles together into atomic nuclei.
2. The electromagnetic force, 0.007 times the strength of the strong force.
3. The weak force, important in the decay of certain elementary particles.
4. The force of gravity, by which every body attracts every other body with a force proportional to the mass of each, diminishing steadily over distance.

As far as we know, these forces apply throughout our universe – although there may be other universes in which quite different forces and laws apply. At the Big Bang there may have been only a single force which then divided; some astronomers are searching for the 'single unified force', the force that links everything. This quest is essentially an illusion, a scientific version of the quest for the Holy Grail: experience shows that tidy discoveries do not last for long – perhaps the current four forces might be unified, only for another four to be discovered.

Another problem has been proposed by some supporters of Darwin's theory of evolution. They are suggesting that the laws of physics may themselves be evolving in order to allow the universe to continue to expand. This idea is consistent with the suggestion that the laws of physics have not always existed. According to current theory they only began to make sense at the 'Planck time' (named after Max Planck), which was 10^{-43} seconds after the Big Bang, at which time the universe achieved the 'Planck density', 10^{93} that of water.

Antoine Lavoisier discovered that air consisted of two gases (oxygen and nitrogen). With this the four-element world-view finally fell into scientific disrepute, although it has survived as an important symbolic component of various metaphysical systems, including astrology.

THE ATOMIC UNIVERSE

The concept of a single material unit, the atom (Greek *a-tomos*, 'cannot be cut'), was originated by the 5th-century BC Greek thinkers Leucippus and Democritus. They believed that the atom was the smallest possible particle and thought,

correctly, that different materials were produced when atoms joined together in different combinations.

Twentieth-century exploration of the universe has ranged from space expeditions and astrophysics to the hunt for the ultimately indivisible particle. It was not until the start of the century that the existence of atoms became widely accepted, by which time some scientists were already speculating that the atom itself could be divided.

The internal structure of the atom was established by physicists such as J.J. Thompson and Ernest Rutherford in the early part of the 20th century. They found the atom to be

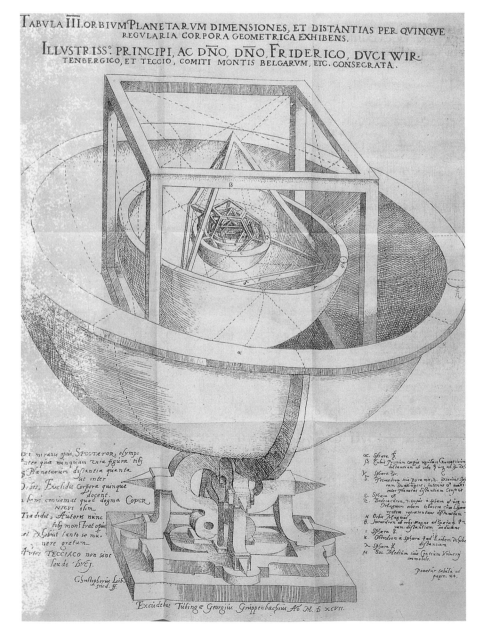

Johannes Kepler, influenced by the Greek philosophers Pythagoras and Plato, believed that the basis of the universe was geometric, and that every planetary orbit corresponded to one of five solid forms, such as a cube or a tetrahedron. This version is from Kepler's *Mystery of the Universe*, published in 1597.

composed of a tiny, positively charged nucleus consisting of protons (positive) and neutrons (with no charge), orbited by a number of negatively charged electrons. The latest evidence suggests that every type of particle has an 'antiparticle', and that these are the basic components of antimatter – mirror images of ordinary atoms, with opposite electrical charges. When both types of atom meet, as they sometimes do in the atmosphere, both are instantly converted into a flash of radiant energy.

Quarks were named by Murray Gell-Mann in 1963 from a line in James Joyce's *Finnegan's Wake*: 'Three quarks for Muster Mark.'

'There could be whole antiworlds and antipeople made out of antiparticles. However, if you meet your antiself, don't shake hands! You would both vanish in a great flash of light.'

Stephen Hawking, *A Brief History of Time*, 1988

THE SUBATOMIC ZOO

Such discoveries opened up deep microcosmic worlds, and in the 1960s it became apparent that on an even smaller scale a whole menagerie of particles existed. In 1963 the US physicists Murray Gell-Mann and George Zweig independently proposed the existence of 'quarks', particles that have no size and that carry a fractional electrical charge: they are simply moving points, with no substance in the normal sense. It seems that the Buddhist belief in the insubstantiality of matter may be borne out by science.

General relativity (see p.217) revolutionized our view of the universe's large-scale structure. Our understanding of the microcosmic world of the atom continues to develop, as we discover more about the strange way in which atoms behave. In 1900 Max Planck suggested that light, X-rays and other waves could only be emitted in fixed-size energy 'packets', which he called 'quanta' (singular 'quantum'). Quantum physics is a branch of science in which all previous preconceptions about the nature of material reality are turned inside out.

THE UNCERTAINTY PRINCIPLE

In 1926 Werner Heisenberg formulated his 'uncertainty principle', which rests on the fact that at least one quantum of light must be used to measure the position and velocity of a particle. This quantum will disturb the particle. Increased accuracy in measuring the position requires a shorter wavelength of light. The shorter wavelength has more energy per quantum, and this extra energy disturbs the particle more. So the more accurately a particle's position is measured, the less accurate the measurement of its velocity – and vice versa.

This is not just a problem of inadequate measurement: it implies a fundamental uncertainty in particle behaviour. Thus quantum mechanics predicts probabilities – not certainties. This effectively sounded the death knell for scientific determinism: the universe can no longer be pinned down to absolute laws. Nor can the observer observe without affecting what is observed.

PARTICLES, WAVES AND WAVICLES

A key feature of the quantum universe is the blurring of the boundaries between energy and matter. Particles sometimes act like little balls, or bullets, and sometimes like waves. The first hint of this duality came in 1801, when Thomas Young shone light through two adjacent narrow slits onto a screen. The fringe-like pattern produced suggested that light was a wave. Einstein's experiments a century later suggested that light came in particles,

Quarks come in six 'flavours': up, down, strange, charmed, bottom and top. Up and down are the commonest. Each quark comes in three 'colours': red, green and blue. Protons and neutrons have three quarks each – one of each colour. Protons have two ups and one down, neutrons two downs and one up.

or photons. Performing Young's experiment with single photons shows, remarkably, that both views are correct: a single photon, fired at two slits, divides in a wave-like way, passes through both slits, and re-emerges as a particle – or what some physicists would call a 'wavicle'.

The particle's ability to be in two places at once has given rise to a theory of parallel universes – the 'multiverse'. Bizarre though this sounds, it at least avoids the logical inconsistencies otherwise inherent in time travel (see pp.217–19).

The other implication of the strange behaviour of subatomic particles concerns consciousness. We know little about the relationship between the physical brain and the mind. But if the working of the mind is related to the particles of the brain, and these can be in two places at once and switch

between physical and non-physical forms, the theoretical possibilities for the nature of consciousness are immense. For example, telepathy may be physically possible.

SUPERSTRING

Both general relativity and quantum theory work in their own spheres, but attempts to create a 'grand unified theory of everything' have so far failed: the maths produces nonsensical infinitely recurring decimal fractions. However, there is one theory that looks promising: superstring. This suggests that particles are really vibrating loops – rather like violin strings – and that their frequency of vibration (the note they play) determines their type. This would surely have appealed to Pythagoras, with his 'music of the spheres' (see pp.225, 262). The

An image made with the Hubble Space Telescope's faint object spectograph, showing a rotating disc of hot gas in the core of the active galaxy M87. As the disc spins, the gas on one side of it (indicated here by a red circle) is speeding away from the Earth, while the gas on the other side (indicated by the blue circle) is approaching the Earth. The extremely high velocity of the gas is the sign of a tremendous gravitational field at the centre of the galaxy – evidence of a massive black hole. The object at the centre of M87 weighs as much as three billion Suns, concentrated in a space no larger than our solar system.

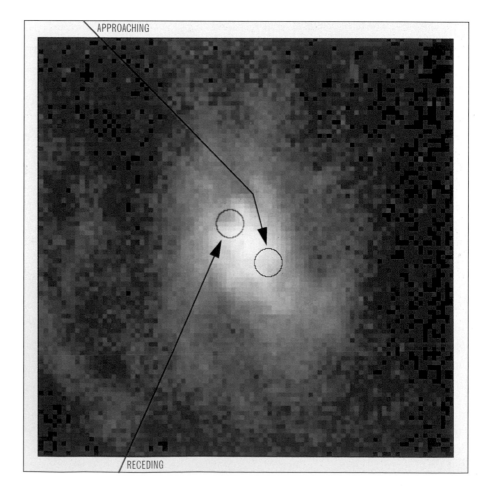

physicist David Gross appeals directly back to Pythagoras with another of his claims – that in superstring theory matter emerges out of geometry.

DARK MATTER

After the 17th century, astronomers decided that space was a vacuum. Now we know that space contains dust and gas – mostly hydrogen. In our part of the galaxy, current measurements indicate that space contains between one atom and 100 million atoms of hydrogen per litre.

Astronomers have difficulty accepting a space that is empty, or almost empty. Some have returned to the ancient Greek concept of 'ether' (a postulated fifth element composing the atmosphere), speculating that space may be made of something, perhaps 'dark matter'. Sound mathematical reasons underlie this conclusion, for when the centrifugal force in the Milky Way, which should throw stars out into space, is measured against the gravitational force produced by its known mass, it is found that about 90 per cent of the mass in the Milky Way must be invisible; the figure may even be as high as 99 per cent.

Those who support the existence of dark matter insist that if it does not exist then the laws of physics that connect mass to gravity are wrong. But there is another interesting conclusion. If the visible universe accounts for only 1–10 per cent of all matter, then it might not even be made of the same stuff as most of the universe. Our solar system might simply be a 'cosmic peculiarity'.

BLACK HOLES

In a sense the darkest of dark matter, because it swallows light whole, is that science-fiction favourite and modern answer to the mythological Hades – the black hole. Black holes have captured the public imagination much as they are said to capture anything that comes anywhere near them. They sound ominous, but they also tempt us with time travel and parallel universes.

Although the term 'black hole' was coined by US scientist John Wheeler in 1969, the idea was first posited in the late 18th century. Then, in 1928, a young Indian, Subrahmanyan Chandrasekhar, calculated that if a star of about 1.5 times the Sun's mass ran out of fuel, it would collapse under its own gravity to an infinitely dense single point. Although Arthur Eddington, the founder of astrophysics, and Albert Einstein claimed that this was impossible, astronomical observations suggest that Chandrasekhar was probably right. For example, the evidence indicates that the star system Cygnus X-1 consists of a normal star orbiting round a black hole, and that there could even be a massive black hole at the centre of our galaxy.

A black hole is a 'singularity': a point in the space–time continuum at which the space–time curvature becomes infinite. This happens because the huge gravitational force of the black hole bends space and time, so that even light cannot escape from it. This could in theory make time travel possible within the hole. Some scientists have speculated that black holes could lead to a fifth dimension. The astrophysicist Roger Penrose suggests that in black holes matter is either annihilated or passes through a 'wormhole' into another space and time (see pp.218–19).

CELESTIAL SITES

In the modern world temples to the stars are becoming fewer all the time. Probably the last official astronomical building in the West to carry any sacred overtones was the Royal Greenwich Observatory in London. John Flamsteed (1646–1719), the first Astronomer Royal (who, although sceptical about astrology, understood its rules), cast the Observatory's horoscope for its founding in 1675 – one of the final acts in Europe in an archaic tradition that the Earth is inextricably linked to the heavens, and that, to maintain harmony between the two, buildings should be designed on astronomical principles.

This practice remains notable in the West in the building of churches on an east–west axis – aligned with the rising and setting Sun. In the East, architecture is brought into the realm of the sacred through the practice of feng shui (a counterpart to Chinese astrology), by which buildings are

ABOVE 'Night work at the Greenwich Observatory' from the *Illustrated London News*, 11 December 1880. The observatory's importance was recognized when the line through Greenwich became the zero meridian.

constructed in harmony with natural earth energies – the same energies that, it is believed, permeate the entire universe. One of the most notable recent examples is the ultra-modern Hongkong and Shanghai Bank building in Hong Kong – designed by the architect Norman Foster, with final features incorporated in consultation with a feng shui expert.

SOLAR AND LUNAR ALIGNMENTS

Megalithic cultures flourished in Britain and western Europe between c.3500BC and c.1000BC, characterized by the stone monuments, or megaliths, that are their legacy. The greatest of these sites is Stonehenge, England, which appears to have been first laid out c.2800BC, and fell into disuse c.1000BC.

Stonehenge was traditionally held to be a Sun temple, a fact that inspired the antiquarian John Aubrey to make the first modern investigations, in the 17th century. In the 18th century William Stukely demonstrated the stone circle's precise geometrical design and in the 19th century the astronomer Sir Norman Lockyer made the preliminary investigations of the stones' astronomical significance. Yet it was the 1960s before retired civil engineer Alexander Thom and astronomer Gerald Hawkins concluded that Stonehenge, together with about 100 other stone circles in Britain, is aligned with the Sun and Moon. Stonehenge itself was a giant perpetual calendar, and could be used to predict the solar equinoxes and solstices, as well as the 18-year lunar cycle and eclipses.

The earliest known such site in the British Isles, dating to the 3rd millennium BC, is Newgrange, Ireland; its name is a corruption of the old Gaelic An Uamh Greine (Cave of the Sun). Newgrange consists of an outer circle of stones weighing up to 30 tons each, with a large and very well constructed mound in the centre. An entrance tunnel

Sunrise at Stonehenge, perhaps the most famous astronomically aligned megalithic site in the world. Astronomy and the regulation of the calendar were clearly of great importance to its builders.

leads to an inner chamber which would have been the focus for any rites associated with the site. The only clue to these is given by the presence of human remains, a Sun disc carved in stone and a shaft through which the Sun's rays penetrate to the inner chamber on the morning of the midwinter solstice. Whatever rituals took place were probably associated with death and rebirth – perhaps the Sun's rays were believed to transport the souls of the dead, carrying them to the afterlife.

EGYPT

More than 1,000 years later the Egyptians made use of similar ideas at the great rock temple at Abu Simbel, built by the pharaoh Ramesses II in the 13th century BC. Twice a year, on 21 March and 21 September, the rising Sun shone deep into the holy of holies, lighting up the three statues of Amun-Ra, Harmakis and Ramesses, all incarnations of the Sun, while leaving the statue of Ptah, the god of the underworld, in darkness. There were almost certainly links between the megalith-builders and the Egyptians, for trade routes existed between Britain and the Nile Delta. Whether such links were direct is another matter; perhaps ideas moved between the two cultures via staging posts in Spain or the Balkans.

The three pyramids at Giza, including the Great Pyramid, were probably constructed c.2690–2600BC, while the step pyramid of Djoser at Saqqara was probably built about 100 years earlier. However, recent studies of the Sphinx by Egyptologist John Anthony West and geologist Robert Schoch have shed doubt on the dating of Egyptian civilization: geological investigation has revealed water erosion that could indicate a possible date for the Sphinx of around 10,000BC. Astronomical evidence indicates that in 10,093BC the eye of the Sphinx was directly aligned with the star Cor Leonis, the Lion's Heart, which is significant because the Sphinx has the head of a man but a lion's body. If true, this would not only revolutionize the history of astronomy but overturn almost every theory about the dating of the earliest human civilizations. At present, however, most Egyptologists reject it.

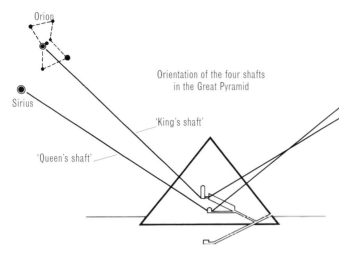

Orientation of the four shafts
in the Great Pyramid

Orion

Sirius

'King's shaft'

'Queen's shaft'

Ursa
Minor

Ursa
Major

Thuban

Draco

SACRED MOUNTAINS AND CELESTIAL ALIGNMENTS

In many cultures a sacred mountain serves to connect heaven to earth, such as Mount Olympus for the ancient Greeks or Mount Kailash in the Himalayas for Hindus and Buddhists. The first pyramids seem to have been built as artificial mountains designed to make the link to heaven in low-lying areas. They were temples, in or from which one could communicate with the gods and goddesses, and pyramids are found in a number of ancient cultures. The Sumerians and Babylonians after *c.*3000BC built ziggurats (stepped pyramids ascending to a flat top); the Egyptians constructed the first 'true', or straight-sided pyramids; while the last great examples were built by the Aztec and Mayan civilizations of Central America.

The 147-metre (481-foot) high Great Pyramid at Giza in Egypt is aligned with a number of stars. The main connections are made by so-called 'ventilation shafts' which run to the outside of the pyramid from the inner chambers. One pointed directly to Alpha Draconis, the then pole star. Others pointed to Sirius, the major marker of the Egyptian calendar, and to the three stars of Orion's belt, the brightest stars in one of the most recognizable constellations. These connections were thought to enable the pharaoh to remain in direct spiritual contact with the

ABOVE **Stellar alignments with the Great Pyramid. The constellation Orion was identified with the god Osiris. Thuban was the pole star.**
LEFT **The pyramids at Giza are one of the wonders of the ancient world. Although tombs, their true function was probably to maintain harmony between heaven and earth.**

stars that spelt out stability and survival in Egyptian belief. According to recent research, the three pyramids at Giza may have been part of a larger pattern, representing the three stars of Orion's belt, while the Nile was seen as an earthly reflection of the Milky Way.

In Central America several sites indicate the way in which pre-Colombian cultures designed their cities so as to reflect the cosmos. Perhaps the greatest astronomically aligned city was Teotihuacan, which was built around the beginning of the Christian era and flourished until c.750; during that period it was the most sacred city in ancient Mexico. The Aztecs later regarded the city with awe and gave it its name, which means the 'birthplace of the gods'; even in the 14th century its reputation was such that the Aztecs still buried their rulers there. Teotihuacan's pyramids rivalled those of ancient Egypt, and the greatest, the Pyramid of the Sun, rose 70 metres (230 feet) from a base the same size as that of the Great Pyramid. We can imagine the priests, decked in brilliant head-dresses and surrounded by clouds of billowing incense, performing the rituals required by the ferocious Sun god – including human sacrifice. The smaller Pyramid of the Moon was 50 metres (150 feet) high, but built on higher ground so that its summit matched that of the Sun Pyramid. Teotihuacan's main boulevard, the Avenue of the Dead, runs 15½ degrees east of due north, and at its southern end lies a third pyramid, dedicated to Quetzalcóatl, the Feathered Serpent. The pyramids are aligned with the surrounding mountains, suggesting that the entire city was seen as the focus of terrestrial and celestial forces. The Sun Pyramid also seems to have been aligned with the setting

of the Pleiades, a constellation that has been considered sacred in many cultures.

In North America archaeologists have identified three successive early cultures, known as the Adena, Hopewell and Mississippian, that built earth mounds and small, flat-topped pyramids typically indicative of human efforts to join heaven and earth. The Great Serpent Mound – a monumental serpentine earthwork – in Adams County, Ohio, has been ascribed to the Adena, which flourished between c.500BC and c.AD200 in the region. At the site of the Mississippian settlement of Cahokia, which was in use until c.1150, about twenty of the original 100 or so earth mounds remain; the principal mounds are aligned with the Sun as it rises over the largest mound at the summer solstice.

In India, Buddhism inherited the Hindu tradition of temples as sacred mountains. Buddhist *stupas* (domed reliquaries) are models of Mount Meru, the mythical sacred Indian peak and cosmic axis. In South-East Asia and China, *stupas* became pagodas, often with seven ornate tiers, which, as in other cultures, may represent the seven traditional planets, the seven days of the week, the seven Buddhist heavens or even the seven stars of the Pleiades. The Buddhist temple is a meeting point of time and space, a model of

Among the Pawnee of North America, communal houses were erected as mirrors of the heavens. The Pawnee pictured the universe as a giant turtle, and the earth lodge was an image of the cosmos:

'You see the head of the turtle is toward the east. That is where the gods do their thinking. While in the west, where you see the hind legs of the turtle, all things are created. The four legs [the four posts of the earth lodge] are the four world quarter gods [that] uphold the heavens.'

V.D. Chamberlain, *When Stars Come Down to Earth*, 1982

eternity, in which, through meditation, the supplicant can gain a brief unity with the cosmos.

Some of the most impressive Buddhist sites are at Angkor in Cambodia, Pagan in Burma and Borobudur in central Java, all of which have now fallen into ruin. The magnificent Shwe Dagon Pagoda in Rangoon, Burma, is still in daily use. According to legend the pagoda is 2,500 years old, although extensive additions were made in the 15th century. The main pagoda is a gilded *stupa*, 98 metres (326 feet) high and visible from all over the city. At its base, aligned with the points of the compass, sit eight planetary shrines – one for each day, with Wednesday divided into two (the morning is ruled by Mercury and the afternoon by Rahu, the Moon's north node). At auspicious moments, advised by their astrologers, devotees perform purification rituals at the shrines, in the process aligning themselves harmoniously with time and space.

The Muslim architects of the 9th–16th centuries, when Islamic culture was at its height, produced some of the most beautiful sacred buildings in the world. Combining rectangular and circular forms that represented the broad structure of the universe, and intricately decorated with geometrical patterns that were often based on planetary orbits, the mosque provided a harbour for the eternal soul in a world swept by the ravages of time.

SACRED DIMENSIONS

Like the Babylonians and Egyptians, the Hebrews believed that human society should be modelled on the cosmos. They also borrowed existing traditions that relied on the number six. The Egyptians divided the sky into 36 'decans', the Babylonians used units of 3,600 years to measure great historical periods, while in some accounts, Plato believed that after 36,000 years the planets arrived back at the points of their creation – and the world would come to an end. Such periods

The 16th-century Blue Mosque, Istanbul, Turkey. The combination of rectangular and spherical shapes represents the union of heaven and earth, bringing the worshipper into direct contact with the eternal.

were especially important in view of the 'ideal' year of 360 days, or twelve thirty-day months. All these figures were considered to embody the sacred principles of the Sun and had a special relevance for the earth's relationship with the heavens.

These sacred measurements are echoed in the Bible – the volume of Solomon's Temple was said to be 36,000 cubits. The dimensions of the New Jerusalem, the ideal city of the Kingdom of God in the Revelation of St John, are based on similar principles. Special mystery surrounds the number 666, the 'number of the beast' in Revelation, although we know from medieval occultism that it represented the Sun. In the early 1920s the antiquarian Bligh Bond, investigating the ruins of Glastonbury Abbey, one of the greatest ecclesiastical sites in Britain, claimed to have found evidence that it was designed after patterns based on the number 666.

Since then other researchers have suggested that a number of major medieval churches, including Chartres Cathedral in France, were designed according to a symbolic astronomical geometry which was lost in the Reformation of the 16th century. The last major British church to be built on such lines was the 15th-century King's College Chapel, Cambridge, believed to have been constructed around the number 26, whose sacred attributes were thought to relate to God.

Among the astronomical features incorporated in Roman architecture was the dome, which represented the vault of the heavens. Plato and Aristotle believed that the universe was spherical – the sphere being the most perfect geometrical form. The greatest complete surviving Roman building,

the Pantheon in Rome, was modelled on Platonic cosmology, and exactly contains a sphere: the distance from the floor to the apex of the dome (43.5 metres/143 feet) equals the diameter of the dome. Seven niches around the hall contained statues of the seven planetary deities. As a symbol of heaven, the dome was incorporated into the sacred architecture of both Christianity and Islam.

COSMIC ARCHITECTS

In the early 16th century Giulio Camillo designed perhaps the most eccentric example of astronomical architecture of the Renaissance. His Theatre of Memory was laid out according to planetary principles, so that each part of the theatre represented a different cosmic truth. It was named after Plato's theory that wisdom lies not in learning facts but in remembering the universal truths that the soul knew before it descended from heaven through the planetary spheres prior to birth. These ideas were taken up by other philosophers at the time, and later revived by the Austrian philosopher Rudolf Steiner (1861–1925).

Steiner was perhaps the last of the cosmic architects, believing, like Plato, that true wisdom consists of 'remembering' ancient truths of which the soul has always been aware. The belief that one's surroundings can affect this led him to lay great stress on his architectural principles. He devised an elaborate cosmology, in which different stages of spiritual development relate to the planetary principles. The buildings he designed, chiefly his headquarters, the Goetheanum, expressed the universal harmonies he found in nature.

6	32	3	34	35	1
7	11	27	28	8	30
19	14	16	15	23	24
18	20	22	21	17	13
25	29	10	9	26	12
5	5	33	4	2	31

THE SQUARE OF THE SUN, the grid for mediaeval magical exercises using the Sun, including sacred architecture.

Total number of figures	36
Sum of a row, column or diagonal	111
Sum of each symmetrical block of four	74
Sum of numbers round perimeter	370
Total sum of numbers	666

COSMIC CLOCKS

Human, animal and plant life is regulated by complex rhythms. Some cycles, such as the chemical changes that take place in our bodies at night, are relatively simple to measure. Others, such as the relationship between the menstrual and lunar cycles, are harder to pin down, so that, according to some researchers, the very existence of a relationship is open to question. Claims of physical connections between celestial cycles and physical processes must be rigorously tested. We may stand at the brink of a new science of 'cosmobiology', but progress is slow and evidence often difficult to obtain.

Central to cosmobiology is the study of cycles, especially the three major classes of cosmic rhythm. Of these, the best understood are those based on the rotation of the Earth – the difference between day and night. These are known as circadian or diurnal (see p.132).

Second are the annual rhythms based on the Earth's orbit around the Sun, which causes the seasons. Such rhythms are reflected throughout human society, and are obvious in the patterns of weather and plant growth. Some evidence indicates that a child's health, intelligence and career may all be influenced by its season of birth; other solar rhythms seem to be connected to the eleven-year sunspot cycle (see p.133).

Third are the lunar rhythms, based on the 'lunar day' of about 24 hours and 50 minutes (the time it takes the Moon to orbit the Earth) and the lunar month of approximately 28 days.

The existence of cycles linked to the planets is possible, although there are so many measurable

This Qing Dynasty woodblock print portrays the Chinese Kitchen God, with, above him, the lunar calendar for 1895. The lunar cycle is of central importance in the Chinese calendar system.

cycles on the Earth that it is easy to make a connection where there is none. Evidence incontrovertibly linking terrestrial to planetary cycles is therefore difficult, but not impossible, to come by. The success of some astroeconomists in matching stockmarket and commodity prices to planetary patterns is one positive example (see pp.254–5).

Is the weather connected to long-term celestial patterns? Long-term fluctuations in solar radiation are thought to have an effect, but science writers John Gribbin and Stephen Plagemann suggest other links. They claim that when Jupiter, Saturn, Uranus and Neptune are aligned on the same side of the Sun, as has happened on nineteen occasions since 1600BC, the result is a sharp disruption in global weather. The clearest such example was the alignment that accompanied the 'mini ice-age' of the mid-17th century.

grain were kept at a constant temperature and degree of moisture and isolated from any outside influence, showed that they germinated at the same season as ordinary seeds.

Confronted with such evidence, scientists in the late 1950s developed the concept of the internal clock. According to this theory, timing systems are written into the very fabric of our existence, being inherent in our biological structures, and thus are independent of changing cosmic environments.

However, evidence of direct cosmic connections emerged from experiments conducted by Dr H. Burr at Yale University, Connecticut in the late

CLOCKS OR INFLUENCES?

There are two possible explanations for cosmic clocks. Either organisms themselves are clocks whose rhythms sometimes match those of the Sun and Moon, or they contain clocks which are triggered by the planets.

The earliest researchers assumed that external, environmental forces, such as light and gravity, were exclusively responsible for connections between terrestrial and celestial rhythms. In later experiments, animals and plants were either subjected to or isolated from any obvious environmental factors. Some of the most famous investigations were carried out by Professor Frank A. Brown in the 1950s. He performed experiments on the fiddler crab, which changes its colour through the day, becoming dark at noon and clear at midnight. No matter what changes Brown introduced into the crabs' environment, their cycle stayed exactly the same. Their colour-changes matched the daily solar cycle even when they were protected against direct solar influences and had no means of knowing the time of day.

Other experiments of Brown's, in which seeds of

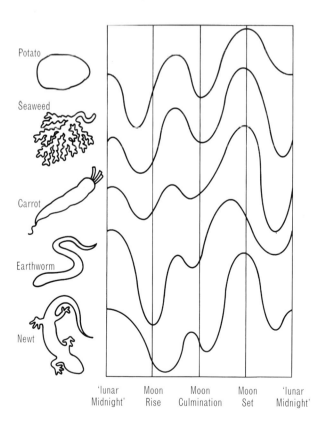

The metabolic activity of plants and animals, measured by oxygen consumption, varies with the lunar day (graph after Frank Brown, _Biological Clocks_, 1962).

Potato

Seaweed

Carrot

Earthworm

Newt

'lunar Midnight' | Moon Rise | Moon Culmination | Moon Set | 'lunar Midnight'

Multiple exposure of the midnight sun in Lapland. Normal solar and lunar cycles break down in the arctic and antarctic circles.

1960s. He discovered that if he ran a wire through a tree, the current produced by its natural electrical potential changed direction at regular intervals. He showed a link between these changes and the phases of the Moon and daily sunspot activity.

Further experiments by Frank Brown appeared to confirm the existence of lunar influences on the metabolic rate of potatoes, carrots and salamanders. His best-known experiment was conducted with the oysters of Long Island Sound, off New York. He sent the oysters more than 1,600 kilometres (1,000 miles) inland to his laboratory in Evanston, away from tidal influences. At first the oysters kept to their natural rhythm, opening and closing according to the familiar tides of Long Island. After about fifteen days, the pattern changed, and the oysters opened and closed according to

when the Moon passed overhead at Evanston – they had 'reset' themselves according to the local lunar pattern, indicating that it was not the tides that regulated their life-cycle, but a direct connection with the Moon.

There are a number of explanations for these and other results, but they all seem to centre on the existence of internal clocks, perhaps evolving aided by a 'genetic memory', and triggered by cosmic signals somehow transmitted in addition to light, heat and gravity.

> 'Persistent research has discovered that the influence of the Moon causes the shells of oysters, cockles and all shellfish to grow larger and again smaller in bulk, and moreover that the phases of the Moon affect the tissues of the shrew-mouse. Even the ant slows down at the New Moon.'
>
> Pliny, *Natural History*, AD77

ELECTROMAGNETISM

According to current scientific knowledge, the only probable means for transmitting celestial information to terrestrial organisms is electromagnetism (the magnetic forces produced by electricity). However, our understanding of electromagnetism is slight, and scientists disagree about its possible effects on human beings.

Astronomers have long known that the Earth's magnetic field varies in strength with the positions of the Sun and Moon, and that sunspot eruptions can cause disturbances on Earth, such as magnetic storms. Such storms have been linked to disruption in radio communications (which use electromagnetic waves). We know the intensity and direction of magnetic fields vary with the lunar day and the lunar month. We also know that certain creatures, including molluscs and pigeons, are highly sensitive to magnetic fields.

Such evidence may indicate a possible mechanism for solar and lunar influences, in which animal and plant life responds not to the Sun and Moon directly but to fluctuations in the Earth's electromagnetic field prompted by changing solar and lunar patterns. Added to the fact that Venus, Jupiter and Saturn are powerful sources of radio waves, and that Mars, Venus and Mercury affect the Earth's electromagnetic field, the idea of wider planetary connections does not seem impossible.

ASTROCHEMISTRY

Although astrochemistry is strictly defined as the study of molecules in space, it also extends to the investigation of the influence of planetary cycles on chemical reactions on Earth.

The first experiments, suggested by Rudolf Steiner and carried out by Frau L. Kolisko, were reported in 1926. Referring to the traditional planet–metal correspondences of medieval astronomy (see box on p.249), Kolisko looked for changes in the rate of chemical reactions involving these metals to determine whether they occurred at critical points in the relevant planets' cycles. With solutions of ferrous sulphate (iron, connected to Mars) and silver nitrate (related to the Moon), she found that the rate at which patterns formed on filter-paper varied according to the relative positions of the Moon and Mars. Kolisko obtained positive results with other planet–metal combinations, and her findings have subsequently been confirmed by other scientists.

Independently Giorgio Piccardi, Director of the Institute for Physical Chemistry in Florence, Italy, stumbled across solar and lunar influences on chemical reactions. Investigating ways to remove encrustations from boilers, he realized that an external force was affecting his experiments, and in 1951 he began to test for possible solar and lunar influences. Specifically Piccardi found that the rate at which bismuth oxychloride precipitates is affected by sunspots. Two of his associates found

The belief that chemical reactions are connected to planetary positions is hardly new – it was the basis of medieval alchemy. The alchemists' specific aim was to manufacture gold, yet alchemy also possessed a profound philosophical dimension. The transmutation of base metals into gold represented the spiritual union of the individual with the Sun (the metal connected to gold), itself representing the light of faith or reason, the soul of the universe. The medieval alchemists were practical astronomers engaged on a philosophical quest to discover the truth about the universe. Alchemy was also the forerunner of chemistry, and the last great alchemist was Isaac Newton. After his death conventional chemistry replaced alchemy in universities.

Illustration of an alchemist at work from a German woodcut of 1519, with the Arien ram next to the Sun. The alchemists' experiments were regulated by astronomy: it was believed that chemical processes varied with time and planetary position.

that naphthalene solidifies fastest at the New Moon and slowest at the Full Moon.

In his search for timing mechanisms Piccardi included one factor until then not considered – the Earth's position in the galaxy. Piccardi called this his 'solar hypothesis'. The Earth turns round the Sun, but the Sun is travelling around the galaxy. The Earth's position with regard to galactic fields of force is thus constantly changing. Piccardi believed

that this variation could explain the seasonal differences in the results of his experiments.

Kolisko and Piccardi opened up a new application of astronomy, revealing fresh truths about our place in the universe. Perhaps we should call the new science 'bio-astronomy'. Its implications are far-reaching: if we can measure planetary influences on inanimate chemical reactions, we may be able to measure them in living bodies containing chemicals.

In 1988 Percy Seymour, Senior Lecturer in Astronomy at Plymouth University, England, and a specialist in cosmic electromagnetism, devised a model to explain Gauquelin's findings. He noticed that the 'heredity effect' was strongest on days of high solar flares – when disturbances to the Earth's magnetic field are most pronounced. Usually such fluctuations would be too weak to affect human heredity or personality, but Seymour argues that planetary and solar influences on the Earth's magnetic field can be 'amplified' many times, and that the resulting disruptions explain the heredity effect.

THE EUREKA EFFECT

Seymour's work suggests that we should look not only at single planetary influences, but also at combinations of planets, on the basis that planetary alignments exaggerate disruption of the 'solar wind' and the Earth's electromagnetic field.

Two British scientists, Nick Kollerstrom and Mike O'Neill, have conducted research that looks at such combinations, taking as their basis the work of John Addey, one of the 20th century's leading astrologers. Addey believed that the separation of any two planets by 72 degrees (a quintile) or 51–52 degrees (a septile) stimulates the creative principle.

Kollerstrom and O'Neill collected birth data for famous scientists, and the times of the

> PLANET–METAL CORRESPONDENCES IN MEDIEVAL ASTRONOMY
> Sun – gold; Moon – silver;
> Mercury – mercury;
> Venus – copper; Mars – iron;
> Jupiter – tin; Saturn – lead

discoveries they had made. They called these times 'Eureka moments', and included major astronomical breakthroughs, such as Einstein's realization that his new theory of relativity accounted for unexplained features of Mercury's orbit. Kollerstrom and O'Neill found that Addey was right – that at Eureka moments there is a much higher than expected frequency of quintiles and septiles.

The 'Eureka effect' research suggests that moments of supreme human inspiration may have a cosmic dimension. Perhaps, as Jung suggested, we are 'psychically' linked to the planets. Such a conclusion supports the ancient Greek and medieval belief that our connections with the planets are spiritual, emotional and intellectual as well as physical. It also suggests that even our expanding knowledge of the planets progresses at moments of planetary significance. The phenomenon is perhaps the best evidence yet in support of the anthropic principle – the theory that there is a direct relationship between human existence and the nature of the universe.

HEREDITY

The French statistician Michel Gauquelin pointed the way to possible physical connections between human life and the planets with his research into planetary heredity. He found that if a parent was born with a particular planet rising over the eastern horizon or culminating (at its highest point), his or her child was likely to be born with the same planet in one of the two crucial positions. Gauquelin began to explore a new branch of astronomy – 'astro-genetics' – in which children might inherit planetary configurations.

WORKING WITH THE PLANETS

Most ancient societies believed that events on Earth were linked in some way to the heavens. It was therefore natural for them to use the movements of the stars and planets as a way of regulating their lives. Farming activities were dictated by beliefs about the stars' role in plant growth and animal husbandry. In the area of health and healing, the planets were used to aid with the diagnosis and treatment of disease. In the modern world, a number of banks and businesses now employ analysts who use astronomical-based techniques to forecast the financial future.

> French law from 1669 until the Revolution stated that timber could only be felled at the New Moon.

AGRICULTURE

In nomadic and pastoral cultures in which the calendar is set by the rising of the Sun or Moon with particular stars it is natural to imagine that those stars have a role in plant or animal behaviour. The Sun's influence was obvious, so might not its role at different times of the year be the result of some influence of the stars to which it was linked? From such observations have developed a range of traditions for regulating the farming year.

> 'If the goat-star [Venus] approaches Cancer the country's crops will recover; if an eclipse occurs on the fourteenth day the harvest of the land will thrive.'
>
> Babylonian Omens

The Babylonians used astrology to indicate the success or failure of the harvest as early as 2000BC. Our oldest astronomical–agricultural calendar is found in the Greek poet Hesiod's *Works and Days* (*c*.750BC). Hesiod advised farmers on using the Moon's phases, as did Cato, Pliny and Ptolemy in later centuries.

The dominant tradition states that crops should be sown, and harvested for immediate consumption, during the Moon's waxing; and harvested for storage during its waning. A variation is that root crops should be sown when the Moon is waning.

The planets were also believed to be influential. Traditional astrology associates each type of plant with a planetary 'ruler', and sowing or planting should take place when this ruler is well placed in the heavens. For example, hops, radishes, rhubarb and ginger are ruled by Mars, and are supposed to flourish if planted when Mars is in Aries, Scorpio or Capricorn.

THE EVIDENCE

There is convincing evidence that plant growth varies with Moon phase. In the 1930s, the chemist L. Kolisko found that wheat germinated faster if sown at the Full Moon than at the New Moon; and Professor Frank Brown (see also p.245) found in 1973 that water uptake by bean seeds was 35 per cent higher at Full Moon than at New Moon – a

In the Middle Ages it was believed that the cycle of the seasons, including agricultural activity, was embodied in the signs of the zodiac as well as the calendar. Haymaking took place in June while the Sun was in Gemini and Cancer, as illustrated by this scene from the 15th-century *Très Riches Heures du Duc de Berry*.

result backed up by later research. However, there is little evidence that the final yield is influenced. Evidence for the Moon's importance in cultivation is increasing in biodynamics, a system based on the work of Rudolf Steiner and refined by Maria Thun in the 1950s in Germany. The system uses the element (earth, water, fire or air) of the zodiac sign occupied by the Moon. Thun related each part of the plant to an element: roots – earth; leaves – water; fruit or seed – fire; and flowers – air. She categorized crops according to dominant part: potatoes – root; cabbages – leaf; corn – seed; broccoli – flower. Each crop must be planted when the Moon is in a zodiac sign of the appropriate element. Thun found that it was the Moon's position in the Indian sidereal zodiac (see p.11) that mattered, not the Western tropical zodiac. The system is used to apparent effect by organic market gardeners in Britain and Germany, and by an increasing number of French wine growers.

> 'The Moon showeth her power most evidently in those bodies which have neither sense nor lively breath; for carpenters reject the timber of trees fallen in the Full Moon as being soft and tender, subject also to the worm and putrefaction, and that quickly by means of excessive moisture.'
>
> Roman philosopher Plutarch, c.AD46–120

HEALTH AND HEALING

Most societies have a host of folkloric traditions which use the stars and planets to diagnose and treat disease. Many customs hold that the Moon and its phases can be used to ascertain both the appropriate treatment and the best time to apply it.

The fathers of Western medical astrology, with its complex methods of diagnosis and treatment, were Hippocrates (5th century BC) and Galen (2nd century AD), and from then until the reforms of Paracelsus (16th century AD) physicians operated according to the same set of assumptions. Essentially they believed that disease was caused by the influence of the stars, from which we get our modern word 'influenza'.

THE FOUR HUMOURS
Traditional astrological diagnosis was based on the theory of four humours, or physiological types (see box). Each had a corresponding fluid – black bile, white bile, blood or phlegm – and disease was caused when these were out of balance. Treatment aimed to balance out the domi-

nant humour in order to restore health, using a mixture of bleeding and herbal remedies. Nicholas Culpeper, the 17th-century herbalist, provides a good example: nettles are 'ruled' by the planet Mars and therefore considered hot and dry; thus they 'consumeth the phlegmatic superfluities in the body of man, that the coldness and moistness of winter hath left behind'.

Treatment could also include the use of talismans (magical objects thought to attract planetary influences), 'virtues' and changes in lifestyle. The Renaissance philosopher Marsilio Ficino recommended that individuals suffering from dour Saturnine complaints, such as depression, might cheer themselves up by wearing gold, the colour of the Sun, or by pursuing Venusian pleasures, such as eating and drinking.

The principle method of diagnosis was the 'decumbiture', a horoscope cast for the onset of the disease or the time of the consultation with the physician. Paying careful attention to the Moon's alignment with the other

planets, every three-and-a-half days the physician either re-checked the diagnosis or changed the treatment. The emphasis throughout was on time, and on matching the patient's individual cycles with the relevant planets.

THE FOUR TEMPERAMENTS
The system of humoral physiology has been brought into the 20th century by the philosopher and educationalist Rudolf Steiner and the psychologist Carl Jung. Steiner investigated the personality types of the humours, or 'temperaments', and saw that each person had a predominant temperament. He related this to physical type and to personality. 'Cholerics' are said to be energetic, impulsive, assertive, commanding, brave, but sometimes despotic; 'sanguines' are chatty, imaginative, adaptable, empathetic, but sometimes vain and superficial; 'phlegmatics' are calm, modest, shy, quiet, faithful, introspective, but often lacking in initiative and slow to adapt; 'melancholics' are inclined to live in the past and be rather pessimistic, self-absorbed and fearful, but may become philanthropic, compassionate and self-sacrificing.

Jung converted the humours into four psychological functions: thinking, feeling, sensation and intuition. Like Steiner, he acknowledged that everyone contains all four, but that in most people one is dominant.

THE FOUR HUMOURS IN MEDIEVAL ASTRONOMY
Choleric – fire – Aries, Leo, Sagittarius – hot and dry
Sanguine – air – Gemini, Libra, Aquarius – hot and moist
Phlegmatic – water – Cancer, Scorpio, Pisces – cold and moist
Melancholic – earth – Taurus, Virgo, Capricorn – cold and dry

COMPLEMENTARY MEDICINE

The past fifty years have seen the proliferation of methods of healing new to the West, many of which are often used with simple astrology, partly because they tend to emphasize spiritual or emotional states as much as physical symptoms. The two most notable are acupuncture and homeopathy. Acupuncture – the ancient Chinese practice of inserting needles into the skin – is a feature of traditional Chinese medicine, a system that relies heavily on the timing factors of Chinese astrology.

Along with medical herbalism, homeopathy is perhaps the most complicated of the Western forms

This illustration from the *De Secretis Secretorum* (*c.*1327), owned by Edward III of England, shows a king with a physician holding an instrument for bleeding on his left, and an astronomer with an armillary sphere (for observing the Moon) on his right.

of 'holistic' medicine'. Like herbalism, its basic assumptions are derived from traditional medical astrology, although instead of the four humours it takes the patient's spiritual, emotional, intellectual and physical states into consideration. It also assumes that certain conditions, and the remedies for them, are strongest at specific times of day.

ASTROECONOMICS

One of the most significant developments in contemporary astronomy is taking place not among astronomers or in observatories, but amongst business people and in finance houses. Astronomically based techniques are increasingly used to forecast the financial future, often with considerable success. These range from the computer-aided matching of financial with planetary data, to more traditional astrological techniques.

Astroeconomics is a method of technical analysis that can have enormous advantages over regular economic forecasting. Astroeconomists work by matching financial data to planetary cycles. Using the latest technology, researchers feed in sets of commodity prices and

'If Saturn governs the lot of fortune, he brings about power based on wealth and the amassing of riches, but Jupiter or Venus that which rests upon favours, gifts, honours and generosity.'

Ptolemy, 2nd century AD

exchange rates, and look for a match with a planetary cycle. In this way, astroeconomists can often forecast general price fluctuations years in advance, where more conventional methods fail.

Almost 4,000 years ago the Babylonians used the planets to anticipate good and bad harvests, which eventually meant higher or lower profits for merchants. In ancient Rome and medieval and Renaissance Europe, most educated people consulted the stars over their financial prospects. The Muslims used points in the sky to examine individual commodities. Astronomy was seen as the best forecasting tool; specialists in its different branches could tell a merchant whether his goods were safe or even locate lost treasure.

The founder of modern astroeco-

nomics was arguably W.D. Gann. Born in 1878 in Texas, he rose from humble origins to become the world's foremost market analyst, developing complex analytical systems based partly on biblical numerology and partly on planetary patterns. Following Gann, another stockbroker, George Bayer, formulated about forty planetary rules according to which financial movements could be predicted. One that has been used success-

The 16th-century astrologer William Lilly, who advised many of the leading figures in England at the time, including, indirectly, both King Charles I and Oliver Cromwell, used to cast 'interrogations' to help his clients. These were horoscopes cast for the moment a question was asked. Lilly would place great emphasis on planets in the second house, the section of the sky often approximately 30–60 degrees below the eastern horizon. He wrote that 'from the second house is required judgment concerning the estate or fortune, of his Wealth or Poverty, of all moveable Goods, Money lent, of Profit or gaine, losse or damage'.

Hong Kong by night. Chinese business thrives on the belief that there is a right time for every action, as indicated by a combination of astrology, feng shui and the traditional philosophy of Taoism. The Hongkong and Shanghai Bank building, whose modern design incorporates aspects of feng shui (see pp.236–7), is seen to the right of the green-capped tower.

worldwide stockmarket crash of 1987 took place on 19 October.

Impressed by such successes, the financial world is taking an increasingly serious look at astroeconomics, and by the early 1990s at least three banks in London were known to be employing astroeconomists.

In Hong Kong, one of the world's great entrepreneurial successes, astrology is an accepted part of everyday life. Chinese business people gain great confidence from their combined use of astrology and feng shui (manipulating natural energies in the landscape) and are repeatedly able to stay one step ahead of their rivals.

Astroeconomics exists almost entirely in the commercial world and is mostly unknown to academic astronomers. Yet its steady development may promise as great a breakthrough in our understanding of our place in the cosmos as does the latest astrophysics.

'Jupiter and the Moon in the same sign indicate the greatest good fortune, bestowing infinite riches... If Saturn is 90 degrees from Venus the natives will lose all inheritance and be reduced to beggary.'

Julius Firmicus Maternus, 4th century AD

fully anticipates reverses in the markets when Mercury moves direct and retrograde – that is, when it appears to reverse its motion through the zodiac.

In the 1980s, Dr Hamish Watson, a former lecturer at the London School of Economics, published work supporting the astrological tradition that the Jupiter–Saturn cycle correlates with ups and downs in the business cycle. Watson was one of a number of astroeconomists who

forecast the long recession in Europe and the USA that began in 1989. In 1986 two other analysts, Charles Harvey and Michael Harding, who had studied Gann's methods, predicted 'a very major correction' in the markets around 19–24 October 1987. In the event the

THE COSMIC STATE

The ancient Babylonian system in which human society and institutions were organized in order to reflect celestial harmonies is described as the 'cosmic state'. This term can also be used with regard to other ancient systems, including the Egyptian, Hebrew, Celtic, Greek, Chinese, Hindu, Maya and Aztec; and even in the modern Western world we find traces of the belief that astronomical ideas shape and influence social concerns.

Even today the ancient traditions of sacred monarchy survive in the coronation ritual. In Britain, the monarch is crowned by the Archbishop of Canterbury, who draws down the blessing of God. The crown is made out of the Sun's metal – gold – and its shape derives from the halo worn by the Greek Sun god Apollo, with stylized Sun's rays radiating from the centre.

BELOW The appearance of Halley's Comet in 1066 was taken as an omen both of the Norman conquest of England (seen here in the Bayeux Tapestry) in that year, and of the excommunication of the Holy Roman Emperor Henry IV in 1076.

THE HEBREW KINGDOM OF THE SUN

Perhaps the most famous example of a 'cosmic state' was the division of the Hebrews into twelve tribes. In fact, the administrative division of peoples into twelve groups was known throughout the ancient world. The Athenians were also divided into twelve 'tribes', and a similar system occurred among the Etruscans and other nations, including possibly the Celts. It was repeated throughout Hebrew history in different forms: for example, the book of Genesis relates that Abraham's son Ishmael was the father of twelve princes, while Deuteronomy records that the entire human race is divided into twelve. When Christ selected twelve disciples, therefore, he was following Jewish

custom based on these ancient ideas, thereby reinforcing the claim that he was preaching universal truths.

The rationale behind this form of organization, in which communities model themselves on the calendar, is rooted in a relative view of space and time: if the Sun's annual passage through the twelve months or constellations symbolically represented the spiritual totality of space and time, then by reflecting this basic principle in social organizations, the order and harmony of society would be preserved.

Such beliefs were central to the Greek philosopher Plato (*c.*400BC). Outlining the basis of a perfect society in his *Republic*, he argued that any rational society should harmonize itself with celestial principles, that

rulers should study astronomy and astrology, and that teams of thirty administrators should each govern for one month.

THE COPERNICAN REVOLUTION

Political theory was so deeply tied to astronomy that any astronomical discovery provoked an alteration in the way people viewed their societies and governments. When the long-held belief that the Earth was the centre of the universe was finally overthrown by Copernicus in the 16th century, a shift in the cosmic state resulted. Autocratic rulers, such as Louis XIV of France, the 'Sun King', used the new idea that the Sun was the centre of the universe to revive the ancient concept that the king held the same position on Earth as the Sun in the heavens, and must be obeyed because his position was sanctioned by heavenly laws.

Conversely, when Kepler and Newton discovered the laws of planetary motion the democrats were encouraged. They argued that if the entire universe, including the Sun, was governed by the same set of laws, all were equal and no king could assert that he was above the law. Eighteenth-century radicals, including the leaders of the American Revolution, regularly appealed to Newton's laws to justify their actions.

The French philosopher Auguste Comte (1798–1857), one of the founders of sociology, was also partly inspired by the latest astronomical ideas. He argued that the same mathematical laws that caused change in the heavens must also cause change on the Earth. The original motive behind sociology was to discover how these laws worked, and to this end the first social surveys were undertaken within a short time of Comte's death.

Nostradamus in his study, surrounded by the signs of the zodiac, an illustration from his prophecies for the eclipse of 16 September 1559, published in 1558. To people at the time, the eclipse signified the death of King Henry II in 1559 and the brief reign of his son, Francis II, who himself died in 1560.

POLITICAL ASTROLOGY

Theories of the cosmic state have long provided the rationale for the use of astrology by politicians. It is well known that in ancient and medieval times monarchs often relied heavily on astrological advice. Although the practice is rare in the modern world outside India and South-East Asia, there have been some surprising 20th-century instances. For example, in 1988 it was revealed that US President Ronald Reagan used an astrologer, Joan Quigley, and that she had advised Reagan throughout his delicate talks with Soviet leader Michael Gorbachev – negotiations that led to the end of the Cold War.

The first recorded instances

THE QUANTUM SOCIETY

The 'quantum society' is the term devised by physicist Danah Zohar and psychiatrist Ian Marshall to describe the similarities between social behaviour and the strange world of quantum physics (see pp. 233–4). In quantum physics the parts can only be understood in terms of the whole. Zohar and Marshall argue that, by contrast, 'reductionist' scientists, who analyze the world into ever smaller components, come up with misleading views of humanity and the cosmos. We are only now grappling with the social impact of the 20th-century revolution in astronomy — it has been argued that 'cultural relativism', in which no culture is seen as superior to any other, is a product of Einstein's theory of relativity, in which the universe no longer has a centre.

of royal astrologers occur in ancient Mesopotamia (present-day Iraq), shortly before 2000BC. At the centre of each Mesopotamian city stood the temple dedicated to the god or goddess who was the city's personal protector. Ur, for example, was protected by Sin, the Moon god; others were dedicated to Shamash (the Sun) or Inanna (Venus). During Babylon's heyday after c.1800BC the entire state was protected by Marduk, a god connected to the Sun but more especially to the planet Jupiter. It was natural to believe that political fortunes could be read in the planet's movements.

After c.800BC, when the Assyrian empire was at its peak in northern Mesopotamia, astrologers formed a sort of elite civil service. Their all-important advice was for the king only, and ordinary people were unable to use their services. Around 410BC, astrologers began casting birth charts both for kings and for the wealthy, and by c.100BC horoscopes were being cast for momentous events in the king's life, such as coronations.

From Augustus (ruled 27BC–AD14) onward the Roman emperors took to astrology with alacrity, believing that it offered them valuable insights into the future, enabling them to gain an advantage over their rivals. Nero's astrologer, Balbillus, was one of his most influential advisers, while some emperors, including Hadrian (ruled AD117–138), were themselves astrologers. However, after Christianity became the state religion in the 4th century, astrology was tainted by its association with paganism and fell out of favour.

In the East, political astrology flourished in Persia and India, and in the 8th and 9th centuries the caliphs of the Islamic empire began to encourage its study in their great institutions of learning, such as the House of Knowledge founded by Harun al-Raschid in Baghdad.

Around the year 1000, European scholars began to study at the Islamic universities, where they rediscovered classical learning, including astrology. In the Middle Ages many of the greatest scholars, such as St Thomas Aquinas and Roger Bacon, turned their attention to astrology, and by c.1200 it was common for rulers at the cosmopolitan courts of Europe to use astrologers. In England, Adelard of Bath advised the future King Henry II in his civil war against King Stephen in the 1140s, while Michael Scot worked for Frederick II (Holy Roman Emperor from 1215 to 1250), casting 'interrogations', or horoscopes designed to answer the emperor's questions.

The 16th century produced two of the greatest

In Rome unauthorized study of the emperor's horoscope was an offence punishable by exile — or even death. The 4th-century astrologer Julius Firmicus Maternus warned young astrologers to avoid this fate: 'No astrologer is able to find out anything true about the destiny of the Emperor. For the Emperor alone is not subject to the course of the stars and in his fate alone the stars have no power of decreeing.'

royal astrologers. One was Michel de Nostradame (1503–66), better known as Nostradamus, who was adviser to, among others, the French queen Catherine de' Medici. The other was John Dee (1527–1608), occultist, astronomer, alchemist, philosopher and secret agent. It was Dee who chose the time for Elizabeth I's coronation, helping to establish one of England's most successful reigns.

Astrology was regularly used in military matters. In the 13th century Guido Bonatti, the first and most famous of all Italian astrologers, set out rules for conducting battles and seizing castles according to planetary dispositions, and established his reputation after some notable successes. Astrology's military use was last seen in Europe during the English Civil War of 1642–9, when the astrologer William Lilly was taken to the siege of Colchester to give encouragement to the Parliamentarian forces – a favourable forecast from Lilly was said to do more to raise morale than a whole additional regiment of cavalry.

By the second half of the 17th century astrology was losing its popularity at court. Louis XIV was the last French king to have an astrologer present at his birth, in 1638. Charles II was the last British monarch to use astrology regularly, employing Elias Ashmole, one of the most notable scholars of his age, to set the time for his speeches to Parliament in the 1670s – an important task in a period when England was constantly in danger of slipping back into civil war.

Since then, monarchs have occasionally shown an interest in astrology, although the only member of the British royal family known to have consis-

---

Surviving Babylonian astrological omens tell us much about the ancient 'cosmic state'. According to one omen from *c.*2000BC, 'When the planet Jupiter turns his face when rising toward the west and you can see the face of the sky, and no wind blows, there will be a famine and disaster will rule. As Ibi-Sin, the king of Ur, went in chains to Ashan.' This tablet records a historical event, the capture of Ibi-Sin by the Elamites. The coincidence of the political event and the astronomical movement would have been recorded, and the next time Jupiter appeared in a similar fashion the astrologer would have warned his king to strengthen his defences.

---

tently taken astrological advice in recent times is Diana, Princess of Wales. In 1952 the British astrologer Charles Carter wrote that Prince Charles' horoscope was not a royal one, a view that has influenced all modern British astrologers. Could Diana's rejection of her destiny as queen therefore be partly seen as a self-fulfilling prophecy started by an astrologer many years ago?

Among the many myths about astrology's modern use by politicians is the belief that Adolf Hitler used astrologers. There is no evidence for this assertion, and everything we know about Hitler suggests that he despised what he saw as ridiculous superstition. Yet a few of the top Nazis did believe in astrology, including Heinrich Himmler, chief of the SS, and Rudolf Hess, Hitler's one-time deputy. The Nazi propaganda minister, Joseph Goebbels, used it cynically, turning out false predictions to mislead the masses. In a similar manner, the British used fake astrological magazines to forecast the defeat of Germany, with the intention of demoralizing ordinary Germans.

According to intelligence writer Richard Deacon, Mossad, the Israeli secret service, use a horoscope set for the date of Israeli independence in 1948 to keep an eye on threats to the country's existence. However, with a few such exceptions, the political use of astrology is generally confined to the Indian subcontinent and South-East Asia, where astrologers are often involved in key moments of state. In 1792 they chose the moment for the inauguration of Bangkok, from which the horoscope of Thailand is now taken. In 1948 they picked the time for the independence of Burma –

4.20am on 4 January 1948. Astrologers for the government of Sri Lanka (then Ceylon) chose the moment – 12.43pm on 22 May 1972 – at which the country became an independent republic. The Indian Prime Minister Indira Gandhi (1917–84) was the most notable of a number of political leaders to use astrology, and it is even rumoured that her astrologers warned her of the danger of assassination but that, as a Hindu and believer in destiny and reincarnation, she went bravely to meet her fate. In India in 1996, the failure of the Prime Minister, Narasima Rao, was attributed partially to the imprisonment of one of his astrologers on corruption charges.

Astrology's record as a political tool shows that it can make correct forecasts some times. It is best used when it offers advice rather than when it makes predictions. Yet an individual's benefit is not necessarily society's gain. Ultimately, astrology is no more than a tool, and has no more integrity than the astrologer, king, queen or politician who uses it.

Astrology has long been a feature of Indian politics. This Sanskrit horoscope of the prince Navanibal Singh is illustrated by the Sun in his chariot.

COSMOS AND CULTURE

The stars have been an endless source of inspiration to artists, both literally and symbolically, from pre-history to the present day. In ancient art, images of the stars and planets are pervasive. The earliest art was religious, and where religion was bound up with the stars people found as many ways as they could to represent the objects of their worship. In the classical world the myths of the planetary gods and goddesses provided a common theme for painters and sculptors.

The first writer to make extensive use of astrology as a literary device was the Roman Petronius (1st century AD), whose *Satyricon* vividly depicted the decadent existence under the emperor Nero. Most educated Romans accepted that the planets and zodiac signs revealed all that was best in human life. With tongue in cheek Petronius portrayed human behaviour as revealing everything that was most ridiculous in the stars.

In the Middle Ages and the Renaissance, astronomy was often the basis of art in both the Islamic and the Christian worlds. Islam forbade figurative art, and beautiful geometrical patterns were created out of the mathematics associated with the planetary orbits. In this way the universe, Allah's sacred creation, was used to create designs which covered mosques and reminded the faithful of his splendour. In Christian Europe the same planetary mathematics, learned from the Arabs, underpinned medieval sacred music. Gregorian chant was conceived as resting on the universal musical principles of the 'harmony of the spheres' (the sound supposedly made by the planets as they rushed through space), thereby helping to maintain God's creation in a smooth functioning order.

The great German mystic, scholar and composer, Hildegard of Bingen (1098–1179), saw in

Pythagoras believed that as the planets rushed through space they created sounds, and that music should recreate the perfect 'harmony of the spheres'. The distance between the planets represented the musical scale.

Earth–Moon – a tone
Moon–Mercury – a semitone
Mercury–Venus – a semitone
Venus–Sun – a tone and a half
Sun–Mars – a tone
Mars–Jupiter – a semitone
Jupiter–Saturn – a semitone
Saturn–Fixed stars – a tone and a half

Although Pythagoras' measurements were wrong, there may have been sound common sense behind his theory. Music is based on timing, or tempo, and it is now thought that its appeal is based on the connections of its rhythms to the complex biological clocks that regulate our brains and emotions. If we can show that these patterns correspond to planetary cycles then we have a common thread running through musical and planetary rhythms.

'The Universe is good not when the individual is a stone, but when everyone throws in his own voice toward a total harmony, singing out a life.'

Roman philosopher Plotinus, 3rd century AD

> 'Countless signs will appear in the Sun, Moon and stars, in the waters and in the other elements as well as in all creation, so that people will be able to predict the disaster that is to come through these signs as through a painting.'
>
> Hildegard of Bingen (1098–1179), for whom the sky was a canvas on which God revealed his plan for humanity.

the stars clues to God's grand design for humanity, past, present and future. Her reading of the Hebrew Scriptures (Old Testament) led her to believe that the apocalypse (Christ's second coming and final battle with Satan) would be presaged by celestial omens. Hers was typical of the medieval mind, which saw the stars as God's messengers, revealing his intentions and wishes through their symbols and images.

WRITING

The first great English poet, Geoffrey Chaucer (c.1342–1400), was also a serious student of astronomy. He applied his knowledge to great effect in his *Canterbury Tales*, relying on the public's understanding of astrology to flesh out his plots and characterization. For example, we are told that the Wife of Bath was born with Mercury in Pisces and Venus in Gemini. The 14th-century audience would have understood the significance immediately: Venus, representing emotions, was weak in Gemini, and Mercury, signifying the mind, was poorly positioned in Pisces. Through his celestial code Chaucer indicates that the Wife of Bath was selfish, over-emotional and unable to think clearly.

William Shakespeare (1564–1616) also used the stars as metaphors and messages. Perhaps the most notable example is *King Lear*, which was in part a treatise on the 'cosmic state', the theory in which political events are regarded as inseparable from planetary cycles (see p.256). The play is, of course, many other things, including a commentary on the nature of kingship and ambition and on the relationship between parents and children. But for Shakespeare and his contemporaries

The Wife of Bath from Chaucer's *Canterbury Tales*.

William Blake, one of the 18th century's great visionaries, did not practise astrology himself, but collaborated with the astrologer John Varley in various experiments. In one of these, Varley would work out the degree of the zodiac rising over the horizon when Blake produced spontaneous visionary drawings. The two men concluded that Blake's moments of inspiration were closely related to the unfolding of universal truths as revealed through the rotation of the Earth and stars. The only surviving example is the 'Portrait of a Flea', which they decided was related to Gemini.

The visual arts in Japan often represent cosmic truths as revealed in nature – as in this Zen garden, which combines raked gravel with rocks, like mountains rising from the sea.

human actions could always be understood through greater universal patterns. The action in *King Lear* opens immediately after a series of eclipses: just as the lights in the sky had been temporarily extinguished, so the light of reason on Earth is to be temporarily eclipsed by greed, lust for power and, eventually, the king's madness. As the play ends, the cosmic order is restored and harmony returns to life. Whether or not Shakespeare himself believed in astrology, it was part of the world around him; the debate on the relationship between free choice and fate was central to Renaissance thought, and Shakespeare participated in it through his dramas.

The works of other writers frequently contained astrological references, such as John Webster's play *The Duchess of Malfi* (1623) and Edmund Spenser's poem *The Shepheardes Calendar* (1579); John Dryden and William Congreve also used astrologers to set the scene. François Rabelais (*c*.1494–1553) and Jonathan Swift (1667–1745) each published satirical imitations of astrological almanacs. William Hogarth, another satirist, included a horoscope in his illustration to Samuel Butler's *Hudibras* (1663–78), and Laurence Sterne used astrology to reinforce his discussion of Martin Luther's life in *Tristram*

Shandy (1759–67). Johann von Goethe, perhaps the greatest German poet of the 18th century, was a devout believer in astrology, and began his autobiography by setting out the planetary positions at his birth.

RECENT DEVELOPMENTS
The 19th and early 20th centuries saw a massive increase in artistic interest in fringe cosmologies, encouraged by the development of spiritualism and the foundation of the Theosophical Society by Helena Blavatsky and Henry Olcott in 1875. An artistic New Age was seen as the natural counterpart to the spiritual New Age prophesied by Blavatsky, and many artists were

Abbey Theatre), of which he was co-founder. One of his greatest works was *A Vision* (1925), a poetic view of history in which human life unfolded in great patterns analogous to the phases of the Moon. Astrology had an equally profound effect on the English composer Gustav Holst. *The Planets* orchestral suite (1914–16) was partly inspired by meditations on his own horoscope and dealt with the 'seven influences of destiny and constituents of our spirit'. Holst was especially influenced by a 19th-century astrologer called Raphael, whose book concerning the planets' role in world affairs led Holst to develop the grand vision of the planets that made *The Planets* such an enduring success.

A handful of writers continued to make clear their deeper commitment to astrology. Henry Miller devoted a substantial section to discussion of the attributes of Saturn in *The Colossus of Maroussi* (1941); the poet Louis MacNeice (1907–63) wrote an astrological textbook. The spread of newspaper horoscopes over the last fifty years has made astrology as familiar to a modern audience as it was in the 17th century, and its role as a literary device has been restored; modern dramas often have characters referring to their birth signs or daily horoscopes in order to establish an element of character or plot.

influenced by Blavatsky's mystical reverence for the universe and her belief in astrology. The Modernist movement drew heavily on theosophy's mystical cosmology, and the composers Arnold Schoenberg and Aleksandr Scriabin, the painters Paul Klee, Wassily Kandinsky and Piet Mondrian, and the architect Walter Gropius all carried theosophical principles into their own fields.

The Irish poet W.B. Yeats also took the new mystical attitude to the stars into his work. A practising astrologer, Yeats was an enthusiastic member of the Theosophical Society, as well as of the more deeply occult Order of the Golden Dawn. Many of the horoscopes he cast are set for important events in the Irish National Theatre (now the

THE SEVEN LIBERAL ARTS
In medieval Europe university education was divided into seven areas, each represented by a planet. They were seen as operating in ascending order, beginning with grammar and culminating in astronomy/astrology, after which wisdom was achieved.

Astronomia (Astronomy and Astrology)	Saturn
Geometry	Jupiter
Arithmetic	Mars
Music	Sun
Rhetoric	Venus
Dialectic	Mercury
Grammar	Moon

SCIENCE AND FICTION

A major feature of ancient astral mythology was the sheer number of invisible beings that populated the universe, from gods and goddesses to spirits, ghosts, demons, gnomes, wood nymphs and leprechauns. There are definite patterns to the stories about such creatures which suggest an important psychological function, echoed in the science-fiction fantasies that have become our modern-day mythologies.

Important in the mythology of the invisible being is the messenger figure, the angel or deity who communicates wisdom and prophecies from the other world, such as the Angel who informed the Virgin that she was pregnant with the son of God. Information revealed by such figures has the sanction of divine authority and so can never be disputed. Another archetype is the celestial parent, usually, a creator god or goddess, such as the Great Mother of ancient matriarchal religion or the patriarchal father god of the Hebrews. It was usual to describe individual gods or goddesses as parents, and in this role they both punished the guilty and protected the innocent.

There is often a close relationship between such invisible beings and the stars and planets. The most important deities, such the Egyptian Nut, Babylonian Anu or Hebrew Yahweh, had power over the whole sky. Yet most invisible beings are just like us, crowding their own world; even the planetary deities, such as Mars and Venus, were driven by human passions.

Why have we created this invisible world? Perhaps we long for companionship. Perhaps the very idea of being alone in an endless, cold universe is unbearable. If the universe were empty of other intelligent life we would be responsible for everything in our power; yet we would also raise ourselves to the level of gods, with no rivals. So we have made a pantheon of unseen companions, some friendly, some hostile, but all superior to us in

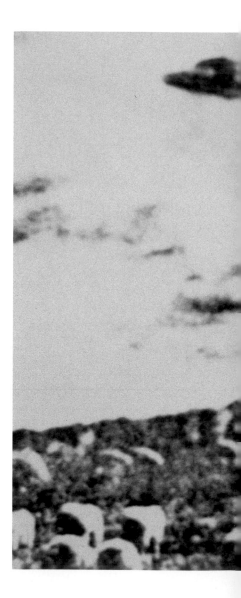

A supposed Unidentified Flying Object (UFO) photographed in Queensland, Australia, in 1954 by W.C. Hull. Some UFO photographs are hoaxes, others optical illusions, while still others remain, literally, unidentified. If we are being visited by aliens, we must ask why they never reveal themselves to people with influence or power. The conclusion is probably that they do not really exist.

knowledge, wisdom and power. They are like us, yet different. Psychologically we might say that they are our shadow, the 'other', that part of ourselves we fail to recognize or long to be.

Modern science fiction has converted the ancient spirits and deities into aliens, yet they have lost none of their power. In classical myth Mars was the god of war, and in science fiction, the Earth is attacked by ferocious Martians. A UFO or time machine is a technological version of a Sun-chariot or winged unicorn, while Superman, the hero from Krypton and saviour of humanity, is an embodiment of the same mythological archetype as Hercules.

SCIENCE, FICTION AND REALITY

Fantastical stories that could be described as science fiction existed long before the Industrial Revolution, but tended to use extraterrestrial settings as vehicles for satire and social comment. In Jonathan Swift's imaginative satire *Gulliver's Travels* (1726), Gulliver visits what are ostensibly far-flung regions of the world, yet he might just as well be on another planet.

By the end of the 19th century, when most of the globe had been mapped, authors were increasingly interested in the theoretical possibilities opened up by advances in science and astronomy.

Jules Verne (1828–1905), one of the first true science-fiction writers, wrote about fantastic journeys to the centre of the world, the bottom of the sea and the Moon. Verne's writing has been called 'scientific fiction' because it explores real science rather than taking liberties with it for the sake of fantasy.

Science fiction has shown a consistent concern with themes such as alien invasion, biological change or catastrophe, space warfare and time travel – with varying emphasis on fantasy. As technology advances in real life, so new motifs appear in fiction – lasers, real-life space travel, robots, the threat of nuclear holocaust, artificial intelligence and genetic engineering. Science fiction deals with the promises offered by technology, but also with its threat, from machines that enslave us to aliens who threaten our existence. A major preoccupation has always been the idea of alien life-forms, and increasing evidence that non-human life does not exist elsewhere in our solar system is

An advertising poster for the film version of H.G. Wells' *War of the Worlds* (1953). On 30 October 1938, Orson Welles famously broadcast a dramatization of the novel in the United States which caused widespread panic: many of the millions of listeners believed it to be a factual report of the invasion of New Jersey by Martians, and fled their homes.

likely to force authors farther out into the stars, making fictional use of sophisticated technology, thought-power or parallel universes.

LUNAR LANDINGS

To early writers looking for a feasible space destination, the Moon, our nearest neighbour, seemed a good candidate. The Greek writer and philosopher Lucian (*c.*AD115–200) set his imaginary travelogue *A True History* on the Moon. Johannes Kepler wrote about a lunar astronaut in his story 'Solemnium' (1631). In Edgar Allen Poe's semi-satirical story 'The Unparalleled Adventure of One Hans Pfall' (1839), the Moon is populated with 'ugly little people', each of whom is somehow intimately connected to an individual on Earth – just as the Moon itself is connected to Earth.

Perhaps the best-known lunar story is by 'the father of science fiction', H.G. Wells. In *The First Men in the Moon* (1901), two men, Cavor and Bedford, travel to the Moon in a sphere coated with a wonderful substance invented by Cavor, known as Cavorite. The qualities of this substance anticipate late 20th-century particle physics and in particular

Paramount Presents "THE WAR OF

Produced by George Pal   Directed by Byron Haskin   Screen
These stills are copyright. They must not be traded, resold, given away or suble

the theory that gravity may consist of particles, or 'gravitons'. Cavorite's essential property is its impermeability to 'all forms of radiant energy' – including gravity. One of Wells' most interesting plot devices (see also box opposite) is his depiction of the Moon as hollow, echoing the 'hollow Earth' genre of early 19th-century science fiction. He places a sea at its centre – a physical impossibility, but an intriguing idea none the less.

geophysical and human problems it has to face, while Kim Stanley Robinson's *Red Mars* (1992) focuses on a project to make the planet inhabitable.

The alien proper in modern science fiction originated with H.G. Wells' Martians in *War of the Worlds* (1898), human-like creatures who had become terrible through the harsh environment of their decaying planet. Wells was concerned as much with moral lessons as with science fiction, attempting to warn his fellow humans about their potential fate if they continued to abuse and exploit the Earth and each other. His Martians had once been like us, before they set out on their course of moral decay; we, therefore, might end up like them.

Wells had heard Thomas Huxley's famous lectures on evolution, in which the Darwinian biologist outlined the idea of

"IE WORLDS" Color by TECHNICOLOR CERT. X

Barre Lyndon   Based on the Novel by H. G. Wells.
hey should be returned to. Paramount Film Service after exhibition.

NEXT STOP MARS

After the Moon, the most popular destination for science fiction voyagers is Mars – although Venus has achieved almost equal popularity as a tropical home for prehistoric animals and cave-people. Recent Martian novels have perhaps been inspired by US president George Bush's announcement in 1990 of plans to send human explorers to Mars by 2019. Ben Nova's *Mars* (1992) is an imaginary account of the first international expedition, with all the

In *The First Men in the Moon*, H.G. Wells' 'wild and desolate' Moon is similar to the real thing; 'We were in an enormous amphitheatre, a vast circular plain, the floor of the giant crater. Its cliff-like walls closed us in on every side. From the westward the light of the unseen Sun fell upon them, reaching to the very foot of the cliff, and showed a disordered escarpment of drab and greyish rock, lined here and there with banks and crevices of snow.' The Apollo astronauts discovered no snow on the Moon, although ice was found in 1996. However, Wells gets some other details right, such as the dark daytime sky, the near horizon (because the Moon is smaller than Earth), and – most effectively – the low gravity.

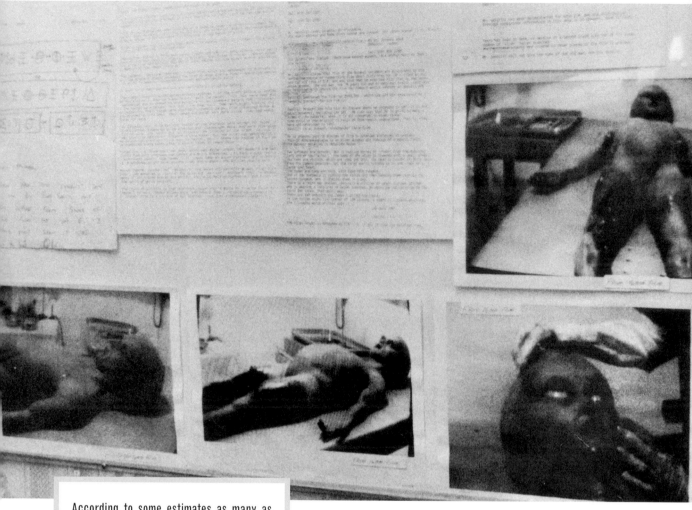

According to some estimates as many as 50,000 people in the USA claim to have been abducted by aliens. A 1996 *Newsweek* poll, coinciding with the release of the alien-invasion movie *Independence Day*, discovered that 48 per cent of North Americans think UFOs are real and 29 per cent think we have made contact with aliens. Other mythologies are involved in this: 48 per cent think that the government is covering up UFO contacts, a figure in line with many North Americans' propensity to see government as inherently wicked.

competition between different species. Portraying the Martians as competing against humanity for land and therefore locked into inevitable conflict, Wells began the tradition of aliens as the invaders from outer space that was later immortalized in Hollywood movies.

ALIENS AND ARCHETYPES

A curious feature of science-fiction aliens is their one-dimensional characters: they are generally either evil, devouring monsters or supremely wise spiritual saviours. There seems to be little ground between the terrifying monster in the movie *Alien* (1979) and the gentle, compassionate extraterrestrial in *ET* (1982). In *Star Trek*, perhaps the most successful of all science-fiction series, each alien species represents a different facet of the human character: the

LEFT **A display of the Roswell 'alien autopsy' featured in the documentary film released in 1995. Although probably a hoax, the film fed popular belief in alien visits.**

Vulcans are embodiments of reason, the Ferengi greedy capitalists and the Romulans murderous killers. As mythology is full of stories of people who come face to face with their doubles, so each race of alien seems to reflect an aspect of ourselves that we need to understand, or with which we need to be reconciled.

UFOS: A MODERN MYSTERY

About fifty years after Wells' *War of the Worlds*, fiction began to blend into fact with sightings of 'flying saucers' or Unidentified Flying Objects (UFOs), a phenomenon that by the 1950s had become an accepted part of modern life. Claims to have experienced visitations from other planets are almost impossible to prove or disprove. Many sightings turn out to be weather balloons or other such objects, or optical illusions caused by, for example, atmospheric conditions. A small number, however, remain unexplained.

In 1954 the psychologist C.G. Jung suggested that collective hallucinations could be responsible. He believed that flying saucer sightings were modern visions, much like ancient religious visions; they were a symptom of the psychic distur-bance afflicting the Western world in an age of total war, the atom bomb and the collapse of organized religion, all of which he thought were symptoms of the cultural upheaval as the Age of Aquarius approaches (see p.105). In other words, as one millennium gives way to another, human beings once again look to the heavens for signs of hope or judgment.

ALIEN VISITATIONS

Following the first UFO sightings came stories that aliens had been sighted. Through the 1950s and 1960s they were usually seen as benign visitors; some people hoped that the aliens had come to teach humanity the wisdom necessary for us to move into the New Age. Such longings drew on the widespread ancient belief that knowledge had been brought by beings from the sky, but also on the best-selling works of Eric von Daniken, whose book *Chariots of the Gods* (1968), a cult classic, promoted the idea that the Egyptians, Aztecs and other ancient peoples had been in touch with aliens.

In the 1980s, aliens achieved a new, more chilling dimension – as abductors. It is perhaps no coincidence that alien-abduction stories began to circulate at about the same time as courts in the US began to take rape much more seriously as a crime, that AIDS was producing a fear of sex, and that an unprecedented degree of child abuse was being brought to light. In this atmosphere, the aliens moved from being kind teachers to ruthless abusers – a switch of roles both reflected and reinforced by the film *Alien*, in which the alien is a sexualized monster who kills her victims by using them to incubate her embryos.

The most celebrated UFO incident is the so-called 'Roswell incident'. This dates back to 1947 when the US Army Air Force allegedly recovered remains of a crashed 'flying disc', together with alien bodies, near Roswell, New Mexico. Around 1979–80 a number of UFO writers started publicizing the incident, accusing the US government of a gigantic cover-up. In 1994 the Air Force eventually responded, refuting ufologists' claims and asserting that the remains were those of a balloon which had been part of the top-secret 'Project Mogul', designed to monitor Soviet nuclear tests. But the official report was overshadowed by a documentary shown the following year, which included footage purporting to show an autopsy on at least one of the aliens recovered at Roswell. The film made global news, yet a number of features, including the amateurishness of the camera operator and the surgeons, suggests that it was a hoax. Although the truth is still not known, the interest generated by Roswell bears witness to our hope that there is other intelligent life in the universe.

REACHING FOR THE STARS

To the ancient Greeks and Chinese, space was a divine realm inaccessible to ordinary mortals. A favoured few were turned by the gods into ever-shining constellations, but for an ordinary human to trespass in the celestial realms was to court disaster through hubris, or presumptuous pride. Thus when the ingenious Daedalus made wings so that he and his son Icarus might escape the Labyrinth, Icarus flew too close to the Sun, the wax holding his wings together melted, and he plunged to his death.

> 'It is in the highest degree unlikely that this Earth and sky is the only one to have been created.'
>
> Roman philosopher Lucretius, *On the Nature of the Universe*, 1st century BC

This story may have passed through the minds of those responsible for the first space flights. Humanity had come a long way since the Wrights' first powered flight in 1905; but could we really reach for the stars and return unscathed?

Human beings' longing for flight quickly expanded into dreams of escaping entirely from Earth's confines. Just as the great Renaissance voyages of discovery were made possible by monarchies seeking wealth, power and glory, so the motives behind space exploration were often mixed. Space exploration had close ties with the military, both in technology and personnel; 'mastery' of space would clearly confer military advantage. Added to this, space became a stage on which the USA and the USSR vied for the premier position – neatly symbolized by the American flag planted on the Moon. Even for humanity as a whole, space exploration was as much a matter of conquest as of discovery.

Icarus Falling by **Paul-Ambroise Slodtz (1702–58). The story of Icarus is more than an early tale of space flight. It is a warning to humanity not to try to reach heaven – or play god.**

> The idea that there are other earths – and other heavens – can be traced back to a Sumerian incantation of the 3rd millennium BC which reads '*an-imin-bi ki-imin-bi*' – 'the heavens are seven, the earths are seven'.

Much has changed since Neil Armstrong's first, historic Moonwalk of 20 July 1969. The urge for conquest has dwindled, and the end of the Cold War has combined with economic pressure – and perhaps even common sense – to convince nations that cooperation is preferable to rivalry and duplication. Scientific discovery has become the principal reason for space exploration, although even scientific motives vary, from the simple desire to learn and understand, through the search for life beyond Earth, to the possibility that we may one day want, or need, to colonize other planets.

ASTRONAUTS AND ROBOTS

The Russians were the first into space, when Yuri Gagarin orbited Earth once in Vostok 1, landing after 1 hour, 48 minutes, on 12 April 1961. Less famous, but more well-travelled, was the first woman in space, Valentina Tereshkova, who orbited Earth 48 times on 16–19 June 1963.

In the popular imagination nothing has equalled the first Moonwalk, even though nine humans have been to the Moon since then. It inspired humanity, and it did so because ordinary people could identify with flesh-and-blood astronauts: they were super-heroes involved in the making of modern myth.

Since then a host of unmanned space probes have travelled to the Moon and planets, and even beyond. Pioneer 10 provided close-ups of Jupiter in 1973, and in 1983 was the first probe to leave the solar system. Pioneer 11 encountered Jupiter in 1974, and went on to fly by Saturn. Voyager 1 flew past Saturn in 1980. Voyager 2 did the same in 1981, and then sent us spectacular photographs of Uranus in 1986 and Neptune in 1989; it is now studying ultraviolet sources among the stars, and searching for the heliopause (where the Sun's influence ends).

The first Venus landing was by the Soviet Venera 3 in 1965. Our first good look at Mars came through robot eyes: Viking Lander 1 landed on 1 July 1976, sending us a wealth of surprising information, including the disappointing news that there was no sign of life. In 1986 the Japanese joined the space programme, sending two craft to investigate Halley's Comet.

THE WAY AHEAD

A major development is the increase in international cooperation. For example, the Hubble Space Telescope, an orbiting observatory launched in 1990, is operated jointly by NASA and the European Space Agency. The most ambitious international project is the Alpha space research station, backed by the US, Russia, Canada, Europe and Japan, and due to be up and running by 2001. The cooperation that made this possible began with the NASA space shuttles Discovery and Atlantis linking up with the Russian space station Mir in 1995.

THE SEARCH FOR LIFE

One branch of the space research programme focuses on the search for intelligent life. If life that had evolved separately from life on Earth were to be discovered it would be the most dramatic scientific discovery of our time, perhaps the most important ever. It would force a fundamental change in our perceptions, opening up to us the real possibility that human

HOW TO DEFINE LIFE

Scientists used to think that life had to be based on carbon; then silicon was included. Then it was thought that all life had to be based on DNA. In 1996 British scientists announced that they had created life that was not based on DNA. But if we define life according to our own experience, then we might not recognize it when it appears.

The Hubble Space Telescope was launched in April 1990 and has enabled us to see farther into space than ever before. Here it is seen berthed for maintenance in the cargo bay of the space shuttle Endeavour.

beings are not special. And that would throw many of the world's major religions into turmoil, for Christianity, Islam and Judaism are all based on the assumption of a unique relationship between God and humanity.

The latest attempt to discover intelligent life is coordinated by the SETI ('Search for Extraterrestrial Intelligence') project. SETI scientists are using radio telescopes to try to detect artificial radio signals. However, any messages would take so long to reach Earth that they would probably have been sent out many years ago – by which time the civilization – even the planet – they came from might not exist any more. If any civilization is sending out radio transmissions now, it will be our distant descendants who pick them up.

In the meantime, there is a chance of very rudimentary forms of life on Mars. NASA scientists in 1996 announced that in examining a meteorite

'It's possible that universes are falling into existence while we're speaking. Somewhere there are trillions and trillions of universes.'

Peter Atkins, Oxford University

from Mars they had found complex molecules, crystals resembling those produced by bacteria, and tiny tubes that could be fossilized bacteria (see pp.166–7).

OTHER WORLDS

We should draw a distinction between our fantasies of extraterrestrial beings, from angels to aliens, and the real chances of other inhabitable worlds. The possibility of other worlds was opened up by Copernicus in the 16th century, and supported by philosophers such as the mystic Giordano Bruno and Thomas Campanella.

However, in the absence of scientific evidence the arguments about life on other planets are mainly theoretical. On the one hand it is argued that the conditions for life as they are found on Earth are so exact that life elsewhere is unlikely. On the other it seems clear that if the laws of physics encouraged the development of intelligent life on Earth they must have done so elsewhere.

The most extravagant version of the life-on-other-worlds theory is the life-in-parallel universes theory. Physicists have concluded that parallel universes are theoretically possible in view of the curious ability of subatomic particles to exist in two places at once (see pp.233–4).

Parallel universes offer the ultimate in space travel – not to the distant reaches of outer space, but to different universes which may be accessible from the here-and-now. But of course, the scientists who believe in parallel universes may be no more than modern mythologers, no different from the Pythagoreans for whom numbers could prove anything, or the mystics whose souls were believed to travel to heaven and the underworld.

> 'In the dreams and fantasies of many modern people, the flights of the great rockets of space research have often appeared as symbolic 20th-century embodiments of the urge toward liberation and release that is called transcendence.'
>
> Joseph L. Henderson in *Man and His Symbols*, ed. C. Jung, 1990

The National Astronomy Observatory, New Mexico, USA. Radio telescopes such as these are trained on the skies, searching for signs of life – a powerful image of humanity's desire to know that we are not alone in the universe.

THE CONSTELLATIONS

A constellation is a group of stars imaginatively connected to form some familiar shape or image. Although the stars appear to be close together they may in reality be many hundreds of light-years apart. Some, when seen through telescopes, may turn out to be galaxies. Virtually every human society has created its own system of constellations. The 88 constellations recognized by modern astronomers are largely inherited from the ancient Greeks, who themselves selected and adapted from the traditions they found in Babylon and Egypt. There was a further spate of constellation creation in the 16th and 17th centuries when European explorers charted the southern hemisphere and astronomers used telescopes to map faint stars that had previously been ignored. Many systems, such as the Chinese and the Native North American, are now dead or dying, but the Western system itself remains a rich repository for a mythic view of the heavens that can be traced back up to 5,000 years.

ANDROMEDA, THE MAIDEN, PRINCESS OF ETHIOPIA

Andromeda was the goddess of vegetation, a form of Inanna, Ishtar and Persephone. Originally she was represented as a young girl wearing nothing but jewellery but gradually, in more puritanical ages, she was clothed in wraps and veils, like Inanna returning from the underworld (see p.153). The central theme of Andromeda's myth is her sacrifice to Cetus the sea monster, as a punishment for the claim by her mother, Cassiopeia, that she (Cassiopeia) was more beautiful even than the Nereids, an alluring group of sea nymphs. Just as Andromeda was about to be devoured she was rescued by Perseus, representing the heroic Sun of spring. On most sky globes she is pictured wearing the chains that had bound her to the sacrificial rock. Andromeda is home to M31, the Andromeda galaxy, a whirlpool of stars two million light-years from our solar system and possibly the most distant object in the sky visible with the naked eye.

AQUILA, THE EAGLE

Nova Aquila, one of the most famous supernovae in recent times, blazed on the night of 8 June 1618, the brightest new star since Kepler's nova in 1604. Such prominence is appropriate for one of the most significant constellations of ancient times. In a tradition dating back to before c.2000BC, Aquila the Eagle joined the Taurus the Bull, Leo the Lion and Aquarius the Water Bearer as one of the four great constellations that governed history. So persistent was this tradition that to the first Christians it represented the gospel-writer Mark. There is something of a mystery here, for Aquila is in the wrong place to be linked with the other three constellations and we can only assume that between the Sumerians of the 3rd millennium BC and the Greeks of 500BC it had moved. Aquila's brightest star is Altair, the twelfth-brightest star in the sky (17 light-years away) which with Vega and Deneb forms the 'summer triangle', one of the most noticeable alignments in the summer sky in the northern hemisphere. Altair is one of the most unusual stars known to us; it is believed to rotate once in 6.5 hours at such a speed that its size is seriously distorted: it may be as much as twice as long as it is broad.

ARA, THE ALTAR

Ara lies just north of Scorpius. It contains no named stars, although it does include our nearest globular cluster, NGC 6397 – 8,400 light-years away. It is often pictured with a flame on top, which may indicate a Persian origin; the Persian Zoroastrians always kept a burning flame on their altars.

AURIGA, THE CHARIOT

Auriga contains a very unusual type of star, an eclipsing binary known as Epsilon Aur. Two stars orbit each other and once every 27 years one blots out the light from the other in an eclipse lasting a full year. Mythologically Auriga has a number of associations. The charioteer is linked to the Sun or any solar hero, driving the Sun daily through the sky. The most popular myth is that he was Vulcan, god of thunderbolts, fires and the Sun – the Roman equivalent of Erichthonius, a legendary king of Athens.

BOÖTES, THE HERDSMAN

Boötes contains Arcturus, the fourth-brightest star in the sky and a mere 36 light-years from Earth. Mentioned by Homer and Hesiod, it was one of the most important stars in ancient astrology – the Roman writer Pliny claimed that its rising was often accompanied by hail storms. The constellation is also known as the Bear Driver, and probably has a mythological connection with Ursa Major, the Great Bear, although the name may also mean Ox-driver.

CANIS MAJOR, THE GREATER DOG

Canis Major contains Sirius, the brightest star in the sky and one of the most important bodies in Egyptian religion. The Great Pyramid was aligned so that the pharaoh's soul might travel between Earth and Sirius, its heavenly home (see p.238). Spell 882 of the Pyramid Texts identifies the pharaoh with the star in the following words: 'O king, thou art this great star, the companion of Orion, who traverses the sky with Orion.' Most authors repeat the story that the rising of Sirius with the Sun heralded the flooding of the Nile, the most important point in the Egyptian year, although in fact this would not always have been the case. In ancient Greece and Rome, Sirius' midsummer rising with the Sun signified the 'dog days', and the star was blamed for bringing unpleasant heat and shrivelled crops. Sirius is also the focus of some modern star-mythology. In 1976 Robert Temple published *The Sirius Mystery*, claiming that, hundreds of years before Europeans arrived, the Dogon people of Mali knew that Sirius had a smaller companion, a dense white dwarf, and that this knowledge could only have come from extraterrestrial visitors. Temple's critics argue that the information could easily have come from French missionaries.

CANIS MINOR, THE LITTLE DOG

Canis Minor's brightest star, Procyon, is a white star 11.3 light-years away. The Greeks believed that it was a malevolent body combining the worst aspects of Mercury and Mars, although, if linked to the Sun, it could signify great honour.

CASSIOPEIA, QUEEN OF ETHIOPIA

Cassiopeia's boastfulness almost resulted in the sacrifice of her daughter Andromeda (see above). As an added punishment Cassiopeia was condemned to circle the celestial pole for ever, sometimes hanging upside down in an undignified posture. Vain to the last, she is often pictured seated on her throne, still fussing with her hair. The constellation contains Beta Cas, the famous supernova of 1572. When this 'new star' appeared, Tycho Brahe proved that it was further away from the Earth than the Moon, overturning a cardinal doctrine of classical astronomy.

CENTAURUS, THE CENTAUR

Whereas the Centaurs were wild beasts (half man, half horse), Centaurus is usually associated with the wise teacher Chiron, whose pupils included Jason, Achilles and Asclepius, the son of Apollo and the greatest of all healers. The constellation includes Alpha Centauri which, at only 4.39 light-years away, is the nearest star to our solar system.

CEPHEUS, KING OF ETHIOPIA

Cepheus was the husband of Cassiopeia and father of Andromeda; his mythic kingdom extended from Palestine to the Red Sea. Cepheus is one of the most northerly constellations. Its most interesting star is Delta Cephei: in 1784 John Goodricke noticed that its brightness varied in a cycle lasting 5.4 days, and after Henrietta Leavitt's research into the relationship between the period of the pulse and the star's luminosity in 1908–12, it became the prototype for the Cepheid variable stars that are used for calculating distances in space.

CETUS, THE SEA MONSTER

The fourth-largest constellation, Cetus was the sea monster sent to devour Andromeda (although sometimes this distinction was given to Pisces' northern fish). It is also the constellation that swallowed Jonah, enabling the disobedient prophet to undergo an initiation, discovering that his true duty lay in total submission to fate and to God's will. Cetus' brightest star is Menkar, from al-Minhar, the Nose. The Greeks were wary of it, claiming it was Saturnine in nature, signifying loss and disgrace. Cetus' most interesting star is a red giant, Mira, which in 1638 became the first known 'pulsating variable' – a star whose brightness varies in a regular cycle.

COMA BERENICES, THE HAIR OF BERENICE

Although this group of stars was not formally classified as a constellation until 1551 (by the cartographer Mercator) Eratosthenes identified it as the Hair of Berenice (or Ariadne) in the 3rd century BC. Berenice was a contemporary of Eratosthenes and was the sister and wife of the Egyptian monarch Ptolemy III. The story is told that she cut off her hair in thanksgiving for Ptolemy's safe return from a campaign in Asia.

CORONA AUSTRALIS, THE SOUTHERN CROWN

Known to the Greeks as a wreath, not a crown, this is how the constellation is often represented on old star maps. There are no named stars in the constellation and no certain mythology is attached to it; it is possible that the wreath is either the crown placed in the sky by Dionysus after he retrieved his dead mother from Hades or, in another version, the wreath he left in Hades in return for his mother.

CORONA BOREALIS, THE NORTHERN CROWN

The semicircle of stars between Boötes and Hercules represents the golden crown made by Hephaestus and worn by Princess Ariadne of Crete when she married Dionysus. Ariadne was also the half-sister of the Minotaur and fell in love with Theseus when he arrived in Crete to kill the monster. According to one account the light reflected from the crown's jewels helped Theseus find his way through the Minotaur's labyrinth.

CORVUS, THE CROW

Corvus was the crow sent by Apollo to fetch water so that he might make a sacrifice to Zeus (the crow was sacred to Apollo). The bird flew off with a cup (Crater) and instead filled it with fruit, waiting for several days while it ripened. After eating the fruit the crow needed an excuse, so it flew back to Apollo with a snake (Hydra), which it claimed had blocked the spring. Apollo saw through the lie and threw the crow, the cup and the snake into the sky

CRATER, THE CUP

Crater was the cup that features in the legend of Corvus (see above). Ptolemy considered its stars to be primarily Venusian, though tinged with Mercury, giving a good humour.

CYGNUS, THE SWAN

Cygnus is usually portrayed as a graceful flying bird, with its head, tail and wings outstretched, and is also popularly known as the Northern Cross. Legend tells us that the Swan was Zeus in disguise on his way to seduce Leda, one of his most notorious assignations. The brightest star in Cygnus is Deneb – the twentieth-brightest star in the sky. It is highly visible on summer nights in the northern hemisphere, forming the so-called 'summer triangle' with Altair and Vega. Perhaps for this reason it appears

to be the focus of some of the 4,000-year-old megalithic stone alignments found in the British Isles. Cygnus is also home to the North American Nebula (so-called on account of its shape), about 3 degrees east of Deneb, and Cygnus X-1, an intense source of X-rays, ten times as massive as the Sun, orbiting the star HDE 22868. One of 300 such X-ray sources discovered by the satellite Uhuru between 1970 and 1972, the discovery finally confirmed Stephen Hawking's suspicions about the existence and nature of black holes.

DELPHINUS, THE DOLPHIN

According to Eratosthenes the dolphin was the messenger of Poseidon (Neptune). It was placed in the heavens as a reward for persuading Amphitrite to marry the god after he had initially offended her. In another story Apollo, god of music and poetry, created the constellation after a dolphin rescued Arion (a poet and musician who lived on Lesbos in the 7th century BC) from mutinous sailors.

DRACO, THE DRAGON

This is the dragon slain by Hercules, and most star maps picture the victorious hero with one foot on the dragon's head. The constellation is the eighth largest, and its stars coil around the celestial north pole. Its brightest star is Thuban, from the Arabic *ra's al-tinnin*, the Serpent's Head, which was the pole star c.2800BC.

EQUULEUS, THE FOAL

This insignificant constellation (it is the second smallest) was listed by Ptolemy in the 2nd century AD, although it was mentioned by Eratosthenes 400 years earlier. Its four faint stars are portrayed as a horse's head next to the much larger Pegasus.

ERIDANUS, THE RIVER

Eridanus, the celestial river, meanders across the sky from Orion to Hydrus, in the farthest reaches of the southern hemisphere. Some classical astronomers associated it with the Nile, others with the Po, although mythically it was the river of life, flowing from the spring at the centre of the world to the ocean that surrounded it. We are told that the Argonauts sailed up Eridanus to discover the smouldering body of Phaeton after he crashed the Sun's chariot. One of Eridanus' stars, Epsilon Eri, features in the science fiction series *Star Trek* as the star around which Vulcan, Mr Spock's home planet, orbits. Aptly, in view of Spock's ultra-cool manner, the Greeks believed that the constellation possessed a cold, dry Saturnine nature.

HERCULES

Hercules was the greatest of the Greek heroes. He had many adventures but, as with his Babylonian equivalent, Gilgamesh, the twelve most important represented the Sun's triumphal journey through the year. Originally the Greeks knew the constellation as Engonasin, 'the kneeling one', and it was not until the 3rd century BC that Eratosthenes identified it with Hercules.

HYDRA, THE WATER SNAKE

The largest constellation, Hydra winds a quarter of the way around the sky, all the way from Cancer to Libra. The snake features in two myths. In one it is the Hydra, the multi-headed monster killed by Hercules, a creature also associated with Scorpio by some modern mystics. In the other it is the serpent that features in the story of Corvus, the Crow. In October 1965 Hydra was home to one of the most famous comets of the 20th century, Ikeya-Seki, visible in daylight when only 2 degrees from the Sun. According to Ptolemy, Hydra possessed the character of Venus and Saturn, conferring an emotional, passionate nature.

LEPUS, THE HARE

Eratosthenes tells us that Hermes (Mercury) placed the hare in the sky because of its swiftness. The Greeks knew the constellation as Lagos and the Arabs knew it as al-Arnab, both of which mean 'hare', but to the Egyptians its stars were the boat in which the great god Osiris (Orion), sailed across the sky. According to Ptolemy, Lepus has the qualities of Saturn and Mercury, conferring a quick wit and a serious mind.

LUPUS, THE WOLF

To the Babylonians Lupus was Ur-idim, the Wild Dog or Jackal, to the Greeks it was Therium, an unspecified wild animal, while to the Romans it was Bestia, the Beast, and was visualized impaled on a long pole held by Centaurus. Although the specific identification with the wolf seems only to date back to the Renaissance, some have suggested a connection with Lycaon, the mythical king of Arcadia who was turned into a wolf as a punishment for feeding Zeus with the flesh of the god's own son.

However, there is no evidence that the Greeks themselves identified the constellation with this legend. Lupus was the location of the supernova of 1006, the only one to be recorded in Europe before the Renaissance. It was said to be three times as bright as Venus and a quarter as bright as the Moon.

LYRA, THE LYRE

Lyra is the home to Vega, one of the bright stars of the northern summer sky and one of the most benevolent stars of classical astrology, sharing with the whole constellation the combined characters of Mercury and Venus. The lyre is associated with Hermes, who invented it, Orpheus, who played it, and Apollo, to whom, as god of music, it was sacred. Vega itself is named after the Arabic al-Nasr al-Waqi, meaning either 'the swooping eagle' or 'the vulture' and the constellation is often depicted as an eagle behind a lyre.

OPHIUCUS, THE SERPENT BEARER

Ophiucus, also known as Serpentarius, is the only constellation to be added to the Zodiac since ancient times. In 1928 the International Astronomy Union redrew the boundaries of the constellations, and extended the constellation to incorporate a section of Scorpio, making it the thirteenth sign in the IAU's zodiac. (This affected neither the tropical zodiac used by Western astrologers nor the sidereal zodiac used by Indian astrologers.) To the Greeks Ophiucus was Asclepius, the god of medicine and son of Apollo, although the constellation is also associated with Hercules who as an infant is said to have strangled two serpents sent by Juno to kill him. According to Ptolemy, Ophiucus was of the nature of Saturn, moderated with a little Venus, conferring a passionate, good-hearted, wasteful and easily seduced nature. The constellation contains two notable stars: Rasalhague, which was important in classical and Arabic astrology, and Barnard's Star, a 'runaway star' which shifts its position to such an extent that in 175 years it will have moved in relation to its neighbours in the night sky by the width of the Moon. Most notable was the supernova of 1604 which Kepler used both to confirm his developing ideas about the structure of the solar system and to make a set of experimental forecasts for the future of Europe.

ORION, THE HUNTER

The three bright stars of Orion's belt are one of the most striking and easily recognized features of the night sky. The whole constellation, including about 77 visible stars, is, from a religious perspective, perhaps the most important. In Egypt it represented Osiris, the country's mythical founder and first king, and one of the forms taken by the god who embodied the entire country. Some of the greatest of Egyptian monuments were aligned with the constellation and once every 24 hours the three stars of the belt culminated over one of the shafts pointing at the sky from the Great Pyramid (see p.238). In the Pyramid Texts the king is addressed with these words: 'Thou wilt regularly ascend with Orion from the eastern region of the sky, thou wilt regularly descend with Orion into the western region of the sky.'

Before c.2000BC the Sumerians knew Orion as Uru An-na, the Light of Heaven, and placed it next to Taurus the Bull: from this it is assumed that in myth the two constellations represented Gilgamesh and the Bull of Heaven. In Persia and Rome, Orion was Mithras, whose struggle with the Bull was central to the Mithraic religion's sacred mysteries. In Greece, Orion was identified with Hercules, and Taurus was the Cretan Bull of his seventh labour.

There are many myths about Orion himself. The son of Poseidon, he had the power to walk on water, but he also inherited some of his father's wilder instincts. He was blinded after attempting to rape Merope, daughter of King Oenopion, but his sight was restored by the rays of the rising sun. In another version he tried to rape Artemis who, in revenge, sent a scorpion, now the constellation Scorpius, to kill him.

Orion's most interesting star is Betelgeuse, a variable star (its brightness varies) which was important in Greek astrology for conferring wealth and honour in war– and which features in Douglas Adams' *The Hitchhiker's Guide to the Galaxy*, the classic work of humorous science fiction. The constellation also contains M42, the Orion Nebula, which in 1880 was the first nebula to be photographed.

PEGASUS, THE WINGED HORSE

Pegasus was the famous horse ridden by the Greek hero Bellerophon, and was the offspring of Poseidon and Medusa, the Gorgon. This is a large constellation – the seventh largest – and contains three stars significant in Greek astrology:Algenib, which was thought to brings notoriety and dishonour, Markab, which signified disgrace and ruin, and Scheat, which indicated extreme misfortune. In October 1995 Pegasus became the location for the first confirmed planet outside our solar system, orbiting the faint star 51 Pegasi.

PERSEUS
Perseus was one of the most famous Greek heroes, and the characters in his mythical adventures are featured in five of the other constellations. His greatest exploit was the killing of the Gorgon Medusa. The most notable star in Perseus is Beta Persei, which is in fact not one star but two, an eclipsing binary, in which one of the two stars in the pair periodically moves in front of the other. Commonly known as Algol, from the Arabic *ra's al-Ghul* (the Demon's Head), Beta Persei was one of the most inauspicious stars in classical and medieval astrology. Perseus is also the home of the Perseid meteor shower, which is thought to be debris left behind by comet Swift-Tuttle, and which peaks every year on 12 August with up to sixty meteors per hour.

PISCIS AUSTRINUS, THE SOUTHERN FISH
According to Eratosthenes, who called this constellation the parent of Pisces, the Southern Fish saved the Syrian fertility goddess Derceto (Greek Atargatis) when she fell into a lake near the Euphrates. The constellation is actually easier to spot than Pisces because it contains the bright star Formalhaut. This marked the winter solstice *c*.3000BC, was one of the 'royal' stars of the ancient Persians and was said by Ptolemy to signify great honour.

SAGITTA, THE ARROW
There are at least three different theories as to the origin of the Arrow. It might be the weapon with which Apollo killed the fearsome one-eyed Cyclops, that with which Hercules killed the eagle that ate the liver of Prometheus, or that with which Eros kindled Zeus' love for Ganymede.

SERPENS, THE SERPENT
Although Serpens technically consists of two parts, Serpens Caput (Head) and Serpens Cauda (Tail), each of which is grasped by Ophiucus, it is always considered as only one constellation. Its mythical origins are lost, but are probably connected to the mythical worm or snake Ourouboros, which represented time or, in the tale of Adam and Eve, the birth of knowledge.

TRIANGULUM, THE TRIANGLE
Known in Babylon as Gis-apin, the Plough, and in Greece as Deltotron (the letter D), Triangulum contains one of the most distant naked-eye objects in the sky – M33, the Pinwheel galaxy.

URSA MAJOR, THE GREAT BEAR
Popularly known as the Plough or the Big Dipper, Ursa Major is the most familiar constellation in the sky. The third-largest constellation, it is identified with one of two characters, either Adrasteia, one of the ash-tree nymphs, or Callisto, who suffered after being raped by Zeus. Legend relates that Callisto was Artemis' hunting companion. One day Zeus entrapped her after disguising himself as Artemis. When Artemis discovered the girl was pregnant she banished her, but worse was to come when Hera, Zeus' wife, turned her into a bear. Eventually Zeus rescued her and placed her in the heavens.

In the northern hemisphere Ursa Major never sets below the horizon, so from an astrological perspective its significance is universal. Shakespeare uses this imagery in *King Lear* when he has Edmund, the play's villain, bemoan the fact that he was 'born under the Bear' – Edmund is 'everyman' and his sins are the sins of us all.

URSA MINOR, THE LITTLE BEAR
The Greeks believed that Ursa Minor was named by Thales, the 'father' of modern astronomy, *c*.600BC, but he may well have borrowed the name from other sources, perhaps Phoenician. The constellation's most famous star is Polaris, the pole star. The star is actually not exactly overhead at the north pole. It will be at its closest in 2012, after which it will slowly begin to move away.

OBSOLETE CONSTELLATIONS
There are some 53 obsolete constellations in the Western system alone, if we take our starting point as the beginning of Greek astronomy in the 6th century BC. Most were always insignificant, but three were of particular importance.

ARGO NAVIS
This was a huge constellation representing the Argo, the boat on which Jason and the Argonauts set off in search of the Golden Fleece. After their adventures were over, Athene placed the boat in the heavens. Nicholas de Lacaille (see below) divided the constellation into three, Carina, Puppis and Vela.

HYADES
Now part of Taurus, the Hyades consists of six stars, forming a distinctive V shape; the most important is Aldebaran. In myth the Hyades were the daughters of Atlas and the sisters of the Pleiades and the Hesperides. The name Hyades may derive from the Greek *uein* ('to rain'), since their appearance coincided with the start of the autumn rains. It is also said that they were the sisters of Hyas, who was killed by a boar while out hunting. Their sorrow was such that they died of grief and were transformed into the rain-bringing stars. Like Adonis (also killed by a boar), Hyas represents the spring Sun; the boar is the summer Sun which brings spring to an end.

PLEIADES
Like the Hyades now a part of Taurus, the Pleiades is the single most important constellation of all, taking all non Western cosmologies into account. People the world over have made the constellation's seven stars the symbolic centre of the universe or the focus of their religion. Both the ancient Greeks and Native North Americans used them to regulate their ritual agricultural year. The Greeks and the Australian Aborigines believed that they were seven sisters. The inhabitants of Polynesia gave the name Matari i Mia, (Pleiades Above) to one half of the year, and Matarii i Raro (Pleiades Below) to the other. To the Maya the seven stars were Tzab, the rattlesnake's rattle.

In Greek myth the Pleiades were the daughters of the nymph Pleione and her lover Atlas, and granddaughters of Oceanis and Thetis. They were the virgin companions of Diana who were carried into heaven to escape Orion or, in another version, because of their grief when their father was condemned to carry the world on his shoulders – they are known as the 'weeping sisters'. The Greek astrologers regarded the stars as inauspicious, combining the characters of the Moon and Mars.

NEW CONSTELLATIONS

NICOLAS DE LACAILLE

In 1751–2 the French astronomer Nicolas Louis de Lacaille (1713–62) visited the Cape of Good Hope, where he studied the night sky and invented a set of new constellations, some tucked into the spaces between the ancient classical patterns, others representing parts of those constellations. His star catalogue was published in 1763.

ANTLIA, the Air Pump, was created in honour of the invention of the air-pump by Robert Boyle.

CAELUM, the Chisel.

CIRCINUS, the Compasses.

HOROLOGIUM, the Pendulum Clock.

MENSA, the Table Mountain, contains part of the Large Magellanic Cloud, one of our neighbouring galaxies, which gives it the appearance of being capped by a cloud, much like the real Table Mountain in South Africa.

MICROSCOPIUM, the Microscope, lies south of Capricorn.

NORMA, the Level, represents a draughtsman's set-square and rule.

OCTANS, the Octant, is pictured as a navigational instrument invented by the Englishman John Hadley in 1731.

PICTOR, the Painter's Easel.

PUPPIS, The Stern, is part of the ancient constellation Argo Navis, the boat of Jason and the Argonauts.

PYXIS, the Compass, lies next to the old Argo Navis; Lacaille saw it as the Argonaut's compass.

RETICULUM, the Net, commemorated the reticle (part of the eyepiece) of Lacaille's telescope. In 1961 it was the subject of a celebrated UFO incident. Apparently a New Hampshire couple, Betty and Barney Hill, were abducted by aliens who supposedly came from a double star system in the constellation.

SCULPTOR, the Sculptor's Workshop borders on Aquarius and contains the south pole of the Milky Way galaxy.

TELESCOPIUM, the Telescope.

VELA, the Sail, is the sail of the Argonaut's boat, Argo Navis.

KEYSER AND HOUTMANN

In 1595–7 the Dutch navigators Pieter Dirksz Keyser (d.1596) and Frederick de Houtmann (1540–1627) charted the southern skies, creating and naming new constellations, first shown on a globe by Petrus Plancius in 1598.

APUS, the Bird of Paradise, was inspired by the birds of paradise discovered in New Guinea.

CHAMAELEON, the Chameleon.

DORADO, the Goldfish, contains most of the Large Magellanic Cloud, a small galaxy about 160,000 light-years away – one of our closest galactic neighbours. In 1987 Dorado was host to Supernova 1987a, the brightest and closest nova spotted so far. This was a breakthrough in astrophysics, as for the first time neutrinos (subatomic particles) were detected from a supernova.

GRUS, the Crane.

HYDRUS, the Little Water Snake.

INDUS, the American Indian, is shown holding arrows and spears.

MUSCA, the Fly.

PAVO, the Peacock, was the bird sacred to Hera, who drove through the air in a chariot drawn by the birds.

PHOENIX is the mythical bird associated with the Sun, which lived for 500 years after being born from its father's body.

TRIANGULUM AUSTRALE, the Southern Triangle.

TUCANA, the Toucan, contains the galaxy known as the Small Magellanic Cloud, one of the most magnificent sights in the sky.

VOLANS, the Flying Fish.

PETRUS PLANCIUS

At the end of the 16th and the beginning of the 17th century the Dutch theologian Petrus Plancius (1552–1622) created a set of new constellations, some in areas left blank by the Greeks.

CAMELOPARDALIS, the Giraffe, is said to be the creature on which Rebecca rode into Canaan for her marriage to Isaac.

COLUMBA, Noah's Dove, represents the dove sent out by Noah to see if the waters of the deluge had receded.

CRUX, the Southern Cross. The stars of the cross's longer beam point to the south celestial pole.

MONOCEROS, the Unicorn, lies in the Milky Way and contains a host of interesting objects, including the Rosette Nebula, a wreath-shaped mass of glowing gas surrounding an open cluster containing the star 13 Mon, Hubble's variable nebula, which changes both its brightness and its shape, and Plaskett's Star, a double star with a total mass 100 times that of the Sun.

JOHANNES HEVELIUS

The German astronomer Joannes Hevelius (1611–87) published a star catalogue, *Firmamentum Sobiescanum*, in 1687, followed posthumously by an atlas in 1690, both including a number of new constellations.

CANES VENATICI, the Hunting Dogs. Its most notable star, Cor Caroli, had previously been named in honour of Charles I of England and Scotland, executed in 1649. The star was said to have shone especially brightly on 29 May 1660 when his son, Charles II, returned to London, restoring the monarchy.

LACERTA, the Lizard.

LEO MINOR, the Lion Cub.

THE LYNX fills a large area of blank sky between Ursa Major and Auriga.

SCUTUM, the Shield, contains M11, an open galactic cluster known as the Wild Duck, after William Henry Smyth's description in 1844: 'this object somewhat resembles a flight of wild ducks.'

SEXTANS, the Sextant.

VULPECULA, the Fox, was the location for the discovery of the first pulsar, PSR 1919+21, by Jocelyn Bell in 1967. Because of the object's regular pulsations, every 1.33 seconds, some thought that it was an extraterrestrial radio message, and it was given the designation 'LGM' ('little green men').

THE DISCOVERERS

Our view of the universe has been shaped by poets, philosophers, shamans and magicians – and scientists. The following chronological list includes just a few of those who have shaped our modern, Western, primarily scientific beliefs about the stars. It is by no means complete. It probably never could be.

Names in SMALL CAPITALS have their own entry in this section.

THALES (c.624–547BC)
Greek sage, regarded as the first astronomer to search for natural rather than supernatural causes of celestial events. His reputation rests on his prediction of an eclipse in 585BC.

PYTHAGORAS (c.570–500BC)
Greek philosopher and mathematician who believed that the universe could be understood through the relationships between numbers expressed in geometrical forms. He synthesized the mystical cosmology of the Druids and priests in Egypt and Babylon devised the theory of the harmony of the spheres, in which astronomy is explained through musical harmonies.

PLATO (c.427–347BC)
Greek philosopher who created a brilliant synthesis of mystical beliefs about the nature of the universe and established the theory of Idealism, in which the physical world is an illusion emerging from the mind of the Creator. He believed that the universe was alive, that the planets were divine and that the study of astronomy and astrology brought the soul closer to God. His ideas were especially influential during the Renaissance. His belief that the state should be organized along the same lines as the stars was very influential on future Utopian ideas and was taken up in the 19th century by COMTE.

ARISTOTLE (c.384–322BC)
Greek philosopher and scientist; a student of Plato and tutor of Alexander the Great, Aristotle began the search for the physical mechanism by which the planets moved, although he still believed that God was the 'first cause'. His ideas were accepted almost without question in the classical world and in Europe from the 12th to 17th centuries and justified the use of astronomy and

astrology to forecast the weather, treat disease and make political predictions.

ARISTARCHUS (c.320–250BC)
Greek astronomer who was the first to realize that the Earth orbited the Sun.

HIPPARCHUS (c.190–120BC)
Greek astronomer and geographer, who compiled a catalogue of about 850 stars which was still in use in the 17th century. He was the first to record the precession of the equinoxes – the gradual shift of the constellations and stars in relation to the Sun's position at the spring equinox.

CLAUDIUS PTOLEMY (2ND CENTURY AD)
Greek astronomer and geographer. Ptolemy's textbooks on astronomy (*Almagest*) and astrology (*Tetrabiblos*) set the standard in both disciplines until the 17th century and were standard university texts in medieval Europe, signalling the triumph of the traditional view that the Earth was the centre of the universe.

ST THOMAS AQUINAS (1225–1274)
Italian philosopher, theologian and Dominican friar. A keen supporter of ARISTOTLE, Aquinas justified astrology to the Christian world by arguing that while the planets influenced the body and physical passions, the soul was still answerable directly to God.

MARSILIO FICINO (1433–1499)
Florentine philosopher; the first person to translate into Latin the complete works of PLATO and the mystical astrological texts attributed to Hermes. These, together with Ficino's own astrological writings, established a mystical, neo-pagan belief in the spiritual influence of the stars as a central part of Renaissance thought.

NICOLAUS COPERNICUS (1473–1543)
Polish astronomer. The first astronomer to challenge PTOLEMY, Copernicus showed in 1513 that the Sun is the centre of the solar system. This discovery was part of the revolution that shook Europe in the 16th century, including the Renaissance and Reformation.

TYCHO BRAHE (1546–1601)
Danish royal astrologer and observational astronomer. Brahe demonstrated

that changes took place among the stars, seriously weakening belief in the old teachings of PLATO and ARISTOTLE.

JOHANNES KEPLER (1571–1630)
German astronomer who became BRAHE's assistant. A devout Lutheran, Kepler believed that God spoke through the stars. As 'mathematician' to the Holy Roman Emperor Rudolph II, he set out to reform astrology, making it more accurate. In the process he worked out the laws of planetary motion, which, with some minor modifications, have enabled NASA to send space probes to the other planets.

GALILEO GALILEI (1564–1642)
Italian astronomer and physicist. The first real observational astronomer, Galileo used his telescope to discover the phases of Venus and the moons of Jupiter, shattering Greek cosmology for good. He worked as astrologer to the powerful Medici family, rulers of Florence, and achieved scientific immortality when he was tried by the Inquisition for his support of COPERNICUS.

ISAAC NEWTON (1642–1727)
English physicist regarded as one the greatest mathematicians and astronomers who ever lived. Newton devised the three laws of motion, synthesizing the work of GALILEO and KEPLER. He is best remembered for his general theory of gravitation, proving the universal law of attraction between separate objects. As a devout Christian, Newton sought to discover God's law working through a combination of astronomy, alchemy, history, prophecy and theology. Newton's demonstration of the existence of single laws throughout the universe had immense political consequences, encouraging the democratic belief that kings should be subject to the law.

WILLIAM HERSCHEL (1738–1822)
German-born British astronomer, Herschel was the discoverer, in 1781, of Uranus, the first new planet. He was also the first astronomer to connect economic rhythms to the sunspot cycle.

GIUSEPPE PIAZZI (1749–1826)
Sicilian clergyman and astronomer who discovered the first asteroid, Ceres, in 1801 – only to lose it again after a month.

AUGUSTE COMTE (1798–1857)
French radical thinker whose System of Positive Polity did more than any modern work to apply astronomical models to human affairs, laying the foundations for all modern sociology and providing a major influence, perhaps as great as that of Karl Marx, on European socialism. Comte believed firstly that the laws of planetary motion discovered by COPERNICUS, KEPLER and NEWTON also governed changes in human society; and secondly that society was in need of a revolution as great as that which had occurred in astronomy. He was the first to argue not only that society should be reformed but that this should be done on the basis of scientific research.

URBAIN LEVERRIER (1811–1817)
French astronomer working on predicted positions for Neptune at the same time as ADAMS.

JOHN C. ADAMS (1819–92)
British astronomer who predicted positions for Neptune in 1845, leading to its discovery.

PERCIVAL LOWELL (1855–1916)
US astronomer who founded the Lowell Observatory in Arizona in 1894. He studied Mars, which he believed was inhabited – and irrigated – by intelligent beings. In 1905 he predicted the position of a planet beyond Neptune, validated by the discovery of Pluto in 1930.

MAX PLANCK (1858–1947)
German physicist who laid the foundations of quantum mechanics (see pp.233–4) with his quantum theory (1900). This states that energy can only be emitted in 'packets', or quanta, and that the size of a quantum is relative to frequency.

ERNEST RUTHERFORD (1871–1937)
New Zealand-born British atomic physicist who developed the theory of radioactive transformation of atoms, discovered alpha and beta radiation, and identified the basic structure of the atom.

CARL JUNG (1875–1961)
Swiss psychologist and one of the founders of psychoanalysis. Jung was inspired by EINSTEIN, who had been an occasional guest at his home between 1909 and 1912, to create a psychic

counterpart to the theory of relativity. In collaboration with the physicist Wolfgang Pauli, who predicted the existence of the neutrino, he conducted statistical tests analyzing the relationship between the positions of the Sun and Moon at the births of married couples. Although the results were inconclusive, Jung's theory of synchronicity, or meaningful coincidence, has become the standard justification for modern astrology.

ALBERT EINSTEIN (1879–1955)
German-born Einstein was the greatest physicist since NEWTON. Denied a teaching post because he was a Jew, he took a job in a Swiss patent office in 1901. In 1905 he was awarded a doctorate degree and published his 'special theory of relativity'. This holds that nothing can exceed the speed of light, that this speed remains constant even if we are moving in relation to the light source, that length, mass and time are all relative, and that mass and energy are equivalent. Einstein's more advanced 'general theory of relativity' (1915) takes gravity into account, showing that space and time are inseparable, and both warped by gravity.

Far from being a closeted academic, Einstein was concerned with the social impact of science. He was also actively involved in anti-war campaigning, and later in Zionism. When Hitler came to power in 1933, Einstein accepted a post at Princeton University, USA, where he stayed for the rest of his life.

ARTHUR EDDINGTON (1882–1944)
British astrophysicist who identified radiation as the basis for stellar energy emission. An expert on general relativity, he helped to prove its validity experimentally.

EDWIN HUBBLE (1889–1953)
US astronomer who demonstrated the existence of separate galaxies and showed that they were receding, so that the universe as a whole was expanding. Moreover, he showed in 1929 that far galaxies were receding at a faster pace – important evidence in favour of the Big Bang theory (see pp.207–8).

WERNER HEISENBERG (1901–76)
German physicist who provided the mathematical basis for quantum mechanics (see pp.233–4). In 1927 he

stated the 'uncertainty principle' (see p.233), vital to the understanding of how subatomic particles behave.

CLYDE TOMBAUGH (1906–1997)
US astronomer who could not afford to go to college, but managed to get a job as an assistant at the Lowell Observatory, where he discovered Pluto by studying photographic plates. He went on to discover star clusters, variable stars, asteroids and nebulae.

SUBRAHMANYAN CHANDRASEKHAR (1910–)
Indian-born US astronomer best known for work on stellar evolution, but also for his radical theory – rejected by EDDINGTON and EINSTEIN but later confirmed by research – that stars over a certain mass would eventually become what are now known as neutron stars and black holes (see p.235).

WERNHER VON BRAUN (1912–1977)
German-born engineer who worked on the German rocket programme during the war. In 1952 he became technical director of the US Army's missile programme and subsequently headed the team that put the first US astronauts in space and on the Moon.

BERNARD LOVELL (1913–)
British astronomer who pioneered radio astronomy and used it to investigate meteor showers and radio emission from flare stars, leading to investigation of stellar atmospheres.

MICHEL GAUQUELIN (1928–1991)
French statistician who investigated correlations between profession and planetary position at birth. He established that certain planetary positions correlate statistically to outstanding professional success. The most significant is the 'Mars effect', linking Mars' position at birth to sporting success. His controversial results are still disputed by most scientists.

STEPHEN HAWKING (1942–)
British physicist who has produced evidence supporting the Big Bang theory (see pp.207–8), done much to lay the foundations of a quantum theory of gravity, and done more than any other single person to prove the existence of black holes (see p.235). He has also helped to make these subjects accessible to the general public.

GLOSSARY

The words in SMALL CAPITALS are cross-referred within the glossary.

anthropic principle the idea that the universe is as it is because we are as we are

antiparticle the basic component of anti-matter – a mirror image of an ordinary ATOM, with an opposite electrical charge. When both types of atom meet, they are converted into a flash of radiant energy

aphelion the point in the orbit of a PLANET at which it is farthest from the Sun

apogee the point in the orbit of a PLANET at which it is farthest from the Earth

asteroid a non-luminous chunk of rock, bigger than a meteoroid but smaller than a PLANET, in orbit round a STAR

atom the basic unit of ordinary matter, composed of a nucleus (of PROTONS and NEUTRONS) orbited by ELECTRONS

Big Bang according to most astrophysicists, the event at the beginning of the universe at which infinitely compressed matter began to expand rapidly into the universe we now know

binary star two STARS revolving round a common centre of mass

black hole a singularity, a point in the SPACE–TIME continuum at which the space–time curvature becomes infinite, and from which, therefore, no radiation or matter can escape

brown dwarf a large PLANET that is just below the critical mass needed to ignite and become a STAR

celestial equator the circle of the sky parallel to the Earth's equator

comet a small, icy object in a frequently very elongated orbit around the Sun, often with a tail

constellation an arbitrary grouping of STARS forming a pattern or figure

declination position north or south of the CELESTIAL EQUATOR, measured in degrees

double star see BINARY STAR

ecliptic the annual apparent path of the Sun around the Earth; the Sun returns to the same place on the ecliptic on the same date every year

electron a negatively charged particle orbiting the nucleus of an ATOM

entropy the tendency of the universe to become more disordered over time

equinox the two points at which the Sun crosses the CELESTIAL EQUATOR, when day and night are of equal length

galaxy a STAR system containing a vast number of stars and a huge amount of gas and dust

graviton a theoretical VIRTUAL PARTICLE

gravity the force by which all bodies in the universe attract all other bodies with a force proportional to the product of their masses and inversely proportional to the square of the distance between them (i.e. diminishing over distance)

horoscope the degree of the ZODIAC rising over the eastern horizon; generally applied to the diagram of the heavens used by astrologers, and to astrological columns in newspapers and magazines

house a division of the HOROSCOPE used by astrologers to study particular areas of activity, such as work or relationships. There are usually twelve houses, according to a number of different systems.

inferior planet one whose orbit around the Sun lies within that of Earth – i.e. Mercury or Venus

isotropy uniformity in all directions

light-year the distance travelled by light in one year

mass the quantity of matter in a body, determining its inertia, or resistance to acceleration

meridian the great circle on the celestial sphere passing through the observer's zenith and the celestial poles

Messier object a non-stellar object, such as a GALAXY, included in the catalogue originally compiled by Charles Messier and added to by others; each is designated by an 'M' number, such as M87

neutron star an extremely dense dark STAR that has collapsed under the pressure of its own gravity

nebula a cloud of interstellar dust or gas

neutron an electrically uncharged particle

neutronium a mass of ultimately compressed NEUTRONS

nova a STAR that suddenly increases in brightness and then gradually returns to its original state.

nuclear fusion the process in which two nuclei collide and form a single, heavier nucleus

perigee the point in the orbit of a PLANET at which it is closest to Earth

perihelion the point in the orbit of a PLANET at which it is closest to the Sun

photon a QUANTUM of light

planet in astronomy, a large body orbiting a STAR; in astrology, usually one orbiting the Earth

positron the positively charged ANTI-PARTICLE of an ELECTRON

precession of the equinoxes the slowly receding position of the EQUINOXES, relative to the STARS, resulting from the Earth's 'wobble' on its axis. Precession has put the tropical and sidereal ZODIACS out of alignment by almost one sign

proton positively charged particle accounting for about half the particles in most nuclei

quantum the indivisible unit in which energy may be emitted or absorbed

quasar a very fast-receding, distant source of energy, STARlike in appearance

radioactivity the spontaneous decay of one type of atomic nucleus into another

red giant a late stage in the lifetime of a STAR, when it becomes relatively bright and cool

red shift the reddening of light from a receding STAR

relativity Einstein's special theory of relativity (1905) gave the relation $e = mc^2$ between mass and energy. His general theory (1915) extended the theory to encompass gravitation. The essence of the theory is the interdependence of MASS and SPACE–TIME

retrograde motion occasional apparent backward motion of the PLANETS seen from Earth's perspective

sign a division of the ZODIAC; the tropical zodiac used by astrologers always has twelve signs

solar wind an outflow of particles from the Sun expanding its corona

solstice the extreme northern- or southernmost position of the Sun in its annual path

space–time (also space–time continuum) the fusion of the concepts of space and time, in which time is treated as the fourth dimension

star traditionally, any bright object in the sky; in the modern definition, a sphere of matter held together by its own gravitational field and generating energy by means of NUCLEAR FUSION

sunspot a cool, dark area on the Sun's surface

supernova a massive STAR that suddenly increases in brightness owing to its collapse and explosion under gravitational pressure (see also NOVA)

variable star a STAR whose brightness varies

virtual particle a particle whose existence can be inferred from effects, but that has not yet been observed

wavelength the distance between two adjacent crests or troughs in a wave

white dwarf a small, cold, dim STAR in the final stages of its existence

zodiac a symbolic or pictorial representation of the STARS or sky. Classical and medieval mystics also believed that the same principles which brought life to the stars animated everything on Earth: humans thus had an 'internal zodiac'

BIBLIOGRAPHY

The following selection will be a help to the beginner in a confusing field.

JOURNALS

SKY AND TELESCOPE (PO Box 9111, Belmont, MA 02178-9111, USA; http://www.skypub.com), and ASTRONOMY NOW (PO Box 175, Tonbridge, Kent TN10 4ZT, England; http://www.demon.co.uk/astronow), are excellent English-language astronomical magazines, available in many countries. THE ASTROLOGICAL JOURNAL, published by the Astrological Association (see Useful Addresses), is a top-quality magazine of serious astrology.

BOOKS

The best authors include Patrick Moore, John Gribbin, Heather Couper and Nigel Henbest. Two authors stand out in modern astrology – Liz Greene on the psychological approach and Michel Gauquelin on the question of cosmic cycles and influences. It is also useful to have an annual astronomical guide. A good one is published by Macmillan (London), edited by Patrick Moore. In the UK *The Times* publishes an excellent annual guide.

BATES, G. AND CHRZANOWSKA BOWLES, J., *Money and the Markets* (HarperCollins, London, 1994)

CAMPION, N., *An Introduction to the History of Astrology* (ISCWA, London, 1982)

CAMPION, N., *The Practical Astrologer* (Cinnabar Books, Bristol, 1994)

DREYER, R., *Vedic Astrology* (Samuel Weiser, York Beach, Maine, 1997)

EVANS, D.S., *Teach Yourself Astronomy* (Teach Yourself Books, London, 1952)

GAUQUELIN, M., *The Cosmic Clocks* (ACS, San Diego, 1982)

GRIBBIN, J., *Companion to the Cosmos* (Weidenfeld & Nicolson, London, 1996)

GUIRAND, F. (ed.), *Larousse Encyclopedia of Mythology* (Hamlyn, London, 1968)

HENBEST, N., *The Planets* (Penguin, London, 1992)

HENBEST, N., AND COUPER, H., *The Guide to the Galaxy* (Cambridge University Press, Cambridge, 1994)

KRUPP, E., *Skywatchers, Shamans and Kings* (John Wiley & Sons, New York, 1997)

MAYO, J., AND RAMSDALE, C., *Teach Yourself Astrology* (Hodder Headline, London, 1996)

MANN, T., *Sacred Architecture* (Element Books, Shaftesbury, 1993)

MOORE, P., *Mission to the Planets* (Cassell, London, 1995)

PASACHOFF, J.M., *Astronomy: From the Earth to the Universe* (Harcourt Brace Jovanovich, London, 1991)

SAGAN, C., *Cosmos* (MacDonald, London, 1981)

SEYMOUR, P., *Astrology: The Evidence of Science* (Arkana, London, 1988)

SHALLIS, M., *On Time* (Burnett Books, London, 1982)

TOWNSEND, R.F., *The Aztecs* (Thames & Hudson, London, 1992)

WALTERS, D., *Chinese Astrology* (Aquarian Press, Wellingborough, 1987)

WORKS CITED IN THE TEXT

ARATUS, *Phaenomena,* trans. G.R. Mair, (Harvard University Press, Cambridge, Mass., and London, 1977)

BARROW, J.D., AND SILK, J., *The Left Hand of Creation* (Penguin, London, 1993)

CAPRA, F., *The Tao of Physics* (Fontana, London, 1976)

CHAMBERLAIN, V.D., *When Stars Come down to Earth* (Centre for Archaeo-astronomy, Washington, DC, 1982)

CROWLEY, A., *The Complete Astrological Writings* (Tandem, London, 1976)

DAVIES, P., *The Last Three Minutes* (Weidenfeld & Nicolson, London, 1994)

GREENE, L., *Astrology for Lovers* (Unwin, Hemel Hempstead, 1986)

GRIBBIN, J., AND REES, M., *The Stuff of the Universe* (Heinemann, London, 1990)

GUTHRIE, Kenneth Sylvan (ed. and trans.), *The Pythagorean Sourcebook and Library* (Phanes Press, 1987)

HAWKING, S., *A Brief History of Time* (Bantam, New York and London, 1988)

HENDERSON, J.L., in Jung, C. (ed.) *Man and His Symbols* (Arkana, London, 1990)

KERÉNYI, C., *The Gods of the Greeks* (Thames & Hudson, London, 1951)

LEO, A., *Esoteric Astrology* (L.N. Fowler, London, 1967)

LILLY, W., *Christian Astrology 1647* (facsimile edition, Regulus Press, London, 1985)

McCRICKARD, J, *Eclipse of the Sun* (Gothic Image, Glastonbury, 1990)

McLEISH, J., *Cosmology* (Bloomsbury, London, 1993)

MANILIUS, M., *Astronomica*, trans. G.P. Goold (Heinemann, London, 1977)

MICHELL, J., *New Light on the Ancient Mystery of Glastonbury* (Gothic Image, Glastonbury, 1990)

PETRONIUS, *Satyricon*, trans. J.M. Dent (Everyman's Library, London, 1996)

PINGREE, D. (ed.), *Vrddhayavana-jataka of Minaraja*, 2 vols, (Oriental Institute, Baroda, India, 1976)

PINGREE, D. (trans.) *The Yavanajataka of Sphujidhvaja*, 2 vols (Harvard University Press, Cambridge, Mass., 1978)

PLINY *Natural History*, vol. 1, trans. H. Rackham (Harvard University Press, Cambridge, Mass., 1929)

PLUTARCH 'On the obsolescence of oracles', *Moralia*, vol. 5, trans. F.C. Babbit (Harvard University Press, Cambridge, Mass., no date)

PTOLEMY, C., *Tetrabiblos*, trans. F.E. Robbins (Heinemann, London, 1940)

RAMESEY, W., *Astrology Restored* (London, 1653)

SANGHARAKSHITA, *A Survey of Buddhism* (Shambhala/Windhorse, Boston and London, 1980)

SCHMITT, H.H., in Neal, V. (ed.), *Where Next Columbus?* (Oxford University Press, New York, 1994)

SPENCE, L., *Introduction to Mythology* (Studio Editions, London, 1994)

SSU MA CH'IEN, *Astrological Treatise of*, in D. Walters, *Chinese Astrology* (Aquarian Press, Wellingborough, 1987)

WATERS, F., *Book of the Hopi* (Ballantine, New York, 1969)

WELLS, H.G., *The First Men in the Moon* (Orion, London, 1901)

WILSON, C., AND GRANT, J., *The Directory of Possibilities* (Corgi, London, 1982)

WOLKSTEIN, D. AND KRAMER, S.N., *Inanna, Queen of Heaven and Earth* (Harper & Row, New York, 1983)

USEFUL ADDRESSES

BRITISH ASTRONOMICAL ASSOCIATION, Burlington House, Piccadilly, London W1V 9AG, England (http://www.ast.cam.ac.uk/~baa) ASTROLOGICAL ASSOCIATION, 396 Caledonian Road, London N1 1DN, England (http://www.astrologer.com/aanet/index.html) The URANIA TRUST publishes an international directory of astrological schools and societies, available from the A.A. or on the World Wide Web (http://www.astronet.co.uk).

INDEX

Page numbers in **bold** refer to illustrations